THE PLURAL PSYCHE

Also by Andrew Samuels

Jung and the Post-Jungians
The Father: Contemporary Jungian Perspectives
(editor)
A Critical Dictionary of Jungian Analysis (with Bani
Shorter and Fred Plaut)
Psychopathology: Contemporary Jungian Perspectives
(editor)

THE PLURAL PSYCHE
Personality, Morality, and the Father

ANDREW SAMUELS

ROUTLEDGE

London and New York

First published in 1989 by
Routledge
11 New Fetter Lane, London EC4P 4EE
29 West 35th Street, New York NY 10001

Typeset by LaserScript Limited, Mitcham, Surrey
Printed in Great Britain by
Billing & Sons Ltd, Worcester

British Library Cataloguing in Publication Data

Samuels, Andrew
　　The plural psyche : personality, morality,
　　and the father.
　　1. Jungian analysis.
　　2. Developmental psychology. Theorised.
　　I. Samuels, Andrew
　　155'.01
　　ISBN 0-415-01759-9
　　ISBN 0-415-01760-2 Pbk

Library of Congress Cataloging-in-Publication Data

Samuels, Andrew.
　　The plural psyche : personality, morality,
　　and the father / Andrew Samuels.
　　p. cm.
　　Bibliography: p.
　　Includes index.
　　ISBN 0-415-01759-9. ISBN 0-415-01760-2 (pbk.)
　　1. Psychoanalysis. 2. Father and child.
　　3. Personality. 4. Moral development.
　　5. Pluralism–Psychological aspects.
　　I. Title.
　　BF173.S2794 1989
　　150.19'54–dc19　　　　　　　　　　　88-18191
　　　　　　　　　　　　　　　　　　　　　CIP

for Rosie

.... sometimes different cities follow one another on the same site and under the same name, born and dying without knowing one another, without communication among themselves. At times even the names of the inhabitants remain the same, and their voices' accent, and also the features of the faces; but the Gods who live beneath names and above places have gone off without a word and outsiders have settled in their place. It is pointless to ask whether the new ones are better or worse than the old, since there is no connection between them....
(Italo Calvino,
Invisible cities)

That which alone is wise both wishes and does not wish to be called Zeus.   (Herakleitos)

Contents

Preface

I hope I've published this book at the right moment. At the moment when the ideas and intuitions are sufficiently coherent to warrant expression but not so integrated and systematized that ossification results. Like any psychological work, the book teeters between developing its own language and the need to use a common language. However, even a common language is a changing language – it must be, to remain alive – and I have tried to explain why certain new words get used and to keep their number down.

This is both an open and a closed book. Open, in that it is concerned with recognizable themes and largely depends on a dialogue with the reader. Closed, in that it is self-referential and self-determining, creating its own world and inviting the reader in. Sometimes the mode of expression is intellectual. But I hope it is never abstract. There is also a good deal of argumentativeness, and this engagement with others, themselves involved in similar enterprises, is central.

When I was at school, I learnt the following maxim from one of my teachers (I think he taught economic history): what now looks to us like the intellectual or ideological discoveries of the past are better understood as *descriptions* of the most progressive contemporary practices. For example, Machiavelli did not write a handbook for princes, containing smart new ideas. Rather, he described what the most enterprising princes were *already* doing. Adam Smith's importance is not that he promoted capitalism, but that he described (and hence understood) what the new capitalists were doing. You could say that such writers were bringing something to consciousness.

I expect this is so with much of this book. What looks like (and, from the emotional perspective of the writer, *really is*) discovery, is description. Discovery is a fantasy. But so, too, is description.

Thinking about the fantasy of description, I'd like to say something about the standing of the case material in the book. I learnt from my first supervisor, Fred Plaut, to be wary of case illustrations that seem to prove or at least strengthen a writer's viewpoint. Be most wary when what is offered is offered merely as an 'example', just to make sure the point has got across. Without going into the epistemological issues, such examples can be grossly manipulative. Yet some kind of fleshy material is needed when the writing is theoretical. How to resolve the problem? I decided to make extensive use of transcripts from workshops I've led on various specific themes. The case material is therefore often not mine (though there are accounts of my own work as well). The advantage is that the reader can share in the freshness and immediacy of my struggle to link my ideas to what the workshop participants brought. I hope the method works and the disadvantages that it has are not too marked.

The Greek word *theoria* means 'looking about the world', 'contemplation', 'speculation' and, in those senses, I am a theorist. But I found that I am also a *theor*. Theors were emissaries sent by the Greek states to consult a distant oracle or participate in important far-off religious rituals. For the past five years, I have been lucky enough to be invited to speak at Jungian congresses and to Jungian societies in several countries. I expect it is a common experience for people who do this sort of thing to come home with far more than they had when they left. I've come back with a vision of the Jungian project worldwide that goes beyond the vision that inspired my book *Jung and the Post-Jungians* and I'd like to say a few words about it in this preface.

Jung and the Post-Jungians had three strands: (1) an account, organized in debate form, of developments in analytical psychology since Jung's death in 1961; (2) a summary of Jung's ideas – necessary to make sense of the first strand; (3) a drawing of parallels with psychoanalysis leading to a claim that Jung should be seen as a pioneering psychoanalyst.

What impressed me, as I did the work for the post-Jungian book, was the way in which the two apparently opposed Developmental and Archetypal Schools have reacted similarly, in an iconoclastic, revisionary way to the tenets of classical analytical psychology. I would not claim that developmentally and archetypally oriented analytical psychologists agree upon their differences; they most certainly do not. But they share a common process.

Gradually, as I mused about this, a pluralistic question arose: would it be possible to link the monotheistic/integrative/*unus mundus*/elitist concerns of the classical Jung with the polytheistic/interactive/microscopic/democratic concerns of the post-Jungians – *without losing the value and heartfelt truth of either set of concerns?* I say this was a pluralistic question, but I had not yet sensed how pluralism, as an ideology, might meet this challenge. When I did, I realized that the subject matter for this book would be far wider than the disputes within analytical psychology.

Pluralism is an approach to conflict that tries to reconcile differences without imposing a false synthesis on them and, above all, without losing sight of the particular value and truth of each element in the conflict. Pluralism is not an exclusively multiple approach because it seeks to hold unity and diversity in balance, making sure that diversity need not be a basis for schism.

In pluralism, I had found the tooth for a book about difference whose goal was neither comparison nor synthesis.

On an experiential level, we have to reconcile our many internal voices so that we can, when we need, speak with one voice. Psychological theories also engage with this phenomenon – exploring how the various parts of the personality relate to the psyche as a whole without losing their distinctiveness. The splits and divisions in depth psychology provide the institutional variation on the theme.

Whether on the personal level, or in the making of psychological theory, or in the political vicissitudes of depth psychology as an institution, in this book I show how pluralism can be used as an instrument to make sure that diversity need not inevitably lead to splits. Here is a brief summary of the book.

In Chapter 1, I introduce the idea of pluralism as a metaphor for and approach to psychological processes and the institutional politics of depth psychology. In Chapter 2 I try to devise a pluralistic model of personality development. Chapter 3 looks at nonliteral meanings of parental imagery (as it appears in analysis).

In Chapters 4 and 5, I focus on the person, image, and body of the father as crucial to the fostering or hindering of psychological pluralism, with special reference to gender identity. Chapter 6 explores whether there are sex-specific psychologies and, then, whether it is valuable or not to take 'masculine' and 'feminine' as metaphors. Chapter 7 throws the concept of gender up against that of borderline personality disorder, leading to reflections on the cultural construction of both.

My interest in the primal scene leads to Chapter 8, which draws together many of the issues raised in the first seven chapters: pluralism, the father, gender, the balance between the literal and metaphorical in psychology.

The book is both a reconnaissance and a celebration of the tension and articulation between literal and metaphorical understandings in psychology. This is exemplified in Chapters 9 and 10, which discuss analysis itself. The clinical emphasis is on countertransference and the role played by the analyst's body.

Chapter 11 is an essay on the hidden pluralism of moral process and Chapter 12 harks back to Chapter 1 in its exploration of the politics of psychological diversity.

I hope that the book stays close to lived experience, inside and outside analysis. But where this does not seem to be the case, I would ask the reader rot to be too critical too soon. For surely the lived experience of analytical psychology and psychoanalysis is that, in the soul's depths, things are not necessarily what we think or feel they are. Nor what we desire them to be.

Acknowledgements

Responsibility for the ideas expressed in this book is, of course, mine. I should like to thank my patients for giving me permission to write about them. I am also grateful to those who participated in the research project described in Chapter 8 and to members of the following groups and institutions for allowing me to transcribe audio tapes of various workshops: the Pittsburgh Jung Society, the Santa Fe group of the Inter-Regional Society of Jungian Analysts, and the Westminster Pastoral Foundation. The feedback from trainees at the Society of Analytical Psychology and the Guild of Psychotherapists has also been very useful.

Several individuals have been extremely generous with their time and energy in commenting on chapters and sections of the book. My debt to them is very great: Michael Vannoy Adams, John Beebe, Giles Clark, Coline Covington, David Curry, Dorothy Daniell, Peggy Jones, Lou King, Paul Kugler, Rosalinda Mammano, Kate Newton, Stan Perelman, Roderick Peters, Fred Plaut, Sheila Powell, Nathan Schwartz-Salant, Bani Shorter, Brian Skea, and Caroline Stevens.

Rosie Parker's engagement with the whole project, at once critical and supportive, has been absolutely essential.

Parts of the book were first published in journals and I am grateful to the editors for permission to use the material and also for the editing that was provided in the first instance: 'The image of the parents in bed', *J. Analyt. Psychol.* 27:4, 1982. 'Countertransference, the *Mundus Imaginalis* and a research project', *J. Analyt. Psychol.* 30:1, 1985. 'Symbolic dimensions of eros in transference–countertransference: some clinical uses of Jung's alchemical model', *Int. Rev. Psycho-Anal.* 12:2, 1985. 'Fragmentary vision: a central training aim', *Spring*, 1981.

'Original morality in a depressed culture' was published as part of a work-in-progress in *The Archetype of Shadow in a Split World* (Proceedings of the Tenth International Congress of Analytical Psychology, edited by Mary Ann Mattoon (Einsiedeln, Switzerland: Daimon Verlag 1987). My thanks to the editor for her contribution.

Material that now appears in several chapters was first published as 'Gender and the borderline' in *Chiron* 1988.

Acknowledgements

Permission to quote from *The Imitation Game* by Ian McEwan (London: Cape 1981) is acknowledged.

Acknowledgements are due to Routledge and to Princeton University Press for permission to quote from the *Collected Works of C.G. Jung*, edited by H. Read, M. Fordham, G. Adler, and W. McGuire, translated mainly by R. Hull. Except where stated, references to Jung are to the *Collected Works (CW)* and by volume and paragraph number.

I should like to thank Mrs Millie Alfandary for her excellent and speedy typing.

1

The plural psyche

This opening chapter is intended as a resource for the rest of the book, capturing and expressing the spirit in which it has been written. Pluralism is an attitude to conflict that tries to reconcile differences *without* imposing a false resolution on them *or* losing sight of the unique value of each position. As an ideology, pluralism seeks to hold unity and diversity in balance – humanity's age-old struggle, in religion, philosophy, and politics, to hold the tension between the one and the many. My use of the term 'pluralism' is intended to show differences from 'eclecticism', 'synthesis', 'parallelism', and 'perspectivalism'. As the chapter unfolds, the distinctions should become clearer.

We learn from political experience that, though societies may aim at harmony and mutual respect, the opposite often takes place. Political pluralism suggests that a fostering of competitive bargaining between conflicting interests produces creative rather than destructive results. However, I am not trying merely to advance pluralism as a desirable state or goal for psychology. My suggestion is that we begin to *use* the idea of pluralism as a tool or instrument to make sure that diversity need not be a basis for schismatic conflict. This instrument would also tell us when a split has become inevitable or even desirable. Pluralism could function as an instrument to monitor the mosaic of the psyche, or that of depth psychology, and help us to carry out repairs when necessary. Not only a goal, also a yardstick.

In our personal lives, we experience conflict; we have to live through it every day. Thus the notion of psychic conflict is central to dynamic conceptions of the psyche. As far as depth psychology as a whole is concerned, the divisions and congeries, organized into schools and studied, or perceived as chaotic and ridiculed, provide the institutional variation on this theme.

On the personal level, we are faced with the pluralistic task of reconciling our many internal voices and images of ourselves with our wish and need to feel integrated and speak with one voice. It is an issue of intense feeling, this intrapsychic process. It has now become an issue of thinking, for psychological theory also seeks to see how the various conflicts, complexes, attitudes, functions, self-objects, part-selves, sub-personalities, deintegrates, psychic *dramatis personae*, internal objects, areas of the mind, subphases, gods – how all of these relate to the psyche as a whole. And what happens when a single part out of many begins to act as if it had the force and weight of the whole? The extent of the list demonstrates the variety of descriptive or explanatory methods, the universality of the problem, and its inherent fascination.

When I use the word 'psyche', I am concerned with a *perspective on psychological processes and phenomena* as well as referring to their totality. This perspective is characterized by an attention to depth and intensity and, hence, the difference between a mere event and an experience is highlighted. Psyche brings with it its own plurality, fluidity, and the existence of relatively autonomous entities therein. Finally, psyche as a perspective hints at meaning and pattern that may be discernible by the individual, but not to the extent of a fixed predestination. The reader will note a tendency to anthropomorphize psyche – for instance, the psyche 'wants' something, or 'yearns' for something, and so forth. This is more than a rhetorical device. Psychological jargon does have living entities locked up in it – sometimes people, but often daimons, animals, or gods. Even the most scientistic classical Freudian will talk of the ego being strong or weak and of the relations between ego, id, and superego as if they were three personages. The reason for this is that psychology theory-making doesn't seem possible without that kind of implicit personification. Jung was the arch exponent of this; his whole psychology takes the form of an animation of inner personages.

A political metaphor, such as pluralism, helps in an evaluation of tensions and oscillations (Zoja 1987) within the psyche. Parts of the psyche are in a state of competition between themselves. Personality, at any one moment, is the outcome of such competition. The questions that then arise are: what kind of access do the various parts of the psyche, the inner interest groups, have to the rest of the psyche? What status and rights does each have? Is there an elite with special privileges? For instance, there is a dynamic between the *puer aeternus* (eternal youth) and *senex* (old man) aspects of a person. The Latin tags refer to differing emotional outlooks and are not intended to be restricted to males. It is not necessary fully to accept these terms from analytical psychology to be able to see how pluralism can be used *instrumentally* to track *senex–puer* competition in the psyche.

The *puer* suggests the possibility of a new beginning, revolution, renewal, and creativity generally. The *senex* refers us to qualities such as balance, steadiness, generosity towards others, wisdom, farsightedness. Each of these positions can become pathological – unmitigated *puer* is redolent of impatience, overspiritualization, lack of realism, naive idealism, tendencies ever to start anew, being untouched by age, and given to flights of imagination. Pure *senex* is excessively cautious and conservative, authoritarian, obsessional, overgrounded, melancholic, and lacking imagination. By the way, these are not simply developmental concepts (though they can be used like that), for even old women and men can be seen to have *puer* (or *puella*) characteristics. Similarly, the *senex* can be seen even in the character of babies. Nevertheless, *puer–senex* interplay takes on different tones according to development phase.

Clearly, the average person will have both sets of characteristics in his or her make-up. A *laissez-faire* approach, involving competition and perhaps some bargaining, might seem an appropriate description of what goes on. On the other hand, at certain times maybe *puer* will rule in *puer's* realm, and *senex* in *senex's*. Each will monopolize, or colonize, whatever seems to fall into its natural sphere of influence. Then there is the possibility that there is some kind of 'governmental' regulation of all of this (for example, by the self). Perhaps the snag with that would be that regulation itself is a *senex*-type concept and, hence, unfair to the *puer*.

Do *puer* and *senex* have equal access to the political 'power' of the psyche as a whole? Perhaps not, if *senex* feels safer to be with and more socially respectable; so *senex* may have some special privileges. On the other hand, *puer* is sexy (though maybe not as *sexual* as he might be), and vibrant, and, hence, popular. The scenario could be prolonged – for instance, we could ask in whose language negotiations are to be conducted – but the example was intended only to show how pluralism works as a metaphor for psychological processes.

3

So far I have been discussing pluralism in relation to the psyche. In addition, a pluralistic approach illuminates the issues of unity and diversity as they affect the various schools of depth psychology. By 'depth psychology' I mean to indicate all psychological endeavours that make use of the concept of the dynamic unconscious. The somewhat old-fashioned sounding term is useful in an age when both psychoanalysis and analytical psychology are deeply split into schools. We need a term that refers to the social fact of a whole field, with all its divisions, and recognizes that depth psychology is itself composed of individual analysts and therapists.

Pluralism is an attitude or ideology that can hold the tension between claims of and tendencies towards unity *and* claims of and tendencies towards diversity: depth psychology as a cohesive discipline in which there are right and wrong viewpoints – *and* depth psychology as containing a multiplicity of valid approaches. A place for ultimate reality *and* for a plethora of phenomena.

The fragmentation and dispute within depth psychology, as individual analysts and groups of analysts fight for the general acceptance of that particular 'personal confession' in which they have invested, seems on the surface to be the very opposite of pluralism. However, using the idea of unconscious compensation (*CW* 6: para. 693f), it is possible to see depth psychology as struggling, and as having always struggled *towards* pluralism. What seems like a flight from pluralism may also be a yearning for its plenitude and an acceptance at some level of a pluralistic destiny for depth psychology. For aggression, so characteristic of debates between analysts, often contains the deepest needs for contact, dialogue, playback, affirmation. (See Chapter 11 for a further account of this aspect of the phenomenology of aggression.)

Many analysts and therapists are committed to dialogue but the psychological difficulties associated with maintaining a tolerant attitude cannot be minimized. Depth psychologists, being people, will continually fail to be as tolerant as they would like to be. In part, this is because of their passionate devotion to their own psychological approach. *But where is a programme to combine passion and tolerance in depth psychology?* We focus on and know about opposites of tolerance – envy, denigration, power, control, and so forth. My intent is to do something positive and realistic with the incorrigible competitiveness and argumentativeness, mining the envious shit for the tension-rich gold it might contain. Competition that is open, psychologically integrated, and valued could lead to a tough-minded tolerance. Through competition with others, we may come to know ourselves and our ideas better and more deeply – a specific example of the importance of the mirroring Other, whose presence glimmers in so many psychologies – Jung's, Winnicott's, Neumann's, Lacan's, Kohut's. This Other is a creative other and needs nurturing for it is closely linked with another other – the convenient receptacle for prejudice and projection, the subject of fantasies of superiority.

Depth psychology is a movement that, historically, has shown itself able to withstand clashes and splits and to generate new hypotheses out of them. This capacity lies alongside the far better-known tendency for the splits to become concrete (institutional) and unproductive. Depth psychology continues to be desirous of entering a plural state but lacks the necessary methodology. It is possible that we are all pluralists but that various forms of omnipotence and idealization encourage us to deny it. The tendency towards multiplicity and diversity is as strong – and creative – as the search for unity or a striving for hegemony. (A further discussion of the use of pluralism as an instrument in relation to dispute in depth psychology may be found in the final chapter.)

As we proceed, we shall see how these two suggestions about pluralism are the same suggestion. That is, *the arguments about the One and the Many in the psyche and the arguments about the One and the Many in relation to the schools of depth psychology are really the same argument.* We have tended always to keep apart the psyche and the social organization of depth psychology. However, the vicissitudes of depth psychology as a cultural movement, the splits, plots, alliances, gossip, and power struggles – all these reveal that, in their professional lives, therapists and analysts are participating in a mighty projection. For, when analysts argue, the plural psyche is speaking. Differing points of view reflect the multiplicity of the psyche itself. Jung once said that the gods have become illnesses. Nowadays, their epiphanies are to be found in our differing approaches to psychological illness as these find expression in the schools of depth psychology. In Winnicott's words, 'we are poor indeed if we are only sane' (Winnicott 1945: 150n). I return to this theme in the final chapter.

A particular interest of mine is to search out how differences of opinion reflect more than differences in the psychological type of the disputants. Granted, some analysts will, constitutionally, tend to prefer, see, and search for multiplicity and diffusion; others will place integration and unity in the foreground. However, in his typology, Jung (*CW* 6) was careful to insist that no one type is better than another and that for an individual to become truly himself (i.e. individuated), *all* typological potentials would have to be realized. In this chapter (and throughout the book) we will see how both of these considerations apply to the discipline of depth psychology: no one kind of approach is *a priori* better, save as a matter of personal preference and loyalty. And to become truly himself or herself, the depth psychologist cannot belong to one school alone. There is an interdependence, with all possible manner of divergence and convergence. The different schools of depth psychology symbolize strands of professional being within a single analyst, so that the exploring of ideological difference becomes an expedition to the interior, a matter of individuation. What gets projected onto the ideological opponent may, in this sense, be the psychological property of the one who projects – and, hence, of great value to him or her. A pluralistic approach provides a framework within which to use projections that are discovered in theoretical dispute. Pluralism sees through schism to embrace a perspective in which various analysts, or the various schools, have to take note of each other, without having unity as a goal; a modular, conversational approach in which different world views meet but do not try to take over each other. It is an emotional challenge as much as an ideological one. As Whitehead said, 'a clash of doctrines is not a disaster, it is an opportunity'.

Problems of pluralism

It is very difficult to hold to a pluralistic attitude. Pluralism may seem utopian in that the simple and reliable mechanism of right or wrong has to be suspended without being completely discarded. Further, it is very hard to feel passionate about being tolerant, to be a radical centrist in depth psychology, to go in for what the parliamentarian Walter Bagehot called 'animated moderation'. Does pluralism condemn us to losing the excitement of breakthrough ideas, which are more likely to be held with a passionate conviction? Boredom would be as great a problem as tyranny. My view is that such a worry rests on a misunderstanding and an idealization of the cycle of creativity. New ideas emerge from a pluralistic matrix and are reabsorbed into that matrix. Ideas do not come into being outside a context; nor does the new necessarily destroy the old but often co-exists with it. Ideological conviction therefore arises from a context of pluralism.

It is well-known that patients benefit when the analyst has conviction (or faith) in his theoretical ideas and clinical practices, no matter how deviant these may seem to be. However, if the debt owed by ideological conviction to a plural *mise en scène* were acknowledged, these benefits might be available together with tolerance of other views, open communication, and the chance to learn from diversity. For, as Yeats said, 'the worst are full of passionate intensity'.

A further problem with pluralism is summed up in this quote from Francis Bacon's *Essays*: 'All things when they are looked upon piecemeal seem *Greater*, when also a Plurality of Parts makes shew of a Bulk considerable. Which a Plurality of Parts effects more strongly, if they be in certain *Order*: for it then resembles *Infinity*, and hinders the comprehending of them'. The danger is that a pluralist would be someone who knows less and less about more and more. A reply would be to say that a pluralist could be someone who knows he or she does not know everything and is prepared to listen to a more informed source (as well as being aware of those aspects of his or her personal psychology that hinder that). Since Bacon's time, we may also have become more suspicious about constructing 'Order' out of 'Parts'.

What would happen if we were able to allow pluralism the same charge as partisanship? To do this we have to go beyond perspectivalism, meaning an apparently detached and dispassionate attempt to explain difference by suggesting that, though the same phenomena are being examined, the perspectives from which this is being done are simply so different that differing theory is an inevitable outcome. Another possibility is parallelism; differing theories are simply different aspects of the same great theory or truth. Parallelism and perspectivalism *are* unexciting and the problem with them as modes of thinking is that they ignore the manner in which all the different perspectives or parallels do have *something* to do with each other. William James made the following statement about this in *A Pluralistic Universe* (1909) and his attack on absolutist, monist, and idealist versions of the world is equally applicable to perspectivalism:

each part of the world is in some ways connected, in some other ways not connected with its other parts, and the ways

can be discriminated, for many of them are obvious, and then
differences are obvious to view.

(James 1909: 40-1)

In fact, as James says, the key word is 'some': 'pluralism
stand[s]...for the legitimacy of the notion of *some*' (1909: 41). The
main theme of *A Pluralistic Universe* is a consideration of the One
and the Many as complementary perspectives. However, the
moment we say that they are complementary, we land in the camp
of the Many. This may be linked to what Miller, discussing
monotheism and polytheism, calls 'henotheism': one god at a time
but, in time, many gods (Miller 1981). The paradox is that pluralism
becomes the only absolute! And the only unity to be found will be
in diversity. What is so appealing about pluralism when formulated
in this way is its anti-utopian tenor: it can accommodate aggression
and monocular vision – monotheism, grand theory, fanaticism –
even that peculiar brand of prejudice that turns out to be genius. If
there is some enormous, single, absolute Truth, it too must
compete. Similarly, binocular vision is also facilitated: dualism, the
conjunctio oppositorum, etc.

One last problem with pluralism that I would like to mention
concerns the risk that we forget how loosely knit depth psychology
is. Then we start to look for differences in an artificial quest for
grounds of dispute. On the other hand, there does seem to be a
pressing need for a field in which to test, in Wallerstein's words,
'one psychoanalytic proposition against another truly different
psychoanalytic proposition' (Wallerstein 1983: 567).

Self and others in a plural psychology

We can see how several strands of James's pluralistic vision apply
to depth psychology. The field of reference is in principle open in
every way, even its depths; we can 'know' the unconscious. Greater
elements incorporate lesser and, significantly, vice versa: 'the
image is a condensed expression of the psychic situation as a
whole' (*CW* 6: para. 745). Crucially, we are morally enriched by
contrast and diversity – without diversity, psychology has no
meaning nor breadth: 'each psychology is a confession, and the
worth of a psychology for another person lies not in the places
where he can identify with it because it satisfies his psychic needs,
but where it provokes him to work out his own psychology in

8

response' (Hillman 1975a: xii). More pluralistically, I would vary this a bit to say 'not only' where a person can identify, but 'also' where he or she is provoked.

Pluralism also resonates with the omnipresence in human ideation of metaphor. By this I mean that the lived world is not fixed or concrete and that symbolic discourse is as tough-minded as any logic. Poesy and science confront each other on equal terms. Depth psychology is less about 'things' than about the relations between things and, ultimately, about the relations between sets of relations. Depth psychology demonstrates cybernetic and systemic features, then. Impact at one point of the psychic system leads to ripples through the whole apparatus. Reflecting on these arguments, the reader may recall my idea that depth psychology, and hence depth psychologists, deeply desire to embrace pluralism and live out its pluralistic fate. However, the situation is even more charged than that.

The depth psychologist has never been able to work in isolation from others in the same field who have a different viewpoint. Leaving aside the question of whether any one analytical approach is more successful than the others (never settled), the arrogance of isolation was never a viable option. The rows within psychology cannot be ignored in a serene, Olympian fashion. Similarly, other areas of knowledge thrust themselves forward. Sometimes, as in the case of physics, the imagery and methodology of the nonpsychological field seem so apt that they quite naturally take over (e.g. Keutzer 1984). Sometimes, psychic processes are revealed as dominant within other disciplines (which has been my discovery in relation to political theory). It follows that a depth psychologist cannot repudiate (deny?) a plurality of study and interest. Even those who feel uncomfortable with pluralism, and render it inaccurately as 'eclecticism', need to recall that the theories with which they feel most at home themselves arose from a pluralist matrix and a competitive diversity of views. For example, the Kleinian corpus was not a single, time-bound, unchallenged, piercing vision. This was something Winnicott noted in a letter to Klein in November 1952 – a quite agonized and remarkable letter. Amongst many other complaints, Winnicott wrote strongly against 'giving the impression that there is a jigsaw of which all the pieces exist' (Winnicott 1987: 35).

Pluralism and praxis

Let's look now at some illustrations of a pluralistic approach to key issues in depth psychology. One distinguishing feature of an analytic attitude is that no one kind of clinical material is considered *a priori* more important than another. The minute details of personal interaction in the session and large-scale symbolic material must *compete* for attention. There is no preconceived caste system of importance. Analysis, as a *Weltenschauung*, offers a strange amalgam of precision and imprecision. The methodology of even attention across a field of reference leads to an ethos of plural interpretation on a variety of levels, vagueness even, and sometimes simply a waiting upon psychological events. Within clinical practice, there is a tension between process analysis of transference–countertransference and content analysis of images and symbols. It is more or less impossible completely to dismiss one or the other of these perspectives. But it can often be very hard to keep the rhythm going (and see Chapter 9, where I attempt to do that).

We see significant differences of opinion in depth psychology regarding the roots of personality, sources of information about them, and ways of translating such knowledge into analytic practice. Depth psychology has generated numerous attempts to understand the blend of innate, biological, archetypal facets of personality with environmental and situational factors. Just to give a flavour: it has been said that rheumatoid arthritis may be a psychosomatic disorder, stemming to some degree from a certain kind of maternal handling. But there is also the possibility that the potentially rheumatoid child is endowed with personality characteristics at birth that give him/her an influence upon the mother that tends to produce the kinds of mothering patterns that have been observed. Perhaps it is nowadays as difficult to accept the idea of a constitutional personality as it once was to accept the influence of early experiences. Finally, multifactorial and interactive explanations can be advanced. Pluralistic attempts at understanding try to make space for all these viewpoints.

As far as sources of information about the development of personality are concerned, there is a difference of opinion in depth psychology between those who advocate the empirical observation of infants and their parents, and those who favour an empathic approach to the adult patient, and to his child side. Then there are those, working as self-psychologists, who feel that the object relations approach is 'experience-distant' (Goldberg 1980). The emphasis on conflict is said to leave out feeling and the presence and function of the whole person. The arguments could possibly be said to be between those who seek truth and those who seek meaning. But truth and meaning seem equally desirable and so a plural attitude is not a luxury; it is a necessity to try to believe in and use apparently antithetical ideas (see Samuels 1985a: 128, 161-2, for an account of attempts to integrate conflict psychology and self-psychology without losing the specificity of each).

Pluralism and eclecticism

Pluralism is intended to be an anti-hierarchical attitude. The objection is not simply to hierarchy itself, but to the presence and influence of prejudged hierarchies: graded, calibrated, a *cursus honorum* of the psyche. All the schools of depth psychology demonstrate just such a hierarchical tendency, whether the good thing (sometimes claimed to be 'fundamental') is labelled 'the self', 'genitality', 'the imaginal', 'the depressive position', 'full object relations', 'separation–individuation', or plain 'individuation'. The list shows that the problem of prejudged hierarchy is not confined to analytical psychology, though my example will derive from Jungian theory, which I know best. This concerns the temptation, consciously and unconsciously, to exploit 'the self' as a concept and as an experience. It is possible to see the relations between the self and the plural psyche too much in terms of the 'order', 'meaning' and 'containment' provided by the former for the latter. If and when this happens, diversity will perish. For the power of the self as the human regulating agency is immense and in it are contained our most precious aspirations. For these reasons, Jung refers to the self sometimes as the 'God-image'.

To rectify the situation, and, in my sensing of it, as a plea for freedom and diversity, we have seen in analytical psychology a countermovement that regards the classical view of the self as leaden and static, with its stress on states of integration and its apperception of conflict mainly in terms of its resolution (Samuels 1985a: 89-132). None of this denies the existence and value of experiences of the self as a 'primary organising force or agency outside the conscious "I"', or as the 'organizing centre of the unconscious', or even the 'totality of the individual' (Redfearn 1985: 9, summarizing Jung). And such experiences *may* be every bit as fluid and mutable as the most ardent pluralist would wish. But such definitions, and even the idea of the self as unknowable, tend to impose (there is no other word for it) their own scale of values, a special hierarchy, upon human thought and experience. We should not forget that there is a psychopathology of the self that manifests as a defensive concern with hierarchy, logic, precision, definition, structure, pattern, regularity, and order at the expense of reversibility, mobility, and interaction. That the perspective of the self and a pluralistic perspective can coexist is shown in Lopez-Pedraza's axiom: 'the many *contains* the unity of the one *without losing* the possibilities of the many' (Lopez-Pedraza 1971: 214).

Now, if we abandon hierarchies of the kind I have been describing, questions arise about what it *is* that structures and organizes the psyche. If there is no superordinate principle (no hierarchy with the self or whatever as its highest and most comprehensive point), and no one element or approach is regarded as *a priori* more fundamental than any other, then how can pattern and meaning come into being? To answer this question, I want, once more, to move back into the social sciences where theorists have had to grapple with similar problems about structure and fundamentals. In his book, *Spheres of Justice* (1983), Michael Walzer suggests that it is necessary to appreciate that human life is not homogeneous. We should stress the relative autonomy of separate spheres of life rather than more inclusive conceptualizations such as 'society' or 'the state'. He goes on to make the crucial point that, in a just world, those who rule in one sphere of it are ruled in another. By 'rule', he means not so much the exercise of power but that people enjoy 'a greater share than other people of whatever good is being distributed' (Walzer 1983: 321). Hopefully, everyone has a turn at this sometime, somewhere, though it cannot be guaranteed. *My proposal* is that, from an experiential point of view, the psyche may be seen as containing relatively autonomous spheres of activity and imagery and that, over time and according to context, each sphere has its dominance. Similarly, from a more intellectual point of view, each school of depth psychology may be seen as relatively autonomous from the other schools and its theory as having its own strengths and weaknesses. It is a case of taking it in turns to be the dominant theorist, and of accepting that, in some ways and in some situations, the other guy has a more utilizable (more true?) theory. Then we may make a bilateral agreement to sing each other's song – not the same as agreeing to disagree and different, too, from being 'eclectic'. For eclecticism means singing selected verses only. Eclecticism ignores the contradictions between systems of thought, whereas pluralism celebrates their competition. Eclecticism does not encourage us to inhabit and work in a foreign system as a means of overcoming tyranny and partisanship.

Eclecticism is surprisingly *in*tolerant in that parts of a theory are wrenched from the whole. In a pluralistic endeavour, the whole theory is used, as faithfully as possible, and together with other theories until inconsistencies lead to breakdown. Then the breakdown itself becomes the object of study. Consensus, which is a prerequisite for eclecticism cannot provide the forum for this process and, paradoxically, crusty dialogue and debate between schools is hindered as much as helped along by consensus, which denies the need for it.

The difference between pluralism and eclecticism is summed up in the architect Louis Sullivan's admonition to his apprentice, which is pluralistic in its recognition of separate spheres: 'Inasmuch as you have problems to meet and solve, let me give you this pointer: Every problem contains and suggests its own solution. Don't waste time looking elsewhere for it' (Sullivan 1947).

Returning to the question of hierarchy, we have to admit that we will always tend to construct *ad hoc* hierarchies based on our feelings. For, at any one time, several thought processes, self-images, and personal myths may be in operation in us. What is such a hierarchy to look like? The weakness of preconceived hierarchies lies in their very *power* to make us feel guilty about our preferences and differences and try to deny them. An *ad hoc* hierarchy differs from a preconceived hierarchy in that the former is capable of seeing itself as one version among many possible versions. Thus the self, for instance, regarded from an *ad hoc* angle, has to have its place in the hierarchy reassessed so that, in its function as 'container' of the scintillae and luminosities of psyche, it competes for importance with those contents themselves. For not all psychic processes are about containment even if they may need a container. And some contents contain their container....

Now that our culture has encountered a version of the outer world characterized by non-Newtonian flexibility and relativity, such fluid passage of thinking is not only legitimate; it is necessary. Nor is it that new. The psychologically oriented political theorist

A.F. Bentley, writing in 1926 of the impact of Einstein's relativity theory on social analysis, had this to say:

> These discoveries ... have set us free – we may at least hope – to envisage social facts, not as verbal dummies supported on creaking frameworks of similar dummies.... Man no longer sits blunt and solid but has become a variable factor of action, in knowledge. Existence, as something definable for any instant, without past or present, has no longer its old deadening effect. ... Man's society, without the unworkable structures of mass and space and time and hopelessly concreted individuals, can now begin to be interpreted.
>
> (Bentley 1926: iv-v)

My intent is to point up the possibility that our concern with hierarchy is truly a search for structure and hence is already conditioned by a whole tradition of thought in the West. That we need, and experience, a structure of some kind in the psyche is not disputed. All the concepts listed earlier perform such structuring. What I do challenge is *whether the actual form of the structure is necessarily the same at all times*, whether, in fact, there is a structure devoid of content at all. If structure and content are mingled, and content changes, then the psyche is to some extent structured by its changing contents at any one time. Over time, some content changes, but not all. For example, this would mean that images, instead of requiring support or structure, would themselves form the evanescent, coruscating networks of psyche. In the next chapter, I term such networks 'imaginal networks'; my aim here is to propose an alternative to hierarchical thinking and its search for structure.

2

Personality and the imaginal network

In this chapter, I take further the linkage between a pluralist approach to competing psychological theories and a pluralist approach to personality. My intent is to work out an *attitude* to developmental psychology rather than to attempt a new developmental theory; in that sense, the reflexive aspects of the first chapter are also continued. By the end of the chapter, we shall be dealing with the topic of personality itself, trying to see how the contents of what I term the 'imaginal network' inflect the personality, without recourse to the idea of a structure prior to and separate from such contents.

The theme is the general impact of past experiences upon present personality and functioning. This is not the place for a survey of the intellectual history of this schism-inducing topic, but it is true to say that many of the uncrossable ravines that have opened up in depth psychology are connected to the subject. What I want to do is to use the pluralist ethos that I have been developing so as to reframe our various theories of the development of personality, enabling a move beyond the limits of the personalistic without losing sight of the humanistic.

A scanning of the literature suggests that the topic of the influence of the past upon the present is relevant both to psychoanalysis and to analytical psychology. The two main branches of depth psychology have reached a point where, at the very least, they are worried and perplexed by the same things. For instance, in his 1984 Ernest Jones Lecture, the literary critic Frank Kermode commented that, for some Freudian analysts, 'the death of the psychoanalytical past [is] a *fait accompli*'. Freud's historical constructions sometimes seem 'delusive' (Kermode 1985: 9). Kermode summarized: 'It is now quite commonplace to deny a

15

genuine relation between what happens in analysis and what happened in the past' (1985: 10). Now, personality as revealed in analysis is, according to most theories of the transference, supposed to demonstrate its origins in the past. If what happens in *analysis* isn't related to the past, then how can *personality* be so related?

The question was also referred to by Padel (1985). He writes of ways in which *diachronic* modes of explanation, which rest on a temporal basis, are challenged by a *synchronic* methodology, essentially a-historical. Clearly, for a pluralistic psychology, both diachrony and synchrony have their interest groups and their separate spheres. The potential of a plurality of understandings, whipped up by context and personal desire, cannot be avoided. Diachrony and synchrony will have to compete, as well as coexist or even co-operate. Importing the term synchrony from Saussurean linguistics reflects the fact that any critique of the claimed naturalness of developmental theory will be influenced by structuralism. However, the tenor of my own ideas is somewhat post-structural and deconstructive. Though the structuralism/post-structuralism engagement is markedly relevant for personality theory, the contents of the chapter do not fit neatly into one slot or the other.

In analytical psychology as a whole, synchronic thinking has a long tradition. Jung's response to the poverty of a historicist approach was twofold: first, said Jung, we are all at least two million years old. Thus what might once have been temporal is by now eternal. Or rather, what looked like personal experiences are, in fact, typical. Therefore, we should take a phylogenetic (archetypal) stance in relation to personal data. Jacoby (1985) has explored the archetypal imagery that is present in theories of development and Fordham (1957: 118) once compared his ideas to a 'cosmic-egg creation myth'. However, this way of thinking is usually *organized* diachronically (e.g. Neumann 1954) rather than synchronically: in stages or phases of development. Perhaps this is inevitable, given the difficulties of devising a synchronous model in any detail (see pp. 22-30, below).

The second strand of the Jungian opposition to reductionism has been to try to balance causal interpretation by prospective and goal-oriented approaches (see Samuels *et al.* 1986: 127-8). However, the problems with Jung's ideas have not been much written about. Elsewhere, I suggested that Jung's idea of reductive analysis was itself somewhat illusory and out of touch with what psychoanalysts actually did (Samuels 1985a: 134-5). Hillman

(1979: 30-2) and others such as Rychlak (1984: 49-53) have pointed out that teleology is itself a causalistic ideology (Aristotle's *causae finales*) and can be used just as deterministically as any other kind of causal viewpoint. What is more, Jungian analysts are aware that Jung's 'final' viewpoint can be misused so as to convert interpretation into sermonizing. It follows that a critique of causality cannot omit teleology.

In his archetypal psychology, Hillman suggests that developmental theories are fantasies in the mind of the theorist (Hillman 1973). Surprisingly, though, for one so committed to an exploration of fantasy and its imaginal world, Hillman is content to leave it there: developmental psychology is a fantasy – meaning unreal, deluded, delusive, false. But we need to work on these fantasies, if that is what they are, for, as I have argued in the previous chapter, the psyche itself may be speaking through its developmental theoreticians. The infant and his or her parents are not only screens for the psychologist's fantasies but for the psyche itself.

What would happen if we were to eternalize developmental theory, separating it from its chronological origins but not eliminating the personal factor? Then we might know more about personality in a state of all-at-oneness, personality as a whole. A patient may come to analysis bringing the information, together with feelings about it, that he or she was separated from his or her family often and early, abandoned even. Now, we know that on one level it is not absolutely crucial whether this happened or not, preferring to give weight to the patient's experience and comprehension of what happened. Later, we may well want to know (and so may the patient) what actually took place. From a synchronous standpoint, it is also not absolutely crucial whether the specific developmental theory that we may use to link the patient's past and his or her depressed present is right or not. But, by it, we are alerted to the patient's personal myth, the tide he or she lives his or her life by, to possible strands and networks of imagery that are at work. Interpretations of the present in terms of the past may have therapeutic value and be helpful in bringing about a sense of coherence and meaning for the patient. *But such interpretations also turn out to be interpretations of the past in terms of the present.* This was something noted by Freud himself in 1898 in an extraordinary letter to Fliess. Freud wrote: 'The mirror image of the present is seen in a fantasied past, which then prophetically becomes the present' (Masson 1985: 320).

Freud's statement is the unexpected springboard for a questioning of developmental psychology and a developmental approach to personality as being somehow natural – with the implication of its being an unavoidable way of going about things. Developmental theories do not tell us what kinds of things they are and that raises the question of what it is that developmental theory actually studies. We may well need a developmental theory that is capable of emerging with general principles but, ideally, this should not predetermine the pattern and cast of our thought. Nearly all developmental psychology tends to be biased towards diachrony: causal, historical, biographical, temporal, chronological, sequential, successive; explanation is by means of *origin*. Origin functions as a centre, guaranteeing a sense of security in the use and user of the theory. The idea of an origin may tempt us to use it as if it were a structure devoid of content; that particular temptation and its emotional and ideological implications are explored in the chapter. While I do not think any depth psychologist can stand outside this developmental tradition, as if in a privileged position, it is nevertheless possible to dispute that there is a self-evident, one-to-one, 'natural' link between past and present. To do that we have to clarify the different styles of developmental theory that exist, and their inter-relation.

Any experienced practitioner will point out that developmental psychology need not (and cannot) be reductive, causal, or mechanistic. When an analyst couches his interpretation in terms that owe something to a model of infantile development, he or she may be seen as employing a form of amplification, rather closely aligned to Jung's use of the word. That is, the model of infantile, psychological processes is being used in exactly the same way as more conventional, amplificatory material might be used (e.g. mythology). This is as metaphor: to make thin material more ample, increase the volume and so make listening easier, and, finally, to enable the patient to see that his problem is in some sense typical or part of a cultural trend. If 'infancy' is a linguistic metaphor that amplifies analytical interaction, or illumines the mystery of personality, then its widespread use becomes understandable. However, *the question of how fundamental infancy is, as opposed to its ubiquity as metaphor, is, perhaps, not really settled.*

Traditional approaches to development are *linear*. Oral leads to anal leads to phallic leads to genital; paranoid–schizoid precedes depressive; deintegration–reintegration gets more and more complex during maturation. Each of these overlapping stages and phases makes its own contribution to ego-consciousness so that any notion of a rigid scale of change, quite foreign to experience, is avoided. So, in sophisticated linear models, personality development is seen as a cumulative process rather than as one stage annihilating its predecessor. Alternatively, the notion of a *spiral* has often been employed to suggest that the developing personality consists of the same elements but with a greater degree of integration aა life proceeds. The linear aspect is less pronounced but, if the spiral is imaged as loosely coiled, new elements derived from the environment may be free to enter it. A more subtle issue is whether development is best conceived of as *continuous* or as *discontinuous*. The psychoanalyst Abrams summarized these viewpoints: 'one stresses understanding in terms of antecedent determinants; the second stresses developmental transformations, i.e. the influence of changing organisation as a result of progressive and regressive processes' (Abrams 1977: 425-6). Hopefully, when a synchronous model is described in more detail later in the chapter, it will be possible to see how development may be regarded as simultaneously continuous and discontinuous.

There is another way to use the knowledge contained in all these analytic traditions – a more pluralistic way. This is by thinking *eternally* and *vertically*. For instance, at any point in his or her life, an individual has a paranoid–schizoid component with its own specific and particular psychology and imagery – splitting, projection, identification, omnipotent control, etc. Though this *may* have been more pronounced when the individual was three months old, that is not the main point. Or, to use another schema of development, at all times in life there's a psychologically active oral zone; issues like dependence, separation, trust do not go away as a person grows up but remain in the psyche in an admixture of the same and a different form. Time, too, takes on a more psychological aspect when looked at in this way. Two-person relating depends, in a way, on three-person relating, probably thought to be 'later' chronologically. For, only when another person is experienced as being in relation with a third person does the individual have to face the fact that he or she is not that first person, and does not own or control them. Thus, the (often unwanted) experience of threeness can lead to the experience of twoness.

Pluralistic developmental psychology is conceived of as a series of interactive models, part-models, and 'modes of experience' (Oakeshott 1933). For example, when anality and genitality

19

interact, sex is dirty. When phallicism and genitality interact, the number of conquests becomes paramount. When aggression is played through the depressive position, argument clears the air and leads to a feeling of enrichment. Play aggression through the paranoid–schizoid position, and the result is argumentative deadlock.

All events and experiences may be regarded as having a simultaneous *and* a successive order. All events and experiences are rooted in their own psychological style and imaginal network. Each style or network has its own attitude to time, its own time-base. Later, we shall see how central is the idea of time to any developmental project. The proposal outlined here differs from most linear models in that, in the linear approach, each successive aspect of a particular theme is seen as contributing to a more complex, if not final version. Thus, as mentioned earlier, the different styles of consciousness attached to the different zones are regarded as contributing to an evolution in ego-consciousness. Instead, it is argued here that each style is virtually complete in its own right, and in constant, competitive interaction with the other styles (see Samuels 1985a: 79-81). The proposal differs from spiral versions of development in that it is not assumed that the person is 'going anywhere'; stasis and circularity are allowed for. After all, the 're' in relationship tells us that things in relationship happen again and again, recurrently and cyclically.

There are certain implications of what has been said for analytical psychology in particular. As far as the Developmental School is concerned, the model depicted goes some way to resolving a contradiction in Fordham's deintegrate theory (1976). When the primary self 'unpacks' its archetypal potentials, these are conceived of as emerging in a pure form, untrammelled by external factors, ready to mate up with environmental correspondences. Little place is made in the theory for the possibility (or probability) that the innate potentials within the primary self are affected by each other *before* they unpack. Not only is too sharp a division made between the innate elements and the outer correspondences but it seems to be assumed that the various deintegrates do not interact; succinctly, the model, apparently dynamic, has a hidden static quality. A more dynamic variant would allow for the influence on personality of deintegrates at all stages of their careers – *in potentia*, in transition, reintegrated – and place greater weight on the interaction of the deintegrates.

As far as the avowedly anti-developmental Archetypal School of analytical psychology is concerned, its position can be reframed or 'seen through' with surprising results. In spite of everything, Hillman has produced a psychology that speaks directly of ordinary, human, personal relationships, especially the childhood ones that it apparently eschews as its subject matter. We might consider a few of the key terms of archetypal psychology: specificity, multiplicity, fluidity, and mobility (Hillman 1983). Each of these also refers to central, core themes in human relationship. For specific people matter to us more than the mean. Indeed, relationship life can be regarded as the unfurling of specificity; for example, the infant relating in ever more personal ways to his or her mother. Or the partners in a marriage experiencing in ever greater particularity just why they are together or just why they must part. Preferences and ambivalences mean that any relationship is already a multiple relationship, for how we see and experience the other shifts with changing circumstances and needs. The relations between people reflect 'movement' in Hillman's sense: autonomously creative, heartfelt, and fluid. *The psychology of the soul turns out to be about people in relationship.* Later, in the next chapter and also in Chapters 9 and 11, we shall explore these paradoxes further.

Hillman has rightly pointed out that there *are* other archetypes than those connected to mother and child and that change is not the only psychological process worthy of note (Hillman 1973). He sees the problem with developmental psychology as being its restriction to the viewpoint of a/the child (personal communication 1985). The whole of the rest of psychology is thereby omitted, together with its enormously variegated population of images and myths. So development is destructive to psychology!

Inasmuch as there is a problem with the idea of 'development', I am sure that this results from a fascination with the numinous image of mother and child. Certain difficulties seem to me to stem from a tendency for subsequent relationships to be regarded mainly or solely as redolent of mother–infant dynamics. The grounds for that viewpoint would be, first, that people tend to repeat patterns of relating and, second, that the mother–infant relationship, being the first relationship, has unusually great influence in this respect. The mother–infant relationship would then be understood as a template for further relations; what is typically present in a person's relation to their mother characterizes all their other dyadic relationships – including, or especially, the analytic relationship. Of course, nobody would actually *claim* that only the mother–infant

21

relationship is important in this way but, as I see it, a habit of mind and a hierarchy have evolved into a consensus that has tended to exclude other kinds of relations: father, sibling, partner, companion, master, servant, rival, God.

Is it really necessary to have *any* paradigm for relationship generally, a guiding principle, a fundamental element? We can explore this question by looking at the emotional theme of *containment*, about which a good deal has been written.

It is often said that one person in a relationship 'contains' the other, or that the relationship contains the people in it. These statements tell us nothing about the range of emotional characteristics of the relationship. For instance, in a friendship, it may well be that the friendship contains the friends. But that does not mean that this friendship is necessarily about containment to the exclusion of such qualities as mutuality, equality, and exchange. It seems to be very hard to restrict the notion of containment to its being one of a range of emotional characteristics that may be present in a relationship. Any dominant part assigned to containment rests on the factor already mentioned: the image is numinous, it has taken a superior place in a conceptual hierarchy and been absorbed into a consensus. Disproportionate usage of the mother–infant relationship in the way I have described intrudes on a pluralistic approach to developmental psychology.

Archetypal states of mind

At this point, we might turn to the task of working out a synchronous and pluralistic approach to development in which the various stages and phases are not regarded either as fading away, or as evolving towards an apparently more mature version of themselves, or as integrating over time, or as behaving in a way that will bring about some final goal. Each element in personality would be *personally eternal*, to coin a phrase. Each stage or phase would be observed as active and interactive in the psyche in its own form and style. Such a perspective could coexist with linear and spiral models, as these were sketched out above, and the differing versions of developmental psychology could be considered together, thus facilitating a pluralist competitiveness between them. A synchronous developmental model would be pluralistic in another sense: it would give equal weight to the multiplicity *and* to the unity of the personality. This would redress the tendency to give greater weight to unity and integration, which is found in both linear and spiral models. There would be no need to insist that every feature of development has a *telos* or goal (see the next chapter for further discussion of teleology).

There is a paradox associated with the very idea of development. We may say that A leads to B, or that B emerges from A. This is certainly a developmental point of view. But, from another, equally developmental angle, for B to come into being, A must exist – not the same as A causing B. Or, though B may seem to come into existence later than A, they may always have coexisted, indeed may guarantee each other's existence. Or, though B may come into existence later, its eventual presence is necessary for A, which comes into existence earlier, to exist in optimum conditions. It follows that there is an interaction between A and B and that *this* is as much a matter of development as the manifold ways in which one leads to the other.

Is it possible to conceive of there being child and adult parts of the personality in a way that does not introduce a rigid split between them? Adult potentials are not caused by childhood – they are present in it. Though adulthood follows childhood, its existence is necessary to provide long-term meaning and identity for the child. If there is no future, then the experience of childhood will be truncated. We can avoid a split between child and adult by conceiving them on a two-way continuum.

There have been several precursors to the search for a synchronous developmental psychology. In psychoanalysis, Balint (1968: 28-9) has written of there being areas of the mind, adding that 'one might equally designate [them] as spaces, spheres, levels, localities, or instances'. Thinking of the idea of the personally eternal, it is interesting to see that Balint images his areas vertically: as 'extending through' the mind from id to ego to superego. More recently, Stern, in his attempt to fuse research-based and psychoanalytic developmental psychology, proposed that, though it is possible to identify four different senses of self, each forming at a certain point and each with its own emotional and social characteristics, 'these senses of self are not viewed as successive phases that replace one another. Once formed, each sense of self remains fully functioning and active throughout life. All continue to grow and coexist' (Stern 1985: 11).

There is also a way in which Freud might be claimed as operating in this paradoxical field of the personally eternal. In *Mourning and Melancholia*, published in 1917, it is striking that internalization of the lost object is regarded as pathological, occurring only in melancholia. In normal, resolved mourning, said Freud then, libido is withdrawn from the object and there's an end of it. When Freud wrote *The Ego and the Id* in 1923, he had evolved the idea that there is an internal world that is built up of images and objects derived from past experiences. From this insight has sprung the contemporary psychoanalytic consensus that what makes a relationship 'good' is its transmutation into a good internal object containing memories and experiences of the lost (or absent) person. When we struggle with loss, we employ the personally eternal to assist us. We relate to, draw on, dialogue with an internal element that, in experience, we treat, *not* as having been introjected or internalized, but as having always been there. The process of mourning is not a giving up of an emotional investment but rather an experiential reorientation inwards of such investment. Nothing dies; all is conserved – that is the hidden dynamic of mourning, in flagrant contradiction of the reality principle!

Jung's concept of the complex also reflects a vertical approach, as well as horizontal or spiral features. Jung was reluctant to link his theory of complexes to a precise developmental schema. Elsewhere (Samuels 1985a: 134-6), I suggested that this was because, consciously or unconsciously, Jung ceded the territory of personality development to Freud. But there are other possibilities, mainly to do with the extreme difficulty of constructing a language that would enable us to use a synchronous model. (I mean that there is a problem for depth psychologists, because others, for instance astrologers, are probably attempting just that: cf. Greene 1984.)

Nevertheless, that the complexes have an archetypal core and hence are always present to some degree means that they are conceived of as influencing a person throughout his or her life. They are eternal as well as personal and emphasis can be laid on their psychological continuity as well as on their development/evolution/change. Crucially for the present purpose, Jung argued that any particular developmental phase becomes an autonomous psychic complex. That is, phases of development do not necessarily fade away nor transform into 'higher' versions of themselves.

As I researched the literature prior to writing this chapter, it dawned on me that the vertical approach, permitting a synchronous model, has had a long and subversive history in depth psychology. *What has not been communicated is the deliberate intention of essaying such an approach.* For instance, in 1975 Plaut stressed that early processes such as splitting not only continue throughout life, but contribute to a sort of individuation radically different from the conventional description that highlights integration. In a previous paper (1959), Plaut had suggested that early consciousness rests on an 'archaic ego'; this, too, never completely fades away. Hillman (1973: 31) quoted Picasso as saying 'I am astounded over the way people let the word "development" be misused. I don't develop; I am.' Picasso's protest illustrates the difficulty most people, not just analysts, have with suspending linear, chronological time so as to let other insights emerge.

Why is it so hard to think synchronically? Clearly, chronological thought is valuable clinically with its capacity to reduce anxiety and increase understanding. But there may be a shadow to chronology in the sense of a general, unconscious feeling of *power* attached to it. If this is so, then the means by which the power is exercised is *interpretation*. Not all of the power of interpretation is negative, for the interpretive act is more often creative (unless a preconceived theory is applied mechanically). But the interpretive act is also highly selective, partial and unconsciously predictive for it is tied in, not only to the interpreter's values, but also to his vision of the future, as the historian E.H. Carr pointed out (1964: 107-8). Carr went on to say that the historian, at least, is known by the causes he 'invokes' for some event or other. Actually, Carr argued, the invoking of a cause is always the result of the establishment of a hierarchy of causes in order to decide which is the most important. As we saw in Chapter 1, construction of a hierarchy of ideas and power are closely connected.

Earlier, when referring to complexes, I mentioned their archetypal core. It may be helpful to expand a little on what might be understood by 'archetypal' over and above what a conventional description of the term might suggest, i.e. noumenal, underlying psychosomatic structures hypothesized as underpinning both images and instincts (see also Samuels 1985a: 23-54 and Samuels *et al.* 1986: 26-8).

In a nutshell, the archetypal may also be seen as a *gradation of affect*, something in the eye and heart of the beholder, not in what he or she beholds or experiences. We can think of the quality of a perception or collection of perceptions, qualities of preoccupation, fascination, autonomy, awe. An analogy would be a filter that is always in place, colouring or otherwise influencing what is seen or experienced. There is a sense in which the filter *is* the experience, or in which the experience is dead without the filter. *The filter is what we term archetypal.* The implication of this is that depth lies in the filter. The filter is a kind of disturbance of attention, distortion even. It is a way of introducing imagery to the world and of imposing imagery on the world so that the world becomes an experienced world (see pp. 39-47, below, the section on the imaginal network).

This account of the archetypal differs from the one referred to by M. Stein (1987: 64) as 'more usual Jungian usage'. There, the emphasis is on a reality said to be 'underlying', a 'structure deeply rooted in the psychic matrix'. Do such structures exist? – or are they not hypotheses, 'theoretical entities', in L. Stein's words (1958: 10), 'put there to do a job'? Does the psyche *have* to resemble a house, with foundations and upper stories? Does the psyche have to resemble anything? Or rather, given that the psyche doesn't resemble anything, should depth psychologists claim that it resembles a house without challenging such an assumption and going on to ask why it is so difficult to accept psyche as psyche? For it is difficult to keep the emotional tendency to import hierarchy under control, as we saw in the previous chapter.

Stewart takes up a middle position with regard to structures, commenting wryly that 'there are structures and structures' (Stewart 1987: 159n). He takes this position because he sees affects as a fundamental 'bridge between body and psyche' and affects are not really the same as deep, underlying structures. Though Stewart does not try to do away with structures altogether, his tendency to work from the outside (emotional expression) inwards is a freeing move in Jungian psychology, avoiding the problems of a too-literal understanding of structure.

Claiming the archetypal as something in the eye and heart of the beholder does not deny that there is a genuine clinical art to spotting profound features in the patient's seemingly banal material, as M. Stein pointed out (1987: 64-5).

Moving on from this version of the archetypal, we can hazard a description of archetypal states of mind. Archetypal states of mind bear relation to phases of development, as in a linear model. But, as they are also conceived of as something present from birth, or before, right up to death, or beyond, *archetypal states of mind invite a vertical consideration.* The suggestion is that there are identifiable psychologies pertaining to each archetypal state of mind. Not *one* psychology, though not ruling that out, but multiple psychologies, probably in interaction, but potentially separate.

It follows that a phrase such as 'the archetypal father' does not imply that human beings are born with a structuring image or expectation of a male personage called father. What does the phrase 'archetypal father' mean, then – if anything? It may be taken as referring us to whatever it is about the image of a father that is archetypal: gripping, numinous, awe-inspiring, even religious in a way, or possibly psychotic. The archetypal bit is within a person as he or she confronts his or her image of the father, or as the general image of father is confronted. *The archetypal father is not in the father at all but in the child's perception of the father* (see Samuels 1985a: 52-3, 261-5). This re-working of the idea of 'archetypal' has advantages when we come to deal with the presence and influence of cultural factors in psychological performance. As clinicians working in an evanescent society, analysts are faced with the problem of evaluating the general cultural version of the images, such as the father image, to which their patients are constantly resonating. For instance, when 'father' is *said* to be about 'authority', inner images of father are bound to be organized around authority. In other words, the clinical approach has to include an analysis of the cultural stereotype. If the patient is describing his or her father, the analyst can scarcely avoid having the cultural parameters in mind. My attitude is that whatever the culture says of a father is true, though not necessarily literally true. It is true in the sense that, as we all live in the culture, our inner conceptions of father must make use of these cultural associations to him. By 'culture', I mean the assemblage, limited in time and space, of the heritage of a community of whatever size – social, material, mental, spiritual, artistic, religious, and ritualistic. Culture carries the connotation of a group that has, at some level, developed its own identity.

Images generated by and within a culture are not, in every instance, archetypal. But they may be of equal importance to the clinician as more obviously archetypal material. The father image that the culture generates is an example of the kind of filter I have just been describing. Things to do with father can only be seen through the filter of father.

Before going on to describe this approach to development in more detail, it becomes pressing to discuss the relations and balance between literal and metaphorical aspects of our descriptions of personality. For it is at the interface of the literal and the metaphoric that we can find a place for the concept of synchronicity in personality development. I used to be very careful to distinguish literal and metaphoric statements about the aetiology of personality; whether I was talking about an actual historical child, for instance, or the-child-in-the-adult, or child as symbol. Now I am much less concerned to make such distinctions and the reasons for that have nothing to do with carelessness. I think I lost something by my precision for, gradually, I have come to see that there are as many connections between the literal and the metaphorical depictions of personality as there are discrepancies. It is very hard to state a general principle upon which these connections might rest and, in this respect, the notion of synchronicity is particularly helpful. Equally relevant is what might be termed the *actuality of the metaphorical*. When the attributes of infancy are employed metaphorically to illumine adult behaviour, the *source* of the metaphor cannot be dismissed. Conversely, the content of metaphorical discourse about the infant has its own impact upon the 'real' infant in historical time – what Freud referred to as 'prophecy' (above). In a way, this suggestion is similar to the discovery in physics that mass and energy are interconvertible: mass standing here for the real infant, energy for the metaphorical infant. In the next chapter, a clinical model based on the actuality of the metaphorical is introduced together with several illustrations of its use in practice.

Let us now return to the topic of archetypal states of mind. One crucial difference between my use of 'archetypal state of mind' and Jung's use of 'complex' is that, in the former case, the possibility that one particular archetypal state of mind might function with the force and authority of the whole personality is taken for granted. From the standpoint of the theory of complexes, such a happening would be regarded as an overwhelming inflation. There is no question of the ego's identifying with an archetypal state of mind, or being unconscious of it, or projecting it, or confronting it – for the person is in it, rather than 'it' being within the person. An archetypal state of mind is conceived as overarching conventional divisions between ego and unconscious, health and pathology. Therapy itself may go on within an archetypal state of mind. To explore all these issues more thoroughly, I shall borrow the numbering approach of Rickman – oneness, twoness, threeness, fourness (this last not mentioned by him) (1951). We should remember the paradox that none of these psychologies is 'earlier' or 'later' than the others, though they can, of course, be depicted that way. Nor is one necessarily any more important for the destiny of an individual than any other. We are in the realm of the gods of the mind; just like the ancient gods, each archetypal state of mind struggles for supremacy but cannot completely annihilate the others. The idea that no one archetypal state of mind is developing into another does not rule out their mutual influence, nor should we overlook the possibility of their working harmoniously side by side.

The archetypal state of mind of *oneness* involves normal narcissism, religious states (oneness with God), nostalgia and creative reverie *as well as* psychosis (in which inner and outer are experienced as one), psychosomatic disorder (mind and body confused as one), and false self-organization – which is a response to invasions of oneness. Thus the state of oneness has its own identifiable pattern and psychology.

So does the state of *twoness*. In health, twoness concerns trust and relatedness, attachment and separation, the capacity to tolerate ambivalence and feel concern. A religious state of twoness implies the sense of having been created, beyond an omnipotent fantasy of having created self and world. Pathologically speaking, twoness dynamics characterizes the schizoid personality and depressive illness.

The archetypal state of mind of *threeness* involves emotional consequences of the differentiation of mother and father, the primal scene, and the Oedipus complex. In health: sexual expression, marriage, procreation, and the communal aspects of religious sensibility. Pathologically: perversion, morbid jealousy, actual incest, an overrigid superego, and certain sexual problems.

Fourness covers whatever it is that enables the four archetypal states of mind to coexist and work together (when they do). It may also be regarded as a form of oneness, as in the famous Axiom of the alchemist Maria Prophetissa: 'Out of the One comes Two, out of the Two comes Three, and from the Third comes One as the Fourth'. However, the integrative thrust of fourness gives it a somewhat different quality from the others (cf. Plaut 1973).

As far as clinical practice goes, an analyst may be able to relate any material to whatever archetypal state of mind or combination of archetypal states of mind seems relevant. For example, if a patient has difficulty in trusting other people, the analyst might *not* think in terms of the patient's relationship with his or her mother, or in terms of the here-and-now transference dynamic. Rather, what would be prominent in the analyst's thinking would be the connections, similarities, and discrepancies between the patient's current situation and the general themes of the archetypal state of mind of twoness, particularly the issue of trust, *just as these are depicted in the literature of developmental psychology.* Or, put another way, trust between an actual mother and infant is one example, a very important one, of the general twoness theme of trust. The mother–infant relationship is not necessarily the blueprint for trust.

Archetypal states of mind affect analytic interaction in that they colour the intersubjective field. Transference–countertransference phenomena can then be considered in relation to the particular archetypal state of mind *as well as* in relation to the patient's past patterns of relationships. The patient's memories or the analyst's reconstruction of the patient's past alert us to the general theme that is relevant. The patient and analyst explore that theme, especially in the transference–countertransference. The crucial question concerns what it is that analysts are doing when they explore the patient's past with her or him.

As I said at the start, the *content* of a synchronous model of development would cause no surprises. What is crucial is the pluralistic use to which existing knowledge may be put. In the rest of this chapter, attention will be paid to the issues that seem to me to be the most problematic but also (or perhaps because of that) to be the most interesting. These are (1) modes of experiencing archetypal states of mind, (2) the possibility of omitting chronology from developmental theory, and (3) how archetypal states of mind are organized and experienced.

Modes of experience

Whether archetypal states of mind are conceived of vertically, as herein, or employed, as they can be, in a linear or spiral vein, they have to have points or areas of contact with each other. To call these contact points 'transitions' runs the risk of suggesting an onwards movement towards a goal; that, as we have seen, is a valid description of events but not the one advanced here. Yet the idea of *transitional features in the quality of affect* is one that deserves to be retained. For instance, the transition between oneness and twoness may be discussed in a linear manner, in terms of the gradual disillusionment of the infant's omnipotent fantasies. Or the transition may be conceptualized synchronously in terms of an emotional interface between omnipotent illusions on the one hand and depending on someone on the other; an interface with which we are familiar. The developmental insight is upended so as to illumine a general, adult, affective situation.

However, because the transitional points express conflict between the various archetypal states of mind, they carry a greater-than-average psychological charge. Referring back to the discussion of the definition of 'archetypal' in terms of affect, the emotional situation at the point of transition between one archetypal state of mind and another is likely to be a prime location of the archetype. The archetype would exist in the cracks between the archetypal states of mind; the archetypal as a liminal, boundary phenomenon. In analysis, the analyst depends on what he or she relates to in the patient's affect to help orientate him/herself. If a patient becomes angry prior to the analyst's holiday break, it is the quality and tone of affect that facilitates the analyst's empathic response to the patient's anger. Is the patient angry at the sudden destruction of an omnipotent fantasy in which the analyst simply does not exist? If so, then it is the puncturing of oneness by the holiday break that seeks a response. Or perhaps the patient cannot see how he or she can cope with the absence of the analyst, and feels let down and abandoned. In that case, the anger is the anger of twoness, of injured trust and dependence-gone-wrong. The patient might be jealous of the person with whom it is imagined the analyst will spend the holiday; such feelings have the stamp of threeness on them.

Maybe two or more of these possibilities can be true at the same time. The patient may feel more comfortable dealing with his emotion in one way than in another, so that the true state of affairs is disguised. It may be preferable to communicate a sense of abandonment to admitting to jealousy, for instance. So what we refer to as conflict between the archetypal states of mind also reflects the patient's unconscious preferences, defensive organization, and self-image.

Certain problems such as sexual difficulties often inhabit more than one archetypal state of mind. Psychosexual disorders may demonstrate a narcissistic personality style, with an absence of whole-person relating. Yet fantasies of being suffocated or swallowed or lacerated speak of problems with and in twoness. Sexual inhibitions and sexualized rage will have oedipal aspects. It is clinically helpful to be able to review such possibilities, not in a particularly systematic way, but as part of an overall analytic attitude to the patient. Whether working with sexual problems or the consequences of holiday breaks, the analyst uses his

31

reactiveness to the patient to learn from him or her which affect has been constellated by the interaction of archetypal states of mind.

Returning to the question of conflict between archetypal states of mind, it is possible to see how a particular archetypal state of mind can act as a hidden presence in another archetypal state of mind, subverting the intention of the 'official' state. A common example of this would be the presence of a twoness dynamic of relatedness and dependence at the heart of a fantasy or experience of oneness. From the *literal* point of view, we know that very early and active two-person relating exists alongside and in the midst of a solipsistic mental style that reflects the fantasies of having created the world and being at one with it. Zinkin (1979), following Buber, suggested that 'dialogue precedes self-awareness' and the question of whether an infant 'really' is fused with the mother causes much heat in developmental analytical psychology. Everything depends on the point of view: from inside, a good fit ensures fantasies and feelings of omnipotence and oneness with the environment. From outside, intense proto-conversation is taking place from, or even from before birth.

It may be that any one archetypal state of mind contains all the others, and even that the apparent existence of separate archetypal states of mind is itself illusory, there being only undivided experience itself. But even if there is something indivisible and complete, which we call experience, we have still to account for our tendency to experience things in a partial, diverse, and affect-laden way. Indeed, even when 'wholeness' is experienced in a mystical manner, the tone varies from mystic to mystic: there are mysticisms of oneness, or twoness, and of threeness. (See Chapter 9 for an exposition of a 'mysticism of persons'.) If diversity were not a fact, then not only would a person have only one experience, we would all have the same experience.

Issues like this form the body of the philosopher Michael Oakeshott's book *Experience and its Modes* (1933). Oakeshott was puzzled by the coexistence of experience as something complete, concrete, and coherent together with 'modes' of experience, inherently partial, which constitute autonomous 'worlds of ideas'. He speaks of an 'arrest' of experience, meaning by that something very close to an archetypal state of mind: an overall tendency to experience things in a certain way. Oakeshott was adamant that a mode of experience is not 'an island in the sea of experience' (p. 71), meaning a limited kind of experience. Rather, a mode of experience is the whole of experience experienced from a particular standpoint. In Oakeshott's project, the particular standpoints are those of different intellectual disciplines, such as science, history, philosophy. For us, the different standpoints are the different archetypal states of mind.

This differs from perspectivalism by virtue of the feeling of completeness engendered by an archetypal state of mind, such completeness aided by the postulate that *all* archetypal states of mind are always in some kind of coexistence. A perspectival approach explicitly ignores the fact that there may be some connection between the perspectives. Here we may see the value in James's paean to the word 'some' (see pp. 7-8, above). Each archetypal state of mind is in *some* way connected to, or involved with the others. That the connections and involvements have a substance and importance is shown in our capacity and desire to experience our personality as a whole. What usually happens is that the struggle between archetypal states of mind is resolved in favour of the state that provides the most complete experience, that is the closest approximation to experience-as-a-whole. Walzer's (1983) comment (see pp. 12-13, above) that justice consists of respect for the values of separate spheres of life comes to mind here and the fate of the apparently 'defeated' states is something that might usefully be explored at a future point.

Neither Oakeshott's 'modes of experience' nor my 'archetypal states of mind' can be organized in a hierarchy so that one may be claimed to be primary or fundamental, either chronologically or experientially. The task of pluralistic philosophy or psychology is to hold the modes in some relation to each other, permitting dialogue between them. What is more, the diverse states or modes are not the result of diverse human faculties or typologies in that all human faculties are involved in any one mode of experience or archetypal state of mind.

It follows that we do not analyse infancy solely because it is, or may be causally primary. Why do we do it at all? Because archetypal themes of the *conditio humana* are most clearly visible when socialization is at its least evolved level. But if analysts take the events of infancy overliterally, then they may be regarded as having trapped themselves in the archetypal state of mind of twoness. Overliteralism is a sign of depressive illness, in which there is a concrete apperception of fantasy upon which harsh self-judgements are based. As depression is part of the phenomenology of twoness, it may be that the psychological perspective of twoness dominates our developmental psychology if and when we take that psychology too literally (Kugler, personal communication 1985). When oneness (or any psychological idea for that matter) is taken overliterally, then it is being looked at with a depressed eye, with the prejudices of twoness.

It is essential to retain the links to pathology that are present in the various archetypal states of mind. Freud noted that psychoanalysis (and analytical psychology, in my view) cannot privilege any of the three endeavours of which it consists: an investigation of unconscious life, a body of theoretical knowledge, and, crucially for our purposes here, a means of treatment. Central to cementing this tripartite division into a whole is the typical move in depth psychology from a consideration of the *pathological*, the abnormal, what lies in illness, to the implications of that on a more general scale. Paradoxically, the individual case is a more profound and coherent phenomenon than the general description. The case contains the norm. That is why depth psychology uses material from patients with difficult, traumatic, or unusual backgrounds so as to highlight issues relevant to all.

Using the notion of archetypal states of mind enables us to engage with the pathological and to grasp the similar dynamics of apparently dissimilar psychological behaviour. The narcissistic person who is obsessed with being left out of things (and hence attains popular acceptance) and the depressed person who feels punished and rejected (whose behaviour compulsively provokes a repetition of such rejection) are both revealed as sharing in the same pool of psychological characteristics. So, too, is the complacent person who knows, or thinks he knows, that he belongs, no question of it (and hence is content to let his personal identity be submerged in a group, a relationship, an ideology, a career). The usefulness of a capacious concept like an archetypal state of mind is that all these depictions may be held together.

If we do not regard adult psychological behaviour as solely and literally derived from infancy, is there a place from whence we might regard it as springing? In biology, Rupert Sheldrake has introduced the idea of morphogenetic fields to explain the evolution of living organisms. Though controversial, his theory has aroused great interest. Creatures 'pick up influences coming from outside them, rather like TV transmissions. To be tuned into these transmissions, the organism has to have the right genetic material....These morphogenetic fields may be distant in time as well as space. They are a transmission from the actual forms of past members of a given species' (Sheldrake 1985: 195). Sheldrake calls the means by which this happens 'morphic resonance'. His further suggestion is that a person's memory may be formed out of morphic resonances between past event and brain, rather than being stored in the brain.

It is possible to speculate that psychological behaviour as we observe it in an individual may have evolved by morphic resonance from previous behaviours of individuals in the past (i.e. vertically), rather than out of personal, infantile determinants (i.e. horizontally). Here the designation of *archetypal* states of mind is important with the connotation that such states have always existed, indeed are a *sine qua non* of being human. Let us take the mid-life crisis as an example. Instead of envisioning this solely as the product of a developmental process, a point on a line of development, we can think as well in terms of an individual's mid-life crisis resonating with all the other mid-life crises there have ever been – sitting, as it were, on top of a huge pile of mid-life crises.

The bonus of establishing a synchronous model of personality development on a sound basis is that *it enables us to have another look at deterministic, causal, reductionist, positivist attitudes to development.* Rycroft (1972: ix) states that he and others have long wondered 'whether it is really possible to maintain that human behaviour has causes in the sense that physical phenomena do or that human personality can really be explained as the result of events that happened to it as a child'. As I pointed out in *Jung and the Post-Jungians* (Samuels 1985a), Jung's critique of what he saw as Freudian reductionism anticipated the growing doubts within psychoanalysis, though teleology does not seem to have interested many (any?) psychoanalysts. By now, it is almost impossible for an analyst of any sophistication to confess to being causally deterministic. Rather, the discourse is of patterns and connections, of hermeneutics, and of linkage via meaning. The main problem with causality is that *causality cannot be wrong* – in Freud's words, it is a retrospective prophecy. If one is looking for infantile causes of adult states, then one will find them. For the adult states decree what infantile states there should have been in order for them (that is, the adult states) to come into being. What many modern analysts cannot stomach is the self-deception and the deception of patients involved when it is claimed that the past 'causes' the present in some kind of 'scientific' manner. *But I am wondering if perhaps we have lost something by this intellectual fashion to be wary of causality.* If the synchronous/vertical model were to be more securely established, then we would have something with which to balance causalistic accounts of personality development. If we want to couple synchronous-acausal models with diachronic-causal models, then *both* ends of the seesaw must be occupied by theories of equal weight. At the moment we are handicapped in that the synchronous model is not well worked out and hence a causal model cannot be given its full-blooded extreme expression either, whether reductivist *or* teleological.

What if, having established a synchronous-acausal model, we once again give house-room to a thoroughly deterministic and causal model? Determinism implies the belief that everything that happens has a cause or causes and could only have happened differently if its causes had been different. Everyday life is only possible given the assumption that behaviour is determined by causes and that it is possible to find out what these causes are. We approach the behaviour of other people, in particular, in the strong belief that there must be a cause for it. As E.H. Carr points out, 'the logical dilemma about free will and determinism does not arise in real life. It is not that some human actions are free and others determined. The fact is that all human actions are both free and determined, according to the point of view from which one considers them' (Carr 1964: 95). Out of this defence of determinism, we may respect Padel's conviction, expressed in the paper referred to earlier (Padel 1985: 26) that it is 'inconceivable that what happened in a patient's past is not relevant to what he or she is experiencing now'. I think that the problem with determinism has been the tyrannical supremacy of chronological time. It is not surprising, then, that people became diffident about owning up to being deterministic. I have been illustrating ways in which the raw materials to effect a redress have been at hand for a long while and that analysts have taken up a wide range of positions in the spectrum. *The more comfortable we feel with a synchronous model, the better chance there is of effectively using a causal-deterministic one in tandem.* Then, as Powell has suggested, an inner dialogue is constellated in the analyst, a form of reverie allowing movements right across the board (personal communication, 1987). We need a time-free determinism.

Time and psychology

Questioning the primacy of clock time has become a cottage industry. Such questioning is part of a general revulsion in Western countries from the unwanted consequences of technology and industrialism and has led to an idealization of a concept of time derived from the perception of natural rhythms, the cycles of the planets, the changes of the seasons, and so forth. Such 'psychic time' is often portrayed as inimical to clock time and a split is thereby introduced. Certainly, the two broad approaches to time are quite different; can they simply be left in permanent opposition?

In this brief section the intent is to draw together some ideas about time which, taken as a whole, would enable us to undermine the role of chronology in an understanding of personality development to the extent that synchronous and diachronic perspectives would have a chance of co-existence. The background stems from physics (e.g. Davies 1984), psychology (e.g. von Franz 1978), and art (e.g. Baudson 1986).

Humanity displays a profound ambivalence about clock time. Though clock time often seems experience-distant, we use it in our practical lives, in art and in religion. Yet we clearly desire to transcend time in a search for immortality. It follows that even if a causally deterministic psychology could be *proven* accurate, it would still *feel* unsatisfactory and unsatisfying. This needs to be said as an antidote to the claim often made by clinicians (e.g. Fordham 1978: 125-9) that reconstruction of childhood experiences in analysis reduces anxiety in the patient and contributes to his or her discernment of meaning in life. The opposite is also true: chronologically oriented reconstructions contribute to anomie and a sense of powerlessness when the patient is confronted with what seem like inevitabilities in her or his neurosis. My proposal is not that analysts cease employing reconstruction but rather that they might also plug into general human ambivalence in relation to time.

An example of the ambivalence is the way memory is used to freeze the temporal past and, in particular, the part played by nostalgia in that (cf. Jacoby 1985; Peters 1985). Here, it is clearly an antipathy to clock time that we observe, employed both for creative and pathological purposes. Creative, in that nostalgic regression enables a person to renew her or himself; pathological, in that nostalgia often contains elements of over-control and character rigidity.

Analysts from Freud on have known that there is a form of time specific to the unconscious, mainly, but not exclusively, encountered in dreams. In dreams, time and space are often ignored and the same may be said of waking dreams and other kinds of fantasy. However, it seems to me that *the moment has been reached for the contradiction in depth psychology between its chronological models of personality development and its knowledge of unconscious time to be faced.* Events in other fields of knowledge may be brought in to help reflection on this hiccough between theory and method. For instance, recent developments in neurophysiology (e.g. Pribram 1971) have led to the proposal that what we perceive as solid reality is built up in the brain on holographic principles. Solid objects are registered by the brain as patterns composed of layer upon layer of waves. Objects vibrate or resonate in tune with the various receptors in the brain. Reality is conceived of as a harmonic arising out of this interaction. Now, if this is true of solid objects, it could also be true of a person's past, their so-called history. A person's perception of the past might also be regarded as a harmonic arising out of the interaction of past event and present perception.

It is interesting to think of the role of the eyes in this. Traditionally, in science and myth, the eyes are an input channel for the brain or psyche. But the eyes are, in many ways, an output channel, the means by which projections are conducted to, and placed in the external world. When we speak of the investment of the world with archetypal expectations, or of the *Ümwelt*, the subjectively perceived environment, or of the discernment of pattern in experiential raw material, or even of deintegration, we should not overlook the eyes as an output channel that facilitates all of these.

We know from a variety of sources that time is not a constant: time is not smooth, but jerky and unpredictable (quantum mechanics); time is experientially relative (the old joke about a five-minute kiss seeming to last for five seconds while holding one's hand in a flame for five seconds seems like five minutes); time can be created, as in the big bang theory; time can be destroyed, as in a black hole; time scales differ according to the 'clock' or 'calendar' being employed – from the Nine O'Clock News to the Age of Aquarius; time is not a unified entity – Kant referred to time in the sense of duration (an intuition) and time as a perspective (a conceptual category). J.B. Priestley suggested that there are at least three ways to represent time that are radically different from the linear narrative of clock time. The first was that, from any given moment, alternative pathways of events are open to a person or group. The story can proceed in parallel forms and, accordingly, have different endings. Second, there is serial time, as proposed by J.W. Dunne. 'On this theory of time we are each of us a series of observers in a corresponding series of times, and it is only as Observer One in Time One that we can be said to die, the subsequent observers being immortal. Mr Dunne had been led to work out this theory by his discovery, which I for one believe to be valid, that frequently in dreams the future is revealed to us' (Priestley 1947: viii). Finally, there is circular time, in which events in human history are sensed to recur.

Samuel Beckett also employs a 'theory' of time, but in a different way to Priestley. John Calder, Beckett's publisher, has suggested that when Beckett's characters invent ghosts or shades that will live on and remember them after death, or when they explore their memories in minute detail, this is his response to 'our fear of anonymity, of being born, going through the trauma of our life span, dying and being forgotten, all record of our having existed soon lost forever. We are more afraid of being forgotten than of dying' (Calder 1986: 13).

In his book *Time and Timelessness* (1983), Hartocollis suggests that, far from being a given or a constant, time shares the same matrices as emotional development generally. Unfulfilled needs in infancy, leading to anxiety and depression, usher in a sense of time. From the idea that time and emotional development enter the subjective world together, it follows that a person's sense of time is affected by his or her emotional condition. Hartocollis writes of the distinct temporal dislocations occurring in differing conditions, such as schizophrenia or borderline personality disorder. In this way, he contributes a voice from depth psychology to the chorus that time is relative.

Experience and organization: the imaginal network

In the previous chapter, I mentioned several problems with the notion of an underlying structure on which images 'hang'. The phenomenological content and specific implication of the image can be overlooked when it is placed in a hierarchy conditioned by what is regarded as the relative importance of the particular underlying structure. But if *structure* is found wanting as an explanation of the organization of images, we still need to detail what it is that enables them to cohere. To this end, I introduce the idea of an *imaginal network*. Any particular archetypal state of mind is formed by experience of some or all of the contents of the imaginal network.

The term imaginal may be unfamiliar. It was used by Corbin (1972) to mark out a place in psyche situated between primary sense impressions and more developed cognition or spirituality. This realm is populated by images and, in every respect, is an in-between state: between conscious and unconscious, between mind and body, and (as we shall see in detail in Chapter 9) between person and person. 'Imaginal' is used in preference to 'imaginary' to indicate a mode of being and perceiving and not an evaluation. There are broad similarities between this idea and Winnicott's 'third area', 'area of illusion', 'area of experience' (Winnicott 1974: 3). Significant differences are also discussed in Chapter 9. The imaginal world, or *mundus imaginalis*, is the locus of unconscious fantasy and archetypal imagery.

A network originally meant any work in which 'threads, wires or the like are arranged in the form of a net'. Modern usage is more complicated and requires a flexible grammar, for the noun is 'network', the verb 'to network' and the gerund 'networking'. In *The Networking Book* (1986), Lipnack and Stamps suggest several ideograms that capture the essence of network as the word is used in its contemporary social and organizational sense. As with pluralism, network offers us both a metaphor for personality and an instrument for monitoring activity within the personality. Once again, the political/social lexicon is relevant for depth psychology. According to Lipnack and Stamps, a network is:

- a physical system that looks like a tree or a grid
- a system of nodes and links
- a map of lines between points
- a persisting identity of relationships
- a badly knotted fishnet
- a structure that knows no bounds
- a nongeographic community
- a support system
- a lifeline
- everybody you know
- everybody you know who...swims, collects coins, sings in the

church choir, watches the children walk to school, reads
Teilhard de Chardin....

(Lipnack and Stamps 1986: 2)

Though networks such as the old boy network are well
known, what distinguishes the contemporary phenomenon of
networking amongst political and pressure groupings of all
kinds is the conscious use of it as an organizational device.
Networks are often described by the acronym SPIN: seg-
mented/polycephalous/ideological/network (Lipnack and Stamps
1986: 5). Unlike a bureaucracy, which collapses when one element
is removed, each segment of a network is organizationally
autonomous and survives the loss of other segments. The word
polycephalous, meaning many-headed, when applied to networks
suggests an organization of peers, or at least a leadership model of
the *primus inter pares* kind. That networks are ideological means
that they depend on a high degree of shared values. One last point
about networks is that they have fuzzy boundaries:

> Connections based on shared values are bound to wax and
> wane as circumstances change for individuals and society.
> Just as we cannot enumerate our personal network, which in
> any case would change by tomorrow, so a group network
> rarely knows the extent of its membership influence and
> resources.

(Lipnack and Stamps 1986: 7-8)

It is not hard to see how the psychology in and of this model of
social organization resonates with what has been proposed so far.
A pluralistic psychology is polycephalous; the moral factor
constantly intrudes; we never completely know the extent of our
inner 'membership, influence and resources' – they are
unconscious. But how can the idea of a network be applied to
images? And, thence, to the nature of personality itself? First, we
have to look at what we mean by image.

A great deal has been written about images, what they are, how
to conceptualize our experience of them, and how to use them in
therapy. There seem to be three major definitional strands:

(1) Images as the mental counterpart (and evoking the goal, in
   Jungian parlance) of senses – sight, hearing, smell, etc. – and

41

instincts – sexuality, morality, spirituality, aggression, and so forth. This would include the unconscious imagery of unconscious fantasy (see pp. 45-6, below).

(2) Imagery as an intervening factor between input and stimulus from the external world on the one hand and, on the other, the subject's output and response. In this definition of it, the image is a hypothetical construct required by the fact that psychological inputs and stimuli differ from outputs and responses. *Something* has to account for the difference.

(3) Imagery as *promoting* feelings, behaviour, and bodily sensations that may occur in the absence of any other direct stimulus save the image. That is, phenomena come into being as if they were the result of direct stimuli but there are no such stimuli present.

It is this last angle on imagery that I want to pursue – the autonomous and self-sustaining nature of imagery, and it departs from the first two definitions by virtue of the creative potency assigned to the image. Images cease to be regarded as psychological analogues of anything (such as instincts), secondary, coded versions of feelings, experiences, and behaviours. Instead, their *transitivity* is highlighted – the capacity of images to make or construct other images, thus crafting experience without direct contact with external stimuli. (Which is not to overlook imagery as functioning in the way suggested in definitions (1) and (2); all three modes could function at the same time.) Transitivity may be possessed by an image to a greater or lesser degree so that it is possible to talk of transitive, less transitive, and intransitive images. A highly transitive image functions as if it had, or were, a transitivity field, operating at a distance and having influence far beyond what is apparent. The term 'transitivity' derives from grammar and therefore its use is more than fortuitous. For if, as Lacan says, the unconscious is structured like a language, then its grammar has to be elucidated.

This particular approach to imagery sheds interesting light on the connections between images and personal relations encountered in analysis. What is the function of the 'other' in terms of the development of imagery? The human psyche needs the other to carry its images in a projected form. Thus people (and objects, for that matter) are sucked into the world of imagery. This is not to deny the reverse process in which aspects of relationship are best expressed, or can only be expressed in imagery. But my concern is with the tendency to meet one's inner world in one's images of persons. For example, a patient of mine generated an image that we called 'the Stone Mother'. This referred to her inner experience of her actual mother and also to her own stony, omnipotent side. (Chapter 3 is devoted to an exploration of the connections between images of persons, specifically parents, and internal dynamics.)

Similar connections can be delineated between imagery and emotion. Causal thinking usually gives a primacy to emotion. We think of this happening in a pictorial, painterly way: you have a strong *emotion* about someone or something that then generates an *image* of them that forms like a painting in the mind's eye. Or a dream image of a person may be interpreted in terms of the affect that is generally aroused by that person. But here again our understanding can be reversed so that it is an image that is seen as powering the feeling, such image not necessarily 'coming from' anywhere.

Analytical concern with imagery arose from this realization that portrayals of 'people' in clinical material were of a symbolic nature. Elsewhere (Samuels 1985a: 118-120), I suggested that there have been two major conceptual shifts in analytical psychology: from a focus on signs (Freud) to symbols (Jung) and then from symbols to images (Hillman), this latter formulation being remarkably similar to Fordham's, allegedly its conceptual opponent. Both Hillman and Fordham are against any preconceived dictionary of instant interpretations, something that both felt had invaded Jungian methodology by the 1960s. Both were aware that the pioneering work that Jung and Freud had done was something of a handicap for depth psychology, particularly if, by regularly abstracting symbols from images, image got lost. For present-day analysts, the symbol is not as momentous as it once was. In Hillman's words, symbols have become 'stand-ins for concepts' (Hillman 1977: 68). It seems to me that the followers of Fordham and Hillman have neglected to bear in mind that there is a necessary balance and interplay between literal personages and autonomous images: the Developmental School overstressing the former and the Archetypal School the latter (and see Chapter 8).

Jung pointed out that what we experience and perceive is not 'reality' but images:

Far too little in theory, and almost never in practice, do we remember that consciousness has no direct relation to any material objects. We perceive nothing but images,

43

transmitted to us indirectly by a complicated nervous apparatus. The consequence of this is that what appears to us as immediate reality consists of carefully processed images, and that, furthermore, we live immediately only in a world of images .... Far, therefore, from being a material world, this is a psychic world, which allows us to make only indirect and hypothetical inferences about the real nature of matter. The psychic alone has immediate reality, and this includes all forms of the psychic, even 'unreal' ideas and thoughts which refer to nothing external. We may call them 'imagination' or 'delusions', but that does not detract in any way from their effectiveness.

(*CW* 8: paras 382-3)

Jung is saying that we experience *reality* indirectly. However, I do not agree with the implication that we experience *imagery* directly (*CW* 8: para. 497). It seems to me that, for once, Jung is overvaluing the ego when he allows for the possibility that experience of images can be direct. For the ego changes its position as it confronts shifting patterns of imagery. It is subject to the differing archetypal states of mind as much as standing in relation to them. The ego experiences through and in images. It is not a case of a single, fixed, stable, observational point in apposition to a moving, unpredictable world; consciousness is as labile as its objects. What is more, the question of whether ego consciousness is truly the only form of consciousness remains open: we speak of body consciousness, self consciousness, even of anima consciousness.

Nevertheless, Jung's idea that *reality is apprehended in images* is strengthened and not weakened by developments in neurophysiology, and particularly by what is now known about pain, seemingly the most direct of all bodily realities. The gate-control theory of pain is a suggestion about the way in which the nerve impulses reaching the spinal cord interact with other nerve impulses and are controlled by further impulses that descend from the brain. The hypothesis was that 'somatic input is subjected to the modulating influence of the gate before it evokes pain perception and response' (Melzack and Wall 1982: 272). The gate-control theory was welcomed by physicians who knew that pain did not behave as it 'should' and by psychologists who knew that pain has its cultural and personal dimensions. Above all, 'the transmission of pain signals to the brain was no longer restricted to a single pathway and it became possible to speculate on the functional relations of any different ascending and descending systems' (Melzack and Wall 1982: 240).

I have quoted from the work of Professors Melzack and Wall, pioneers of pain theory, because of the need to emphasize that the indirectness of perception and experience, and its typical portage via imagery, does not imply a downgrading of the body – anatomy, physiology, medicine. Indeed, as Achterberg (1985) has shown, there is now a vast body of literature attesting to the overlap and interpenetration of body and image. That bodily sensations are also images is a theme that runs through this book and, indeed, is an extension of what Jung intuited when he introduced the concept of the psychoid unconscious: a level of reality in which the psychological and the physiological, and even the inorganic, are alternative aspects of each other (see Chapters 8, 9 and 10).

The necessary indirectness of the imaginal world has always been known to mystics. Meister Eckhart:

> Every time that the powers of the soul come into contact with created things, they receive the *created* images and likenesses from the created images and absorb them. In this way arises the soul's knowledge of created things. Created things cannot come nearer to the soul than this, and the soul can only approach created things by the voluntary reception of images. And it is through the presence of the image that the soul approaches the created world: for the *image is a Thing which the soul creates* with her own powers. Does the soul want to know the nature of a stone – a horse – a man? She forms an image.
>
> (quoted in Underhill 1961: 6)

Achterberg points out that the indirectness of imagery, what she calls its 'invisibility', puts it in the very good company of other great issues: 'learning, motivation, memory and perception.... Even though one cannot observe "learning" or "motivation", but only changes in behaviour as a predictable consequence of some stimulus, laws have been developed to describe how these factors operate' (Achterberg 1985: 144).

This remark of Achterberg's leads us to consider the questions of unconscious imagery in general and nonfigurative imagery in particular, for both of these are invisible to the consciousness of subject and observer alike. These issues are important for the idea of the imaginal network because of the need to go beyond what is consciously known and not to be confined by what can be portrayed in images derived from real life. Clearly, we are affected by images of which we are not conscious, and it is probable, or even likely, that the contents of unconscious fantasy do not adhere to formal pictorial conventions. If we were to ask what such imagery 'looks like', we would be asking altogether the wrong question, thereby making imagery an analogue of something, as in the first definition mentioned earlier. This is what the Kleinians have done by asserting the bodily cast of unconscious imagery and fantasy. They *seem* to be on safe ground, and it is true that they have fleshed out one segment of the imaginal network. But it is a highly spasmodic, partial, and challengeable version of imagery, *still following the pictorial painterly conventions*. Images need not be 'like' anything. We only know of the presence of the imaginal network from its actions, and we only know its actions from our being disturbed by them and their contribution to our archetypal states of mind.

The art critic Adrian Stokes addressed this problem of unconscious imagery. He wrote of a 'representation or imagery...[where] likenesses are not involved' (Stokes 1972: 123). Further, according to Stokes, the work of art is 'a strait-jacket in regard to the eventual images it is most likely to induce' (p. 124). This insight (actually from a Kleinian source) can be claimed for a deliteralized developmental psychology in which the zones, phases, stages, and areas are regarded with an imaginative appreciation of the emotions involved so that they do not become strait-jackets. But, at *the same time*, the zones, stages, phases, and areas have also to be taken literally. For there are *some* links between the literal and the metaphorical ways of seeing things in developmental psychology.

In a letter to a friend, written in 1933, Picasso wrote that:

> There is no abstract art. You must always start with something. Afterward you can remove all traces of reality. There's no danger then, anyway, because the idea of the object will have left an indelible mark. It is what started the artist off, excited his ideas, and stirred up his emotions. Ideas and emotions will in the end be prisoners in his work. Whatever they do they can't escape from the picture. They form an integral part of it, even when their presence is no longer discernible.
>
> (quoted in Cooper and Tinterow 1983: 266)

What could be a better expression of the relation between the literal terminology of developmental psychology and its metaphorical nature and usage? As I said earlier, metaphor cannot be divorced from the roots of its content even though those contents have been absorbed into a wider and less literal understanding – in Picasso's words, become 'prisoners in the work'.

If we are to achieve an articulation of the literal and metaphorical approaches to developmental psychology, it will have to be by means of a simultaneous apperception of them, leading to the possibility of their joint use. Simultaneity of perception was something that fascinated the cubists. Braque and Picasso developed a way of representing three-dimensional figures and objects (the literal) in two-dimensional terms (the metaphorical) while providing, 'without recourse to illusion, a true depiction of the space involved' (Cooper and Tinterow 1983: 84). They did this, as they stated in 1911, by shifting from a perceptual to a conceptual approach to reality. 'Figures and objects are analysed into a succession of facetted shapes which, individually, serve no descriptive purpose, though when assembled in an organised manner they evoke a figure or an object seen from several points of view' (Cooper and Tinterow 1983: 13). In these senses, cubism was also attempting a pluralist grasp on reality, working with the literal and the metaphorical aspects of that reality. Serendipitously, Juan Gris referred to cubism, not as a 'manner', but as 'a state of mind'.

3

Parental images and the self-monitoring psyche

This chapter takes up the concern of the last one with metaphorical interpretation of developmental material – in particular, parental images. The overall idea is that parental images may be understood as a form of self-monitoring, even of self-diagnosis, generated by the patient's psyche and communicated to him or her (and to the analyst). Although the suggestions about parental imagery are presented in an orderly way, this is *not* intended to be a systematic and comprehensive presentation. The ideas arose pragmatically, and then, when I had developed a pragmatic model, I could see how it connected with a good deal of theory that is well known. So these are clinically based theoretical speculations.

As I said in the previous chapter, I am less interested in the undeniably important personal/archetypal division in terms of understanding parental imagery than I am in the literal/ metaphorical division. Images, narratives, and memories of the actual parents *are* an inextricable mixture of the personal and archetypal. However, the metaphorical approach (that images of the literal parents refer to the individual in some way) is also something that is basic to analytical psychology. But the lack of detail about this intrigues me. In order fully to understand parental imagery, we have to consider its function and *telos*.

I do not mean to propose that what follows might replace the reconstruction of the patient's infantile relationships, or to overlook the fact that parental images that crop up in analysis may be the outcome of the transference–countertransference relationship. Nor am I forgetting the possibility that parental figures, in dreams perhaps, may be understood as representing parts of the self. I am suggesting that parental images, images of the real parents, may be understood as autonomous contents (or figures) of the unconscious, not necessarily referring to specific elements in psychic structure. The parental images bear unconscious contents for the individual to face rather than merely representing something. If this is so, then, in Jung's words, 'the essential thing is to differentiate oneself from these unconscious contents by personifying them, and at the same time to bring them into relationship with consciousness....It is not too difficult to personify them, as they always possess a certain degree of autonomy of their own' (Jung 1963: 211). Now Jung was referring to his own images at the time of his confrontation with the unconscious in 1913-14, the great images of Philemon, Salome, Elijah, and so forth. But it seems to me a great pity to confine this perspective on personified imagery to large and fascinating images. My suggestion in this chapter is that exactly the same approach can be taken to quite ordinary analytical material concerning the parents (likely, anyway, to be large figures for the individual) without losing the value of the other approaches. Just as synchrony cleared a space for diachrony, so what is being sketched here respects other points of view whilst adding a further range of possibilities. I should add that I am not sure to what extent these ideas apply outside of analysis. My observations were made in the analytical setting so I can only speculate about whether one's everyday thoughts and images of one's parents are things which, in Jung's words, 'produce themselves and have their own life' (Jung 1963: 207).

(1) What is described to the analyst as a negative parental attribute or aspect can be understood as representing something positive that the individual needs to develop in him or herself, or possibly as a kind of unconscious agenda, suggesting emotional difficulties that need to be worked on in analysis. If a passive man talks about a negative, aggressive father, it is possible to strip away the negative connotation the patient or the analyst might give to aggression. The negative aspects of aggression are not denied, indeed they may be worked with in many ways that are familiar. But an additional understanding involves looking at the quality the patient describes *as if it were part of a text.* Then we might say: does the fact that the patient is talking about an aggressive father to the analyst suggest something in addition to the transference about what the focus of the work might be. The patient's psyche is setting its own agenda and the parents are its messengers.

This could be seen as a special example of what we know about shadow projections – that they often carry something of value for the individual. My suggestion is that the negative attributes of images of mother and father, about which we hear a good deal during analysis, are functioning as a form of guidance for the progress of the analysis as a whole. The parental images are self-generated *monitoring* images, *diagnostic* images. This does not imply something precise or dogmatic, to be followed to the letter, but rather a suggestion of a whole range of possibilities. The images still refer to parents (personal and archetypal factors being mixed). But there is this extra self-monitoring dimension. So when the patient dreams of a parent figure with a certain negative quality, as well as thinking in terms of transference, the analyst might wonder what would happen if the negativity were to be suspended temporarily and explore the resultant agenda with the patient.

(2) Parental imagery also tells the analyst something about the individual's parenting capacity, broadly conceived. I do not simply mean the ways in which her or his capacity to be a real parent and to have children reflect how she or he was parented, though that comes into it. I mean the individual's whole eros-attitude, or lack of it – their whole 'therapeutic' attitude to the world, including themselves. I am referring to self-parenting and also to genuine relationship capacities, to political views and attitude to the environment, to a general level of humanity or humanitarianism. All these are somehow encapsulated in metaphorical form in what the patient relates to the analyst about the parents he has experienced in his life. This could be a reason why the images everyone has of his or her parents, even when they are dead, change so much in the course of an analysis. It is not just because patients forgive their parents or see their parents' better side or understand what they have projected onto them. The parents the patient tells the analyst about are also representative of all those aspects of 'parenting' mentioned just now. As this process evolves and is enhanced in analysis, so the images of the parents come to seem more positive, more and more rounded, more and more like real people. In addition, idealized positive images may shift towards a more ambivalent tone.

As with the previous hypothesis, certain theoretical notions are relevant, though, once again, the theory followed on the clinical experience. In 1975, Searles wrote a paper called 'The patient as therapist of his analyst'. The argument can briefly be summarized: an inalienable part of being human is to be a 'therapist'. Neurosis and psychosis involve different degrees of damage to that human capacity. A neurotic or psychotic is damaged in the ways we know of but, in addition, the capacity to be a therapist is damaged. It follows that the healing of a mentally ill person requires that the patient work on and improve the capacity to be a therapist – what I am referring to as the parenting capacity and see as represented in parental imagery. Searles suggests that the patient can help the analyst to be a better parent for him and hence to be a better analyst. In analysis, there is only one person on whom the patient can practise his or her capacity to be a therapist – namely the analyst. A crucial part of 'getting better' is for the patient to be a therapist to the analyst. Here, 'good object relations' are expressed in terms of caring for people, which is one parenting capacity referred to in parental imagery: the kind of parent that is imaged suggests the level of parenting (therapeutic) ability possessed by the patient. I suppose that being able to control compulsive urges to parent others is also a part of personal growth.

A further theoretical consideration concerns the image of the 'Wounded Healer' (Guggenbühl-Craig 1971; Samuels 1985a: 187-91). Again, this can briefly be summarized: what often happens in life is that the wounded and the healing/healthy parts of the personality are split off from each other. In a sense, this is how we reach a situation wherein there are patients and analysts as separate classes of persons – patients are officially wounded and analysts are officially healed. Of course, every analyst knows that in addition she or he has been wounded. The patient, on the other hand, is wounded, but also has a healthy element and a capacity to be a healer (compare with Searles – in both theories, healing and health are more or less synonymous). Looked at from this perspective, what happens in analysis is that gradually and implicitly the analyst's wounds come more and more into the foreground, as an inevitable counterpoint to a strengthening of the patient's healthy/healer side. So both analyst and patient are re-constituting within themselves the image of the Wounded Healer in its complete form. Both analyst and patient may be said to be relating to this unified image of the Wounded Healer as well as to each other.

What is important from the clinical angle is the way in which the patient's psyche selects parental imagery from the imaginal network to inform the analyst (and the patient) about how they are progressing in terms of bringing the split between health and wound together and, in particular, the level of 'parenting' of which the patient is capable. If the patient describes a parent in positive terms, then he or she may also be referring to the capacity to be such a parent – to self, others, and the environment. Therefore, when things are going generally well in analysis, we would expect to hear ambivalent reports about parental attributes and characteristics, speaking of the patient's struggle to develop object relating and concern.

(3) This last hypothesis has to do with the primal scene and primal-scene imagery and will be stated rather briefly because the topic is taken up at length in Chapter 8, which is devoted to it.

Here, I want to suggest that primal-scene imagery functions as a kind of psychic fingerprint or trademark. How the patient images the parents together, or how coupledom in general is envisaged (not forgetting the analytic dyad itself), are excellent indicators of the state of play or overall situation in the patient's psyche at any one time. This can be harmonious, disharmonious, one side dominating the other, one side damaging the other, patterns of exclusion, triumph, defeat, curiosity, or total denial – all the great primal-scene themes, in other words. All these are telling analyst and patient something about that overall internal situation. The primal scene is *a self-generated diagnostic monitoring of the person's character at any moment*. That is why images and assessments of the parental marriage change so much in the course of an analysis. The parental marriage is not what changes in the majority of instances. Nor is it merely an increase in consciousness on the part of the patient that makes the image change. The image changes because the patient's inner style and attitude are changing. And the specificity of the image communicates what that style might be.

In Chapter 8, I have tried to work out in more detail what kinds of primal-scene imagery refer to particular strands of psychopathology in the patient. As I said at the outset, this chapter is not intended to be a systematic or all-embracing theory. Rather, it is essentially a form of clinical pragmatism, designed to be used alongside other models. However, just to give a general example, if a person has a bland, sexless image of their parents together, then this reflects something about that person as a whole, their awareness of their own conflicts; their entire psychic style is encapsulated in the primal-scene image. My intention is to draw attention to the possibility that a variety of different meanings (or even different *kinds* of meanings) are locked into parental imagery.

Before making some suggestions as to why these three propositions 'work' – that is, have clinical value – I would like to give two skeletal illustrations of the phenomena and processes I am describing. Later in the chapter, there are numerous further illustrations.

An analyst presenting her case at a workshop led by me on the theme of 'Working with parental images' said 'I never know whether I'm going to see this patient because the father agreed to pay for the analysis but keeps reneging on his promise. He keeps reneging on the deal.' Now, this was a warm-up statement to what she intended to present. Consciously she did not regard this as a part of her presentation. For she hadn't seen this as parental *imagery* at all, but rather as a fact, a simple, literal fact. Of course, it probably was a fact, and even true. The father had agreed to pay but reneged on the deal. But using the ideas outlined above threw up all sorts of possibilities in the *image* of a father who reneged on a deal. Was the patient trying to get out of a lousy deal *she* had made, or was she overcommitted and should renege to lighten her load, or did she have to resist the temptation to renege on a deal, or was there a deal she should now renege on? What kind of a deal had she done or tried to do with herself that was now in danger of being reneged on? Or, using the second of the three hypotheses, wherein parental images refer to parenting/therapeutic capacities, we could ask what kind of a 'therapist' is it who reneges on deals? It turned out to be a rich example even though it was not intended to be one. And an understanding in terms of transference–countertransference dynamics was by no means ruled out – rather, such an understanding was enhanced. What is significant about the example is that the account was absolutely factual but *at the same time* a metaphorical interpretation was extremely useful.

Another broad illustration is probably more controversial. If the patient is talking about a sexually abusing parent, the reference might *also* be to the patient's own sexual attitudes; for example, their need more often to take the initiative in sex or to enact their sexual fantasies to a greater degree. There is no need to rule out the actuality of incest or ignore the destructiveness in order to reach its symbolic layers (see Chapters 5 and 10). In terms of self-monitoring, perhaps the patient's psyche is suggesting that the patient needs to cross some kind of taboo line, maybe not in the sexual area at all. We strip away negative value judgement and feeling and regard the imagery from the standpoint of what it is that the patient might have to work on in analysis. Similarly, talk of a sexually abusing parent could be regarded as setting an agenda in terms of countering exploitation, correcting misuse of power, mix-ups between power and sex, and so forth. I am suggesting that we do not confine ourselves to working on the negative feelings the patient has about the parent; the pain, misery, distress, and anger. However, there is a risk that a more metaphorical understanding could lead to a collusive denial of such feelings. Assuming that the analyst feels reasonably sure that this is not the case, then the extra dimension concerns what the psyche is trying to tell us by giving us this particular image. As I said in the last chapter, the literal and metaphorical perspectives can coexist in the analyst's mind as well as compete for interpretive primacy therein.

The giving and receiving of plural interpretations is a highly problematic technical issue. It may be that the differing interpretive views will have to be spaced out over time so as to make their assimilation easier. On the other hand, the impact of interpretation is on an inner-world level and not through intellectual understanding. It is difficult to see how such impact would be interfered with if an interpretation were plural in nature. Unless the unconscious can only deal with clear-cut messages. The difficulty that may exist with plural interpretation could be more to do with adherence to what are felt to be the technical rules of analysis. We might also recall E.H. Carr's comment, mentioned in the previous chapter, that, for a historian, whatever he offers as an interpretation of events is always the outcome of the establishment of a hierarchy of interpretations. Note that Carr is not going on to say that all interpretations save the main one are discarded. So, to an extent, all interpretation is plural interpretation.

It is often possible for the analyst to make her or his uncertainty or multiplicity of viewpoints the central plank of an interpretation and, methodologically speaking, this may be more satisfactory than crudely offering the patient several options and letting him or her choose! Many single-strand interpretations are themselves concerned with intrapsychic conflict and internal dissension; in such cases, plural interpretation may be stylistically closer to many-layered psychic reality. The risk of intellectualizing need be no greater than with single-strand interpretation, and could even be less.

The weakness of plural interpretation is undoubtedly that it could degenerate into infinite and unreal tolerance and acceptance of any viewpoint whatsoever. But, as I argued in Chapter 1, it is as possible to experience a charge from the plural (tolerant) as it is from the singular (incisive). In any case, we would hardly want *all* interpretation to be plural or, conversely, to have to give up the chance of making a different interpretation of the same material in another session.

To conclude these brief remarks on plural interpretation, I would like to speculate as to the effect on the transference of making such interpretations. Negatively, the analyst may be seen as woolly, hedging his bets, not providing value for money, and so forth. More positively, the idea of analysis as a partnership would be promoted, without its acquiring a radiance of spurious equality or becoming a two-person discussion group.

We can now turn to a discussion of the reasons for the clinical validity of these hypotheses.

Although the capacity to have an internal life is inborn, much raw material for such inner life comes from the individual's first encounters with the outer world, which, to a great extent, means his or her parents. The dynamic between consciousness and the unconscious, which is common to all, means that from the earliest times the individual will, unconsciously, employ images stemming from relationships with the actual parents to carry parts of the psyche. The capacity to select and employ such images is a function of the self. Relations with parents become part of inner processes and, ultimately, part of the psychical apparatus – part of psychic structure. This sheds light on why the incest connection is potentially valuable as well as containing enormous dangers (as we shall see in Chapter 5). One function of sexuality in relationships is to make them psychologically important to the individuals concerned. Close physical relations with parents are necessary for the parents to become part of the inner growth and structure; sexuality fosters and facilitates that closeness. The overall reason why parental imagery performs this kind of monitoring, diagnostic function for the psyche is, then, *that it has always done so.*

This explains, to some extent, why a focus on parental imagery is justified. For it could be claimed that all imagery, and indeed, any manifestation of the unconscious, performs the same functions of self-monitoring and self-diagnosis. While this is true to a certain extent, I feel reasonably sure that there is something specifically self-referent in the monitoring/diagnostic sense about parental imagery. It follows that the imagery that concerns me the most is of the parent–child relationship.

The question is still left open of how it can be true that an account of a father who reneges on a deal is a factually true statement and yet has additional metaphorically derived meanings. Here, I do not think it sufficient to invoke the self as an organizing agency or principle. Rather, it is the psyche itself that is in action: a perspective on phenomena characterized by an attention to depth and intensity (see pp. 2-3, above).

Anyone who writes poetry or paints will have more than an inkling about it. As I suggested in the previous chapter, at the core of any metaphor there is something that is not part of the metaphor. It is used in the metaphor but it is not the metaphor itself. As Jung pointed out, the parents, who are real people, are used imaginally by the psyche to express itself in a metaphorical way (*CW* 5: para. 507). But, thinking of the psyche as a kind of poet or artist (*pace* Jung, who would not do it), the psyche cannot just switch off or disregard the raw material it has elected to use. If the psyche wants to communicate its inner state by means of parental imagery, it will do so. But what it cannot stop happening is the real parents shining through, as it were. The original literalism of the actual parents suffuses and infects the metaphor (Picasso's 'indelible mark'). The metaphor is thereby undermined. And the converse is also the case: all concrete, actual, literal, parental images have a metaphorical potential, waiting to be activated. Metaphor cannot divorce itself from its material; all material has an implicit metaphorical usage waiting to be discovered. All of this is also true for transference images: communications from the psyche that cannot be divorced from the raw material employed – in this case, the figure of the analyst.

En passant, we can see that the debate between Freud and Jung about the real or fantasized nature of primal imagery can never be conclusively resolved. For I am not saying that metaphor is more important than literalism. I am trying to demonstrate that they can function *at the same time*. The exciting aspect of this is that one is bringing together reductive and synthetic approaches to analysis – something Jung often *sought* to do (Samuels 1985a: 269-70). The means, theoretical and practical, by which such a twinning might be effected are not something Jung wrote much about.

A last clinical subtlety concerns the use in analysis of the analyst's countertransference imagery. As this is the subject of Chapter 9, I will make only a slight reference to it here. The kind of parent the analyst fantasizes him/herself to be for the patient – that is, the kind of parental image the patient constructs in the analyst – may also be subjected to the hermeneutic I am describing in the chapter. This would lead to understandings other than those couched in terms of projection of internal objects. Rather, the parental images constellated in the countertransference may also be looked at in terms of the psyche's self-monitoring: as agenda-setting, as evocative of the patient's parental/therapeutic capacities, or as depicting the situation in the psyche as a whole.

Clinical illustration

The following case illustration comes from another workshop on the theme of this chapter. It is extracted from the analyst's presentation that she had written out.

'G. was a borderline patient. In his first session he said it was his girlfriend who suggested he go into analysis since he was unable to hold onto the money he earned as a teacher. Within a few days he would spend it all on drinks, clothes, and luxury goods, alcohol, hashish, and cocaine. The patient was extremely greedy. When he took cocaine he was unable to stop until he had used it all up. So he would have to borrow money from his mother and aunts. His father would pay for his rent and basic expenses. G. said his father was violent, dictatorial, vulgar, a businessman whose only concern was making money. But, poor soul, he couldn't help it! Hence, G. was tolerant, ever so kind, friendly, gentle. He would never oppose other people, and he would not let himself get involved deeply in relationships.

In a dream, G. is admiring a gorgeous scarab. He would like to share that beautiful sight with his neighbour who is hugging him in a sadistic, crushing manner. The association is with his father – who is unable to recognise the beauty of life or its positive aspects; he is a violent man.

Later in the analysis, G. attempted suicide. When he came for his next session, I found myself giving him, with affectionate concern, an emotional picture of himself: all the anger, hatred, desire for revenge, and contempt for himself and others that must have driven him. Intuitively, I realised that this was the right course of action to take. So I let him know more than once how arrogant he was, and that nobody could possibly hurt him as much as himself.

Two dreams: (1) Two beds next to one another. I am in one, my father is in the other. He is the centre of attention. I feel overwhelmed and impotent. (2) My father tells me that my mother has cancer of the breast and uterus. I feel embarrassed and suspicious. It is as if he were saying that she is no longer any use to him on the sexual level.'

Who is the father that G. talks and dreams of? What happens if we treat him as an image, a metaphorical representation of certain aspects of G.'s psyche, even of psyche in general? What positive elements are projected into the father but subsequently described in negative terms? Aggression seems the obvious possibility – but this would have to be an aggression shorn of its penumbra of destructive and contemptuous tones. What G. seems to seek is a form of oedipal confrontation, other than merely spending and wasting his father's money.

The horrific primal-scene dream in which his mother is damaged by cancer and hence rejected as a sexual partner is important. True, it is a problematic fantasy that sex is destructive. But he is unconsciously owning his aggression and, now that the muddle between sexuality and aggression is revealed, maybe they can be disentangled.

The analyst felt herself to be acting as a sternly loving mother after G.'s suicide attempt. But in her confrontational style, and her admittedly fed-up attitude, she was responding to transference pressures to be a certain kind of father-figure for G. Here, the metaphor of parental image as representing a person's therapeutic/parental position is relevant in a strikingly concrete way: the analyst is modelling a parental attitude (i.e. attitude towards himself) that, by now, after some time in analysis, would be accessible to G.

Further illustrations

The next six examples have been transcribed from an audio recording of another workshop on the same theme. There is a uniformity in the material presented that may be accounted for by the operation of a kind of group associative process in which each case sparked off thoughts in the participants about cases of theirs that seemed similar. The structure of the workshop was that I gave an introductory presentation of these ideas and suggested that, rather than doing a form of overall supervision, which would scarcely be possible in the short time available, we should focus on trying to integrate the material of my presentation with the clinical material of the participants (who were not asked to prepare case material in advance). Readers will note how often I had to rein myself in and not shoot off into a more general (and probably deeper) discussion of the case. The advantage or these procedures was their permitting of a focus; the disadvantage, that many of the more profound analytic issues had to be overlooked.

Analyst A (female): What if the patient is talking about a priest rather than a father as such? I've got a new patient whom I've seen twice. She's a Catholic teaching in a Catholic school. She's been talking a lot about a relationship with a priest. The message she gives me is that she feels the priest has broken the seal of confession. It seems to be about whether what she's doing with me is confidential or not.

AS: Well, I'm sure you've thought of this in terms of transference already so I won't say much about that. I agree that the ideas I've outlined could work when the image is of a parent- figure rather than an actual parent. Let's look at this in terms of the priest's qualities being extracted from their matrix of feelings and value judgements. Now, breaking the seal of confession means talking to a third party about something you've heard in secrecy. It may well be that her unconscious is exploring whether *she* can tell you things told to her in confession *not* whether *you* can keep silent about things she tells you. Perhaps she needs to break secrecy about something, tell something to a third party, which hitherto she has been keeping behind the seal of confession.

Analyst B (female): I've got a patient whose father actually died when he was six. He finds it hard to have relationships. He's a bit of a *puer aeternus*. He seems to cut the father out completely. There's a lack of the erotic altogether. He always comes regularly to analysis but there's no relationship. He only relates on a social level. There's very much the lack of a parent there on almost every level.

AS: From a psychodynamic viewpoint, he hasn't internalized an image of his father. But if we look at this in terms of his style of relating to self and others, then we might be able to see in more detail how it is he cannot be a father to himself or to others.

Analyst B: Well, in terms of his attitude to the world there's something missing. He brought in two photographs of his father in the war.

AS: My idea might be useful here. Even though these are photos of a man who really existed, now we have some specificity for an *image* of the father – a military father.

Analyst B: It was rather a romantic soldier picture.

AS: Now we're beginning to get something about the precise missing qualities in this man. The father image is of a kind of warrior–hero. Perhaps a psychodynamic view would be that this is an idealization or persecuting ego-ideal which he cannot live up to. But what I would ask in addition is: what are the positive qualities of a warrior–hero? Without my being too scholarly about it, a warrior–hero is trying to get away from mother. Now we know that the warrior–hero can't really get away from mother but he's trying to do it. Maybe this is a bit of agenda-setting: separation issues. You said the man is a *puer*. One of the things about the *puer* is that sometimes he takes excessive risks (as does the warrior–hero). Perhaps where all this leads to is that this man needs to take a risk. Much as we despise martial and heroic qualities these days from a liberal point of view, these are perhaps what this chap has to work on, especially risk-taking.

Analyst C (male): A patient of mine is homosexual. In our second session he told me that he felt his mother would have been much better off if she had never married the husband (sic). He has no image of love or affection between the parents. The father actually died when he was 12 and he says his memory of his father is of feeling very uncomfortable when the father was close to him, just not liking it as a boy, being physically close to father. He says things like that when his father was still alive, his mother was able to earn more money than him.

AS: His split parents tell you something in detail about his split state. He's not only valuing one parent more than another but he's surreptitiously looking down on one parent. Saying I don't want to be physically close to father is one thing but then he compares the two parents: mother earns more, mother is more potent, mother shouldn't have married father, etc. He's saying father was a wet – is he putting down his own male potential? Maybe – but maybe there are qualities in the image of the father which haven't emerged yet which constitute an agenda for your work together. I was wondering if whether, by a kind of unconscious symmetry, the son who tries to avoid physical contact with the father brings into being, or constellates, a father (man) who *does* want physical contact with his inner son. Now that would be an agenda to work on....

Analyst D (female): I want to talk about a female patient of mine. She's not homosexual, she's not actually sexual. It's to do with the self-parenting thing that you mentioned. She talks a lot about her concern for her parents, especially when they retire in a few years time. She's always talking about what they're going to do. She's someone who has had extremely inadequate parenting. She speaks about not being able to see herself as separate.

AS: She tells you about an image of the parents as people who need parenting and she's going to be the one who does the parenting. We can stick with the image of the parents who need parenting and help with planning for their retirement. She's telling you something about what she needs from you: help in connection with the future, help in retiring from something. She's asking for holding, for boundaries, and for structure. Maybe, too, there's something she needs to retire from....

Analyst D: Yes, she's a very driven person, a career woman. Sometimes I even wonder why she's come, so perfect is her defence. Also, she's very cut-off from problems about her future.

AS: It would be easy to get misled by her bossyboots act, apparently able to be a parent to the parents.

Analyst D: But in fact the parents don't need her input. They're a totally independent couple and take no notice of her.

AS: But that's what I'm getting at, it's her image of them as needing her that's important. It's parenting of a certain specific kind that is being referred to: planning-ahead parenting. She's talking really about not having internalized a certain kind of mirroring, a subtle kind of mirroring which doesn't just mirror the situation as it is but also mirrors potential, mirrors the future, mirrors that eventually the baby will walk, that kind of thing. It's what we mean when we refer to the mother carrying the baby's self – she holds an image in her mind and in her reverie which has futurity and the realization of potential in it. That's what she wants to discuss with you – her missing sense of the future. Why are you smiling?

Analyst D: I'm smiling because I've just written about this patient in terms of a lack of mirroring. I'm smiling at mirroring.

Analyst E (male): I have a patient who told me about her mother being very strong. Very domineering and had lived alone and brought up her two daughters. The husband left when the patient was a year old. The image is of a mother who is able to stand alone and my patient is very frail and fragile. She's in her mid-thirties and desperately wanting to make a relationship. It's all around her own strength and whether she can stand alone or whether she needs relationships.

AS: Surely you don't see those two as polar opposites like she does – standing alone and needing someone? Maybe you have to stand alone before you can relate. Achieve unit status before entering genital relationships. That's a possible agenda, the split between independence and relatedness. But there's also a kind of parental/therapeutic attitude involved, isn't there? She has a secret, unconscious, domineering, and controlling attitude to her object world which is in contradistinction to her frailty and vulnerability.

Analyst F (male): I've got a patient who sees her mother as being in need of being taken care of. The mother is very paranoid and diagnosed schizophrenic. The patient is working on her fears about looking at her own child bit. Somehow, we are managing to care more for that child in her.

AS: But the image of the paranoid mother is also setting an agenda for the analysis. Not her fear of regressing, etc., but her fear of *you*. The patient may be more paranoid and persecuted than she's letting you know. I mean by you but it could be general.

Analyst F: Yes, it is becoming more apparent how persecuted she is by me.

AS: The image of the paranoid mother is a true image. But it also sets an agenda for this woman, it's the outcome of the self-monitoring process I have been describing. I don't think you have to *do* anything as a result of this dialogue. Understanding is often enough.

The next three examples also came from a single workshop.

Analyst G (female): The patient is a 23-year-old female. Her father is a hard-headed and judgemental man, a Unitarian minister. Her mother is artistic and interested in ghosts and spirits.

AS: How does she describe the parental marriage?

Analyst G: Her father is an alcoholic but won't admit it. Her mother is an overeater.

AS: How does she see the *marriage*? That isn't really an answer to the question, but maybe that's the whole point – she hasn't got a coherent attitude or maybe what her attitude is is difficult for her to admit to. The judgemental, hard-headed qualities she sees in her father could be on her therapeutic agenda?

Analyst G: She certainly is a confused, disorganized, late kind of person.

AS: Or maybe those hard-headed attitudes are her own attitudes towards herself, her therapeutic attitude towards herself.

(Then there followed a group discussion about Unitarianism.)

AS: What does a Unitarian psyche look like?! Maybe because the Unitarian Church rejects the Trinity, such a psyche would tend to be rather dominated by one image or theme of imagery, maybe in a psychotic way.

Participant: What is going on reminds me of family therapy when each family member gets associated with one emotion or other.

AS: Yes. And I think there's the same interest in what it means if a person cannot image their parents' marriage. People who can't image their parents are giving you very rich material but it's difficult to work with because you're working with an absence and not a presence. You can sometimes get into the missing parental imagery by seeing and listening to how the patient talks of other couples.

Analyst G: She doesn't – oh, yes she does – her sister is getting divorced. And she's interested in my relationship. As she walked out the door one day she noticed my ring and congratulated me. She asked the date of the wedding and I told her. When therapy resumed after the holiday I took at the time of the wedding, she asked me if it had really happened!

AS: She asked someone who was getting married on a certain date if it had really happened.... That's a very aggressive swipe, isn't it? As well as a profound wish it hadn't. You see, the problem is to *notice* the primal-scene material. That's hot material, what you told us.

Analyst H (female): I've got a patient who says her father existed only to facilitate her mother and agreed with everything her mother said. She dreamt of there being two bathtubs in a bathroom. In the dream, there is another child, who is retarded and possibly has no arms and legs and head. The parents are paying all the attention to this child. She remembered her childhood eczema and the baths she had to take in relation to that.

AS: There are so many possible understandings of this – her negative self-image (retarded, etc) and a sense of exclusion from and longing for parental affection and attention. Also jealousy. But I also wonder if she might be a more intact person than either you or she thinks she is. The looking-after parents of the dream *also* refer to her own self-parenting capacity. Maybe she can only meet this strength of hers via a dream as it is for some reason unacceptable to consciousness.

Analyst H: I am not sure but I would say that stuff like that comes out in all kinds of ways – she has talked about going childlike in order to get some attention.

Analyst I (male): The patient I am thinking about had an older sister who died seven years before the patient was born. Her parents were very aged when she was born. There is a family myth that, on the night she was conceived, her father had a dream in which the dead daughter appeared to him and said that she would give them a new baby.

AS: The primal scene is the dead daughter fertilizing the father, then?! That's quite a gender mix-up.

Analyst I: Well, not on the surface, that doesn't seem to be her problem. But the mother and father ceased to sleep together after she was born and the daughter slept with the mother. She hated it. She was told by both parents that they were not having intercourse. Her mother wanted her to be a nun and encouraged her spiritual life. She had a close relationship with the local priest who inspired her. She managed to get him to agree that she could take Communion as early as five years old. He gave her secret instruction. Her presenting problem is that she wants to be held and have a close partnership with a man but either she idealizes nonavailable men or finds ones who are not up to it.

AS: She goes for weak men?

Analyst I: I would say more for philistines or ones who can't understand her spiritual life.

AS: It's a good example to discuss because it's so multifaceted. It's her father's material on one level, his dream. Even then, it can be understood metaphorically as hers. She has to be some kind of spiritual fertilizer to men just as the dead sister has to be some kind of sexual fertilizer. There's a connection between the father's dream and the men she has to give spiritual and cultural stimulation to. There's also the image of her in bed between the two parents. They could stand for parts of her which haven't come together. What kind of problem in integration is it? I am thinking about her self-healing capacities. Her father has an 'annunciation'. What happened at the Annunciation? Gabriel brings a message to Mary foretelling a virgin birth. There's some kind of denial of her parents' sexual connection and, perhaps, her own sexuality.

Concluding Note

As a concluding note I would suggest that we have to think in terms of rounding out the usual connection that is claimed between past and present in analysis: that the here-and-now transference–countertransference dynamics enable a picture of past patterns of parent–infant relating to be described. For, in addition, if we want to find out about the patient's present internal dynamics, we have to listen in a certain way to what we are told about the parents they had in the past, or still have. Analysts are aware that what they are told about the patient's parents is the result of numerous operations of selection, mostly unconscious. It seems to me possible that self-monitoring in the forms I have mentioned, and probably in many other forms as well, may be a motive power behind the patient's selectivity: clinical material concerning parents conforms to the self-monitoring, self-diagnosing needs of the psyche at any one moment in time. *The parents are messengers.*

The illustrative material is intended as a contribution to the working out of a synchronous developmental psychology that itself would have a place in a pluralistic approach to the development of personality.

4

A relation
called father

Introduction

The next four chapters are linked in that they explore, on the one hand, the evolution and facilitation of psychological pluralism in the individual personality as well as in the prevailing culture and, on the other, the consequences of a failure to achieve such pluralism. The main thread of this exploration concerns gender identity, broadly conceived, and, in particular, *the father*.

In this chapter, an analysis is made of the neglect of the father in depth psychology. That is followed by an attempt to find meaning and purpose in incestuous fantasy and behaviour. A new concept is introduced, that of there being a state of *unconscious gender certainty*. When this is rigidly split off from a degree of gender confusion, the formation of a flexible and plural sensing of gender by individual and culture alike is hindered.

In the following chapter, the role of the father in the emergence of gender identity in his daughters and sons is discussed and illustrated with clinical material. It is proposed that clinicians begin to think of an optimally erotic relation between father and daughter, and of the father as the one who transforms the aggression of the son into something positive and creative.

Chapters 6 and 7 take us onto the cultural level. In Chapter 6, I consider the emergence in analytical psychology of a profound concern with the 'feminine principle'. Whilst potentially a valuable development, this concern is skewed by its expression in a style that is analogous to that displayed by an individual who is in the grip of unconscious gender certainty. Hence, pluralism and flexibility are downplayed and even damaged.

Chapter 7 works on and around a similarity in tone and 'smell'

between (a) current debates about the factors at work in the
formation of gender identity, and (b) arguments within
psychoanalysis concerning the aetiology, phenomenology, and
treatment of borderline personality disorder. The part played in
such disorder by gender issues is foregrounded, leading to a review
of ideas on the father's role in borderline personality disorder,
which rounds off the four chapters.

The image of the father

We have reached a very interesting point in the evolution of
analytical thinking. A wheel has turned full circle, for the father
was the key parent in the early days of psychoanalysis – the
tyrannical, castrating, oedipal father. Then we got hooked – validly
and necessarily – on the mother; now we're coming back to the
father. He is still often the prohibitive father but also, increasingly,
the positive father; the facilitating, empathic, mirroring father who
aids imagination, creativity, and psychic health generally. And out
of that patrix we are starting to see the father cropping up in the
aetiology of all kinds of disorders where he just didn't seem to have
a place previously – anorexia, for example, and alcoholism (Shorter
1983; Leonard 1982). So, although it is not just the positive father
who has reclaimed centre stage, the positive father may be regarded
as a new element in the picture.

In a way, this is puzzling because, just as psychological thinking
touches the image of the positive father, so a great deal of cultural
and social criticism has at last caught up with the image of the
negative father: patriarchy, a phallocentric culture, male violence,
male sexual abuse of children, male chauvinism. Perhaps depth
psychologists, not for the first time, are engaged in something
subversive. At the moment when the image of father in the social
world and his authority therein are under attack as exclusively
negative, we, in our limited ways as analysts, are struggling to
preserve a balance. There is certainly a subversive element in what
I have to say about the father, and particularly when I come to the
positive, erotic father.

In Western countries, a shift is undoubtedly taking place in
parental ideals and aspirations; the implications are profound even
if the change may be little more than cosmetic, behaviourally
speaking (see Lewis and O'Brien 1987). For, from the standpoint
of depth psychology rather than social science, the internal world,

in the sense of images and feelings, is the primary area of study. And, if there *is* a discrepancy between aspiration and behaviour, what better topic could there be for the psychologist to study?

An apparently increased sharing of parenting functions is not, in my opinion, the main issue. The main change has more to do with the coming out of the closet of the father's physical *involvement* with his family, more than 'providing' for it. Changing nappies, taking a hand in feeding, going to the swimming bath, these are symbols. The symbols refer to a situation in which it is no longer shameful (i.e. feminine) for a man directly to express his deep involvement with his family, and the darker side of that is the wrong kind of involvement with the family that has found its way into prominence. This lies behind the preoccupation with incest and child abuse, which, as we would now probably all agree, is far more widespread than had been thought. My suggestion is that it isn't those statistics, just as it isn't changing the nappies that's the issue. Behind the pain, misery, and guilt of actual incest lies a fascination with the father in the family. The newspapers and the media that concentrate on incest are expressing this general fascination with the image of father physically involved with his family; positively when he takes the kids swimming, negatively when he touches their sex organs in the swimming bath.

We need to explore incest because, like it or not, incest and the father are irremediably linked – which is not to deny 'maternal incest'. Freud and Jung split more dramatically over the incest question than over almost anything else. Freud spoke for the literal, the instinctual, the causative; Jung for the metaphorical, the psychological, and asking 'what's it *for*?' Summarized briefly, Jung's view was that the unconscious aim of incest fantasy was not a desire for intercourse with a parent, but a symbolic expression of a longing for the rebirth of oneself through contact with the 'parental soil'. A wholly different meaning for regression then emerges: a movement back to a regenerative source for the purposes of personality enhancement and enrichment (*CW* 5 and cf. Kris's aphorism (1952) 'regression of ego in the service of ego'). My aim is certainly not to say that Jung was right and Freud was wrong and, indeed, that summary of Freud does not necessarily pertain in today's psychoanalysis. But the tension that Freud and Jung *personified* between the literal and the metaphoric aspects of incest is one that is with us today, so that when we encounter clinical material around this theme, the tension will be at the heart of our reactions (see Samuels 1980).

Jung's ideas about metaphoric incest sometimes seem divorced from ordinary family realities. The underlying question, as it seems to me, is 'How do we grow?'. We may reply by saying that maturation is the outcome of a psychological, biological, and cultural interaction, or something anodyne like that. But the elephant's child continues to ask, *exactly* how does it happen? One answer is to focus upon the depth aspects of relationships in general and relationships with parents in particular. Getting really close to somebody who is more developed than you psychologically (whatever that 'more developed' might mean) leads to some kind of enhancement or enrichment of the personality by virtue of the extreme closeness. The idea that a person actually grows *inside* by relating in a very close way with people *outside* who have qualities he or she has not yet manifested is at the heart of psychodynamics and object relations. But we have to ask what it is in our general human make-up that enables us to get that close in the first place. In other words, if you're a parent and I'm your child, and I need to be close to you to grow, something more than my dependence on you has to make that happen between us. It cannot happen in consciousness because neither of us can bring it about by will-power. *The psychological function of incestuous sexuality is to facilitate the closeness of love.* Desire in a relationship guarantees the importance of that relationship to both participants. It can go tragically wrong, it can get acted out, it can possess generation after generation of a family. *But incestuous desire has the function of providing the fuel for the means by which we get close to other people and, hence, grow: love.*

These reflections can be put into a clinical context, not a specific example, but rather something so general that all analysts will presumably recognize it. What is the function of the sexual transference? What is *it* for? And what is the function of the normal reciprocal sexual countertransference (see Searles 1959)? Not neurotic, not problematic, not acting out, just reciprocal. The patient (of whatever sex) expresses desire for the analyst (of whatever sex), who cannot help but be stirred in some way. What's *that* for? What happens incestuously in a family between parent and child may also happen in a piece of psychotherapy or analysis. One vital function of the sexual transference and the sexual countertransference, looked at like this, is to enable the patient to use the analyst for his or her growth (and vice versa). Such transference–countertransference is not a secondary eroticization of something else, such as the feeding relationship; as we shall see in Chapters 5 and 10, it is absolutely primary growth stuff.

However, the idea that a father might play a part in this process, or in other developmental processes seems to excite resistance. In a paper on borderline phenomena, admittedly written some time ago, Mahler (1971) records her impression – 'just an impression', in her words – that the preoedipal father has a role in the separation–individuation process. And yet, as so often in psychodynamic writings like those of Winnicott, this role is conceived of *in relation and reaction to maternal influences*. For instance, according to Mahler, the father is the 'awakener from sleep', the sleep of symbiosis, or the protector from an overwhelmingly suffocating mother. Now, it has to be granted that the relation of father to child has in it certain social and psychological elements of indirectness and I shall return to those in some detail in a moment. But this cannot explain or justify the continuing marginalization of the father in the analytic literature, as if he had no pattern of relationships with his children worth exploring in its own right. Elsewhere (Samuels 1985b), I have tried to *redress* this imbalance; here, I should like to *analyse* it further. It is worth trying to understand *why* the imbalance exists because speculations about it may themselves throw up insights about 'the father' that can be played back into practical analysis. The argument that I would like to rehearse is of the father *as* gender.

A relation called father

Citing the father *as* gender is intended to do more than grab the reader's attention. For gender is the psychological and cultural analogue of biological sex; this implies a foregrounding of the cultural dimension. As far as extrauterine life is concerned, the relationship of father and child may be seen as arising out of two other relationships: the pair relationship between man and woman, and the primal relationship between woman and infant. Please note that I am not saying that the tie of blood is irrelevant or that the relation of father and child is less direct in an emotional sense, or less meaningful to both of them than is the relation of mother and child. *But it is signified and acknowledged in a different way because it is constructed in a different way.* It therefore carries a different set of implications. To say that the father–child relation arises out of the interplay of two other relations is to recognize that it is mediate and cultural in its essence. Some kind of common connection of father and child to the mother is what brings the father–child relation into being. As we know from anthropology, it is not necessary for the biological father to be 'father' and there is widespread cultural variation over this. In all cultures, though, the woman who gives birth to the infant is 'mother'. The actual presence or absence of a father does not alter the overall dynamics of the description, though individual experience would, of course, be affected (see Samuels 1985b: 40-1).

Paradoxically, that the relationship called 'father' is a *created relationship* gives to it immense psychological and cultural significance (hence my insistence earlier that this is not a secondarization of the father). The created relationship called 'father' becomes the germ for an entire system of cultural organization based on kinship. For kinship is not 'natural', and certainly not universal in its shape or pattern. Our concern is with the psychological aspects of kinship and how they affect gender issues and here we may come to understand the problem analysts have with the father: *the father is too psychological*. The father relation is not a biological fact and, because depth psychologists as a whole cannot get their connection to biology sorted out, they tend not to be too confident with purely psychological facts. We struggle to work with *psychological* facts and this explains the appeal of Lacanian psychoanalysis to feminism: the psychological and cultural factors in the emergence of the child as a sexed subject are given the greatest weight (see Mitchell 1974).

A fascinating by-product of this discussion is the impact the psychological and cultural relation 'father' has on the biological relation between woman and infant. Just as the father relation arises out of the interplay of the two biological relations of man–woman and woman–infant, so the process may be envisioned in reverse. The (cultural and psychological) relation 'father', or its image where the father is absent, impacts on the (biological) relationship of woman and infant, converting and transforming it into the kinship relation of mother and child (remember, kinship is not 'natural'). Here again, I am not claiming that maternal feeling is the *result* of the transmutation of biology into culture by the father. What I am saying is equally fundamental, though. A cultural edifice called 'mother', which would include 90 per cent of developmental psychology, could only be approached by means of an application of the *idea* or assumption that relations can be cultural and psychological. The father relation, which is in its essence cultural and psychological, is the paradigm for our capacity to regard any relationship from a psychological point of view. For example, our tendency to regard, and limit, woman as mother is not based on biology; rather, it has as *its* paradigm the father relation, which is primarily approached psychologically and culturally. *The biological weakness of the father relation gives it its psychological strength*. For the father–child relation has to be *declared*. Indeed, whole chunks of patriarchal culture rest on this particular aspect of male vulnerability. We don't know the father is the father until we can apply the psychological idea and image of father. An image produces a relationship, it's pure psychology and tremendously difficult to handle. What is more, once we accept that 'father' is a cultural phenomenon, we are close to entertaining the idea that 'mother' is also a cultural phenomenon, not necessarily 'natural' for women. As our culture decrees that motherhood *is* natural for women, it cannot afford to look too closely at the father, lest he give the game away.

The role of the father in the formation of gender identity

Elsewhere, I have argued that differences in the life experiences of women and men do not necessarily mean that females and males can be said to *function* quite differently, psychologically speaking. The argument is expanded in Chapter 6. My intention has been to refute the suggestion of an inborn gender complementarity of women and men (or, in Jungian terminology, innate 'opposites') which leads us to create an unjustified psychological division (Samuels 1985a, 1985b). My argument now will be that paternal deficits contribute to a certain kind of ossification around gender, which I call *gender certainty*.

Later, in the next chapters, when I discuss the case of Margaret, my use of the terms 'gender certainty' and 'gender confusion' will become clearer. I am not primarily interested in the conventional, psychodynamic idea that gender certainty often masks gender confusion – though it certainly can. My concern is more with the uncovering of a secret and unhelpful gender certainty in the unconscious, a denial of the potential of animus and anima. Such unconscious gender certainty may be present either when the surface gender identity is confused and chaotic or when surface gender identity seems certain. In the latter case, the content of unconscious certainty is not the same as that of conscious gender certainty. When gender certainty is conscious, the image an individual has of womanhood or manhood that is displayed to the world via their persona differs from the image buried deeper in the unconscious. That image, with which the individual is unconsciously identified, is a rudimentary idea of womanhood or manhood, one quite unmediated by the actual parents. In a sense, gender confusion is itself stoked up by these half-formed, powerful, idealized, archaic images of gender. With gender certainty as the yardstick, any ordinary human state of gender identity will seem confused. The existence and operation of gender certainty plays a key role in the feelings of gender confusion in the patient.

As far as clinical judgement is concerned, Broverman *et al.* demonstrated as long ago as 1970 the part gender-role stereotypes play in clinical assessments of mental health. By means of questionnaires given to clinicians, they confirmed two hypotheses: (1) clinical judgement concerning mental health differed according to the sex of the patient and these differences faithfully followed current gender stereotypes; (2) behaviours judged healthy for men portrayed an 'ideal standard of health' whereas behaviours judged healthy for women did not. The authors wrote of a 'double standard' when it comes to diagnosis.

We turn in the next chapter to a study of the part played by 'father' in the formation of gender identity. Please note that no attempt is being made to 'knock' theories that stress other factors, such as the role of the mother, in personality development. Rather, an attempt is being made to concentrate on the father and highlight his function and contribution.

An approach that restricted the father's role to the preoedipal phases of development would be as insipid as one that focused only on oedipal dynamics. Though we should be careful not to abandon completely the distinction between preoedipal and oedipal aspects of the father–child relation, maturation does not really take place in discrete stages or phases. Development is not necessarily a linear or (chrono)logical business. As we saw in Chapter 2, there is a psychological sense in which three-person functioning precedes two-person functioning. Concisely, the child's recognition of and relation to the father and her/his discovery of the relation between father and mother make it impossible for her/him to continue to maintain the illusion of a fusionary or symbiotic relation to the mother. Intimations of threeness usher in genuine twoness (see also Chapter 8).

Another justification for taking into account both the preoedipal and the oedipal father comes from the work of the Kris study group of the New York Psychoanalytic Institute on borderline personality disorders. This group studied borderline patients in an intensive way and concluded that there is no one phase of development, no one structural defect, no one kind of trauma that is responsible for borderline disorder (Abend *et al.* 1983: 222-8). The group also concluded that all the borderline patients they considered 'showed evidence of severe Oedipal problems...[and] intense triangular conflicts'. Of course, this somewhat reactionary group of classical Freudians seeks to downplay early object relations theory but, it seems to me, their conclusions are amply documented and well argued. It's possible to glean something of value from the internal Freudian dispute: the insistence by the disputants within psychoanalysis that borderline disorders are either two-person or three-person illnesses points up the struggle the borderline individual faces as he or she struggles to come to terms with the pre/postoedipal divide, the primal scene, and, in particular, apperception of the father.

The study will be divided conventionally: father and daughter, father and son. This is intended to reflect the differences in the experiences of boys and girls that were mentioned previously. A considerable amount has been written about how the different experiences of the sexes with *mother* lead to significant differences in gender and social roles and stereotypes. For example, Eichenbaum and Orbach wrote that:

> all mothers learnt from their mothers about their place in the world. In each woman's experience is the memory – buried or active – of the struggles she had with her mother in the process of becoming a woman, of learning to curb her activities and to direct her interests in particular ways.
>
> (Eichenbaum and Orbach 1982, p. 31)

Chodorow (1978) considered that the different nature of the preoedipal experiences of females means that a woman's sense of self is 'continuous with others' and this is what enables them to be empathic with an infant – unlike males, who are treated as an 'opposite' by their mothers (Chodorow 1978: 26).

What follows in the next chapter may be seen as an attempt to draw together some ideas about the consequences for gender and social roles and stereotypes of the father's relation to his children of both sexes. There is one caveat, though. We shall have to take care to see through any conventional division:

father–daughter———>sex; father–son———>aggression.

Concluding reflections

The problem of gender certainty is not simply the problem of compensation or overcompensation for gender confusion. Gender certainty may be regarded as an underlying psychic reality, experienced as a self-image and lived out to a greater or lesser degree. Gender certainty and gender confusion are not 'opposites'. Together, they constitute a strategy for coping with the stress and anxiety of human sexual fluidity and diversity that is represented by gender. But when the two halves of the strategy are split, the result is unsatisfactory and unsatisfying.

For instance, when Kernberg (1975) writes of a premature Oedipus complex, he can be seen as referring to the failure of an individual personality to hold the balance between certainty and confusion in relation to gender. Oedipal dynamics can lead either to certainty or confusion, and this is particularly so when oedipal prematurity forces relations into a heterosexual mould. Aggression also plays its part in both gender certainty and gender confusion. In the former, the other gender is inferiorized; in the latter, gender itself is annihilated. The problem of gender difference presents as a problem of 'animated moderation'. How to find a way of not being *too* gender certain or *too* gender confused – somewhere in the middle, just a little mixed up. Here, the role of the father will turn out to be critical.

Not knowing too well puts us under great strain. For the world we live in has firm gender-bound opinions about what is normal, abnormal, or appropriate sexual behaviour, what the discrepancies are between masculinity and femininity, and where a person stands on the sexual spectrum. The world is not neutral as regards gender; gender certainty is rewarded if it accords with the general view. Earlier, I referred to the father *as* gender; if that is so, then, given that men claim to represent humanity, women *are* sex. The idea of 'woman' and the idea of an innate, biologically based, sex-bound psychology are really the same idea. The cultural formation of the father relation gives to men the province of culture and to women is assigned the province of biology.

But culture is not a constant; it is a pluralistic network and that pluralism will find its gender form. Like all pluralisms, gender pluralism involves some kind of competition, or even a division of the field. Sexual preferences and orientations, and their gendered associations, are in a state of competition. Sexual fantasies are not politically neutral.

When we think about sexual behaviour, we encounter the paradox that something biological shows the most marked cultural variation. It seems to me that what is important about the huge range of sexual activities of which we are aware is its *very existence*, not whether particular activities are appropriate or even have meaning. Why has such a range of sexual activity come into being? The advantage of admitting a huge degree of ignorance, particularly in the clinical, analytical setting, is that this is the attitude most likely to come to the aid of the middle ground between gender certainty and gender confusion. We are confused about the degree of confusion, certain only of a lack of certainty. *There is also a pleasure in not knowing.*

However, analysts are tempted to operate under the delusion of normality when it comes to gender. Exposure to the fluidity of gender is rewarding and pleasurable, though undoubtedly anxiety-provoking. Exposure to gender fluidity is exposure to an anxiety-spewing monster – not for the inflated achievement of slaying the monster, but for the experience of exposure of one's self, one's gendered self. The small-minded way is to propose sexual or gender normality for the patient when that is a far-off thing for the analyst. It would be morally wrong for the analyst to use the patient's gender vicissitudes to detoxify his or her own, ignoring the capacity of desire, like psyche itself, to change.

5

The father
and his children

Introduction

As indicated in the previous chapter, what follows is an attempt to draw together some ideas about the consequences for gender and social roles and stereotypes of the father's relation to his children of both sexes. In particular, there is a focus on the father's contribution to the child's achievement of a satisfactory and satisfying balance between gender certainty and gender confusion and how this theme is marked out in the clinical situation.

In a sense, all that is being attempted is a *description* of what ordinary, good-enough fathering looks like, with specific regard to daughter and son. In no sense is *prescription* or *proscription* being advanced. It seems to me that phenomenological work is what is lacking in depth psychology's approaches to the father. I readily concede that this is only a sketchy beginning.

Father and daughter

In my practice, I have been seeing several women who occupy a cultural and psychological position somewhere between the traditional and the contemporary; I expect that this is a problem with which my readers are familiar. Two emotions stand out. First, the patient's sense of failure at fulfilling neither the ancient nor the modern womanly ideal, sufficiently pervasive to undercut any coherent sense of identity. Sometimes the rage and frustration at the sense of failure boil over into aggressive (or sexual) outbursts. Second, in several patients there was what felt like a greater than usual conscious and unconscious preoccupation with motherhood, whether in its presence or absence in their lives, such preoccupation heavily colouring the women's images of femininity and gender identity. Motherhood is absolutely equated with womanhood and, whatever confusion or weakness in gender identity there might *seem* to be, the woman *knows for sure* what a woman is *in principle*. She has identified and is identified with the gender certainty of a 'feminine principle'; she is mired in it and it is causing her to feel confused. Interestingly, though, at the same time she may share in the social downgrading of motherhood – at the conscious level, anyway – a further example of certainty at work.

Over time, I became aware of a common thread of experience for some of these women in relation to their fathers, and a common and troubled attitude to their mothers. I have developed an interest in how the father, overtly different from his daughter, has something to do with the degree of success she has in coping with the eventual discovery of the covert differences from her mother. These remarks on the daughter–father relationship arise from the need imaginatively to root ourselves in what happens in lived and bodily personal experience. It is that rootedness that helps to keep the so-called literal and so-called metaphoric in articulated balance. Incidentally, I am not intending to neglect all the other familial relationships (for example, mother and daughter) in this account of womanly experience; the focus is deliberate so that we can learn something more about the father.

Let me begin with a clinical vignette. Margaret was eighteen when she came to see me. (All names and details of patients have been changed.) She turned up for our introductory meeting exactly one week early and the next day her mother telephoned to ask what had happened at the session because, later that evening, Margaret had taken an overdose. In fact, I sent her away because I was with another patient and so I had had only doorstep contact. She managed, then, to communicate her desperation. Margaret was the second youngest of four children and her mother had had some experience of Jungian analysis that she put to good use by interpreting her children's dreams and in other 'professional' ways. Working with Margaret, I was struck by how often it was her mother's opinions that were being voiced. Above all, her mother's view, as relayed by Margaret, was that motherhood is the acme of womanhood and that she, Margaret, was *such* a worry and a failure, because of her lack of interest in things maternal, babies in general, and her younger brother in particular. We could say that Margaret 'knew' for sure what a woman was supposed to be, and, out of this gender certainty, judged herself harshly. The problem in analysis was how to build on her vague recognition that there was more to womanhood than motherhood.

Margaret's father was described as an alcoholic with a tendency to become violent. He was said to be completely in awe of his wife and to regard the children as her domain. His attitude to Margaret's education was that it should fit her for marriage. In general, he was dismissive and disapproving of Margaret. Truly, the mother image held sway over this family.

Margaret's ambition was to be a writer but she could not manage to fit this into a scale of values in which motherhood was at the summit; it was *either* be a writer *or* be a mother. Unconscious attempts to denigrate motherhood as a means of feeling less inferior took the form of fantasies of being a boy and, in her dreams, her hostility towards her mother and, perhaps more significantly, the *idea* of motherhood began to emerge. It took me some time to see how aggression against mother was, for Margaret, a way ahead. She dreamt: 'The whole family was on holiday – it might have been in Venice for there were small canals and white pavements and glass shops. One night S. (elder brother) murdered Mummy and K. (younger brother) in their beds – Mummy stabbed first and then K. who was lying next to her. I was so upset I went shopping in an American supermarket crying really loudly, not knowing how to contain my grief. I tried to pay for the chewing gum I had bought but I saw the packet had been half-eaten. I tried to fill it up from other packets. A man said to me, "It's good to cry".'

We discussed the dream in terms of her freedom, when 'disguised' as her brother, to slay mother and, by implication, the mother 'trip' that had been laid on her. It did not feel right to her to limit our understanding just to aggression against her personal mother. She commented that it was odd that she did not simply buy a full packet of gum as a replacement; it had to be *that* packet. She associated this with being 'stuck' with who she basically was in outline, but perhaps new contents were possible. I threw in the idea that gum isn't nutritious, to which she responded that chewing gum was vital for her concentration when writing – 'Why do you always talk about food', she said, 'when I want to talk about work?' In such a way, in the transference-countertransference, unwittingly but necessarily, I embodied the mother who seeks to limit her adult identity to that of the maternal woman.

After that dream she became depressed for a while and prominent in the transference during the depression was a yearning for paternal acknowledgement. She said she had 'lost' her father for ever, now, because he would have nothing to do with a mother-murderer like her, being so much under his wife's thumb. My tentative formulation was that, to the extent that Margaret was suffering from a depressive illness, the sense of mourning referred to paternal deficits in the area of gender-identity formation. In Margaret's case, her gender certainty hid her emotional impoverishment; she had to become *confused* at depth before she could get free. But even the very existence of gender *certainty* as an unconsciously live and powerfully self-destructive factor within her was itself hidden behind a *confused* and androgynous persona, and required analytical elucidation. This is a radical revision of the conventional kind of formulation that would be content with having reached the confusion.

In the previous chapter, I tried to translate Jung's ideas about incest fantasy into an ordinary familial context. Such fantasy concerns personality enhancement and enrichment. If incest fantasy is acted out, it becomes destructive. But if it isn't there as an actual, concrete, tangible, bodily feeling in the real family, the literal family, then I do not think the kind of growth a girl can get out of her metaphoric relation with her father will take place (or a boy from his mother, for that matter). This is the implication of the idea that sexuality fuels the device that renders relationships into the stuff of inner growth. In Robert Bly's words, 'the divine is connected with matter' (Bly 1986). Jung's 'ultra-violet' needs to link up with his 'infra-red' (*CW* 8: paras. 414-20). Plain speaking about the body and about sexuality is neither prurient nor titillating nor embarrassing; it is necessary.

Now, boys probably do have an easier time of it than girls, because their mothers are so used to being sexual in relation to children of either sex that they are not as frightened of their incestuous sexuality towards their sons as fathers generally are towards their daughters. I am thinking of the erotic aspects of pregnancy, childbirth, feeding, and so forth. This cultural phenomenon can be seen readily in everyday life. There are typical ways in which fathers force the psychosexual development of their daughters into a distorted format by virtue of their not being able to cope with the erotic involvement. The first and most obvious way is actual incest. The father may not realize what he is doing because he has a personality and background that make it impossible for him to hold the balance between the sexual and symbolic, the literal and the metaphoric.

The father and his children

A brief illustration of the interweave of paternal deficit and gender certainty comes from my work with Penny. She was referred to me as 'borderline' and presented as a noisy, demanding, even hysterical, highly 'instinctual' person. There was a history of prolonged sexual abuse – with the man next door. She reached a place in the analysis where she could see that this man had appealed to her because of a 'total gulf' between her and her father. Two memories came to her, and she just couldn't make up her mind if they were connected or not. First, she saw her father in the bath with an erection. Second, she recalled her mother saying to her father, 'If you do that again, I'll leave you.' After the memories came, she was very angry with me indeed. One session, she got up and sat in the desk chair, which is located behind my usual chair (she does not use the couch on a regular basis). She told me what she would like to do to my head with an instrument, and this became an expressed fantasy of what she *was* doing.

I knew that this was a violent woman. She had had military training in unarmed combat and, once, leaving a session, she had deliberately run someone down with her car. But I was not frightened. In fact, I had the most pleasant, warm sensation in my lower legs and feet, as if seated before a fire. I went on to have a vision of a small and comfortable living room in which we were both sitting. In my mind's ear, I could hear the rustle of 'my' newspaper. I was smoking my pipe anyway. I said, 'You're watching daddy read his paper. It's pleasant. Part of you wants it to go on for ever. Part of you wants him to look up and acknowledge you. The tension is what is making you angry. You're smashing my brains up because that settles the question of whether I'll notice you of my own accord.' For the first time, she and I could grasp the *telos* of her exceedingly dramatic and demanding behaviour. Her aggression towards father enabled her to avoid finding out what he felt about her, perhaps avoiding finding out what he was doing that caused her mother to threaten to leave him. I had experienced an embodied countertransference that spoke both of her strategy and the difficulties with it (see Chapter 9 for a fuller account of embodied countertransference and analytical visions).

Penny, like Margaret, knew what a woman was supposed to be like. She had done more than Margaret to break free of this via her life in the military, and she was older, in her late thirties. The vital assistance that her father might have supplied had to be sought from the neighbour in an overliteral, concrete, and, ultimately, unsatisfactory form. The period of work I have been describing with Penny preceded what I can only describe as a classical Freudian analysis of her oedipal dynamics as these were expressed in her compulsion to go out with married men who were not fully available for relationship. Space does not permit more than that brief report of how things developed.

Listening to Penny's story, we might once again reflect that the father who baths his daughter and the father who touches her up in the bath are the two sides, substance, and shadow, of a central phenomenon: the involved father. But there are many more ways for fathers to damage their daughters and, as I have been trying to show, actual incest is the tip of the iceberg. Numerous problems met with clinically stem from an *insufficiency* of kinship libido or incest fantasy, not an excess of it. The father who cannot attain an optimally erotic relation with his daughter is damaging her in a way that deserves therapeutic attention. This can be seen happening in so many ways: excessive prohibition about her activities with boys, a mocking of her sexuality, making fun of her infatuations with rock stars, which is all part of the incest theme – she's trying to grow by close contact with Michael Jackson. If the father says 'take that dreadful poster down', and he's the kind of father I have been describing, then he may be seen as inflicting a certain kind of incest damage upon his daughter. Mockery, strictness, and plain uptightness are reflected in a lack of physical involvement from the time the girl is a little baby. Lack of physical contact between father and daughter is an enormously important factor in the personality disorders, whether narcissistic or borderline. I would suggest that we begin to think of *an optimal erotic relation between father and daughter and, hence, of the pathology of a failure to achieve that*. Eventually, the daughter and her father have to renounce their admitted longings for each other, and such mutual renunciation is itself an affirmation of the daughter's erotic viability.

I must stress that this 'erotic playback', as I call it, is not dependent on whether the father is recalled as having been nice and understanding towards his daughter, though a loving father is more likely to be an optimally erotic father than, say, a physically violent one. But I have encountered numerous women who have had the erotic playback from fathers who do not fit a liberal, bourgeois description of a 'good' father.

My idea is that the father's literal, erotic playback to his daughter permits a pluralistic breaking out of the bondage of the metaphorical equation: woman = mother. The equation is equally binding on a woman whether 'mother' is highly valued or not. That ambiguous equation is quite the most powerful element underlying the belief, in both women and men, gender progressives and gender conservatives alike, that there is a distinct 'feminine' psychology. The erotic can act as a kind of liberation for the daughter so that she can begin to explore a plurality of other, nonuterine female paths for herself, and maybe paths that cannot be sexed or gendered in advance: for instance, the spiritual path, the vocational path, the path of solidarity with the travails of other women, the path of an integration and use of the aggressive impulse, the path of sexual expression – the individuation of the lusty woman who can begin to think in terms of going where she wants to go and coming when she wants to come. Eventually, a positive estimation of motherhood may evolve but on an individual basis. Erotic playback promotes an attempt to challenge and overthrow the constricting aspects of the notion of a separate 'feminine psychology' or 'feminine principle'. On the personal level, a tight and rigid 'knowledge' of what femininity is – what I have called gender certainty – is a key element in how a lack of erotic playback deploys itself.

Brenda did not see her father until she was five or six because, as a German alien, he was interned in Canada during the war. Her first meeting with him, as she related it, was when lying in the bath, aged about six, and this strange man came in to be introduced as her father. She said, 'If you're not nice to me, I'll call you Uncle' and he immediately began to tick her off for being cheeky. It seems that her father did not take time to reintegrate himself into the family but tried to impose his authority from the outset. Her mother, who was Jewish, felt responsible for her gentile husband's fall from grace in Nazi Germany and for his subsequent internment. That was why she put up with his authoritarianism for many years, before leaving him when Brenda was grown up.

For a long time, I had little idea of why Brenda wanted analysis. My hunch was that all was not well in her main relationship but I decided to wait and see what materialized. Gradually, it all came out. Her partner was a struggling painter while she herself was a high-flying academic. She complained of underfunctioning in the work situation, not her actual intellectual work, but the administration of the department and relationships with colleagues, especially men, were not going well. She felt perpetually on the brink of a huge explosion of rage and spoke of fears of going mad.

In presenting the following dream of Brenda's, I am not trying to communicate a breakthrough or anything like that because we did not make much progress in our work together. She dreamt: 'I'm

in a large, whitish, Georgian house, neglected. Neglected garden.
Stairs, steep, very narrow, uncarpeted, wooden. On either side
white-painted tongue-and-groove, very high enclosed small
landing. A door, also tongue-and-groove, hardly visible, tightly
shut. Finally, at the top, a small room – bedroom? – and beyond it
an open door to the bathroom. Large bath with water in it, more like
a mini swimming pool. Cut-out, black, wooden seats floated in it,
like clouds. To one side of the door a plastic curtain. I look behind
it to find an ordinary bath. Noise from another room. I go in. A
larger bedroom, light. A large bed. Many men and women
intertwined. Lazy, sensual, one woman sitting back on her
haunches, a man kneeling, facing her. He puts out his hand and
pinches her breast – lightly – and I feel that it must be a rather
painful sensation. I'm both drawn towards the scene and slightly
repelled.'

These were Brenda's associations to her dream:

> The house is like a country equivalent of some friends'
> London house; similar mixture of being a fine house but
> rather crumbling. The stairs – rather puritanical, narrow,
> white. Reminds me of C.'s (partner's) parents' sort of
> decoration, but also we have tongue-and-groove panels round
> our bed. But the way the door merges with the wall, that's
> definitely C.'s parents' style. That door – so firmly closed –
> the bedroom door of my parents' room, closed, the Saturday
> after-lunch (or was it Sunday?) ritual, 'We don't want to be
> disturbed ...'. The bath – when I was about fifteen I stayed in
> Bremen and was taken to a country schloss. In the garden was
> a little sunken bath with a submerged stone bench at either
> end. I thought – think – that it was the height of sensuousness.
> The plastic curtain and bath seem rather ordinary, utilitarian.
> The bedroom – it was relaxed, easy, co-operative but...I don't
> know what I didn't like. The breast? My nipples are very
> sensitive, when they're touched I feel vulnerable, for what
> starts as pleasure can suddenly become pain.

Our dialogue about the dream and associations covered three
general areas. First, her parents' marriage – its exclusiveness,
togetherness ('tongue-and-groove') and her mockery of it ('ritual').
Second, that the bath was the 'height of sensuousness' implied that
her rebellious initial utterance to her father gave her pleasure of a
kind. Third, and connected to the last idea, there is a link between

sensuous pleasure and vulnerability, for instance when supine in the bath with the other upright (her sensitive nipples).

Brenda's lifelong fight with her father was the sole source of erotic playback, and it was not enough. She tried hard to keep her aggression out of her marriage and under control at work but was consumed by a terror that there would be a catastrophic explosion. What she found difficult to face was the sense of satisfaction she attained via her aggressive impulses and fantasies. In the analysis at least, she did not discover ways of achieving intimacy other than aggression. For, when negative feelings towards the analysis and towards me began to surface, she withdrew.

The various strands of this chapter can start to come together now. There is something destructive for women about the belief in a distinct 'feminine' (or 'masculine') psychology. Gender certainty forms the oppressive heart of much neurosis. Women have suffered enormously from narrow definitions of what it means to be female, from the requirement that they be unaggressive and selfless creatures who relate, who are responsive to the needs of others, who react but do not act. Here, psychological illness may even be regarded as a kind of protest about such a requirement. True, as *mothers*, maybe something like that has to be done. But as *persons* women can sniff out other vistas and ways of being. Strange as it may seem, it is the young female's apperception of herself as a sexual creature, facilitated by her erotic connection to her father, that enables her to spin through a variety of psychological pathways, enjoying the widest spectrum of meanings inherent in the ideogram 'woman'. The father's first fertilization helped to make the female baby. His second helps to bring forth the female adult, who is then free to drop her father when and if she needs to. There would be little point in replacing a 'femininity' that pleased Mummy with a 'femininity' that pleases Daddy. And the female adult can, now more than ever, be a multifaceted woman–person, free not only *from* symbiotic relating with her mother, but free *to* grow in all manner of unpredictable and exciting ways.

Father and son

There are two quite distinct but compatible ways to view the father–son relationship: in terms of intergenerational conflict or in terms of intergenerational alliance. It is the peculiar genius of Freud's Oedipal theory that, in it, such a dual viewpoint exists.

Unfortunately, as the emphasis in psychoanalysis has been almost exclusively upon the prohibitive, castrating father we have heard, as I noted earlier, less about the alliance with his son. Yet the interplay of alliance and conflict is crucial to any kind of organic cultural development. Indeed, conflict and competition between father and son is itself not always negative, for it indicates change, improvement, progress, vitality, and a healthy check on both reaction and revolution. The overt alliance provides a framework within which all this, competition included, can happen. There is also a connection between past and present, for the father–son link is nothing if not historical and the image of the elder telling (almost) all he knows to the younger is a compelling one. It is as if father and son strike a bargain, at least in my commonplace rendering of Freud's theory of identification. If the son gives up his claim on the mother, he will receive help and facilitation with his life tasks. Only when it is used in an excessively defensive way does identification lead to a submergence of the boy's individuality in the image of his father.

The castrating father of Freud's theory should not be ignored, though. For the incest taboo to be effective, and this has to be the case lest all culture sink into a familial miasma, the older generation has to be well muscled. This is not the place to discuss castration anxiety in depth, but Jones's (1927) concept of aphanisis is relevant. The term means the removal by the same-sex parent, not only of the means to express sexual desire, *but also of the capacity to feel desire itself.* It is a brilliant attempt by Jones to verbalize what it is that the oedipal child is afraid of and, hence, what gives the prohibition its power.

The reader may recall my idea that one task in analysis is to see how the cultural stereotype resonates with the inner images of the patient. In a son, the cultural stereotype of the father suggests a figure incarnating conscience and functioning as a repository of values and ideals. Thinking about that, a remarkable scenario develops. The father's function in relation to the son is to turn incestuous libido away from sexual expression with the mother and into new directions, so that a spiritual enrichment may ensue. But the father expresses his opposition to instinctual incest in the most virulent instinctual form – castration, aphanisis, or other terrible punishment of the son. *That* father may be represented in myth as a bull, a creature whose potency and virility mingle with its other terrifying and violent features. Instinct serving spirit is being used to drive out instinct serving sex. The spirit is also 'instinctual', as it were. This paradox suggests that, in terms of the son's internal father image, we must face the reality that a degree of emotion or passion is necessary alongside spirit. Many male patients, including several borderline individuals, complain that this is what their otherwise unobjectionable fathers lacked. *A passionately spiritual father is different from one whose dry concentration is on conformity; the whole flavour of prohibition varies.* The passionately spiritual bull father is not the same as a bully, a father whose self-image rests on the defeat of his son.

The clinical material I have to offer about the 'dry' father is somewhat unusual. Eric was an actor. His demeanour was passive–aggressive, his ambition zero, and his value system that of a conventional English gent. Eric's mother was strongly in support of his analysis and gave him a schematic biography of his early life to bring to show me. I set out below the parts of this that relate to the parental marriage. Eric was very much a mother's boy. His presenting problem was a phobia about pubic hair and violent fantasies about dismembering women and inserting their cut off limbs into their vaginas. As Pontius (1986) has pointed out, such fantasies involve the creation of a 'male–female superhuman' and, reading his mother's account of her marriage, one can see why Eric was impelled from within to create a replacement for it as the source of his being. I am aware that the mother's account is highly partial; that is the point of reproducing it.

(1) Advised by V.'s (her husband's) psychiatrist not to marry him as he was considered a depressive with psychological impotence.

(2) Eric result of only intercourse during first year of marriage; this a means only of producing a child and not of love-making, which V. considered dirty.

(3) Eric worshipped by me not only as a miracle in itself but perhaps also as a means of sublimating lack of sex life.

(4) At age 6, Eric given a puppet theatre by his godfather inside which he was amazingly artistic. Said he wanted to be a ballet dancer. V., already not a full man himself, was adamant this was not what a man should do. A row followed between us in front of Eric – I had so much sexual frustration that I could be very bitter towards V. although or because I loved him so much I wanted him very badly. I had no sex life at all after I conceived T. (Eric's sister).

(5) Quite wrongly, I had to make too many decisions due to V.'s passivity.

(6) Children sent to boarding school at V.'s insistence.

(7) V. keen for Eric to enjoy sports and walks but all they did together was discuss history, which they both adored. Eric not 'sporty'.

(8) V. had depression and psychoanalysis all our married life (sic).

I should like to discuss Eric's situation in terms of his father's failure to use paternal reverie as a container that might facilitate the transformation of Eric's aggressive fantasies and impulses towards women into something that might be integrated and, eventually, used creatively. Each of the terms 'reverie', 'container' and 'transformation' has origins in Bion's (1965) extension of Kleinian thinking. However, these terms are usually employed in relation to the mother. We do not have much idea about what paternal reverie is like.

In overall terms, the father–son couple work on the establishment of a *telos*, or purposeful goal for aggression. This involves the recognition, at a nonverbal level, of the intentionality of aggression. Aggression cannot have existence save in relation to an object of aggression and, where the object of aggression feels like the mother, the father's transformative influence is in the general direction of highlighting the *affect* and downplaying the *target*. What is at stake is *the integrity of aggressive development*. We can put this into language of the heroic quest. The father may contextualize heroic endeavour as something other than the slaying of a mother–dragon. For that act can lead to a metaphorical slaying of the whole creative unconscious. The father may be able to accentuate *heroic process* rather than specific *heroic achievement*. This would involve the need to expose oneself to danger, not once but many times, a lifelong process beginning in childhood. The deliberate exposure to danger, *and not the danger itself*, is the valuable part of the son's heroic quest. If there is a victory, this is decidedly not a once-and-for-all event; it is not the sort of victory to get inflated about.

As far as the integrity of aggressive development is concerned, it does not really matter that much whether the child's self-image at any one time is of aggressor or victim, provided he has ample experience of both of these positions and is not trapped in one or the other. The father structures a spectrum of aggression, ranging from victim to aggressor. Because of projective identification, the victim can *become* a threatening object and vice versa. The fluidity and interchangeability are vital if aggression is to remain a benign force, capable of utilization via transformation. Generally speaking, the father aids his son in the transformation of aggression by his reverie, handling, and play. Of course, in practice, both the parents do this together and, when the mother performs the particular function of the transformation of aggression, she can be recognized as doing some fathering – just as fathers are often said to do some mothering. *'Mother' and 'father' are also metaphorical statements.* What particularly needs emphasizing, though, is that transforming aggression is not the same as either a parent 'managing' it by helping a child to remain psychologically intact when under terrific internal pressure occasioned by rage, or a parent 'surviving' the child's aggressive onslaught. Transformation, as used here, does *not* refer to those achievements. It is an on-going process of relationship involving loss of egohood by both parties in order to bring to consciousness and fulfil a psychological need hitherto unrecognized.

Let's look at one specific aspect of aggressive transformation, wherein Eric and his father failed completely. This is the shift in the quality of aggression from a manic–heroic–separation style to the aggression of ordinary oedipal rivalry, permitting a pluralistic intertwining of the two styles. This shift requires a fostering within the father–son relationship. The father 'offers' himself as a target for the son's aggression, not in an all-knowing way, but as part of an authentic struggle whose outcome is not certain, even though its value as process is tacitly agreed. The father–son alliance (or the mother–daughter alliance if we consider this area of experience from a female point of view) upon which cultural consistency depends is a further transformation arising from the recognition by both father and son that neither can gain absolute victory. The delusion of victory is often encountered clinically, particularly in borderline symptomatology.

One particular problem, often met with in analysis, concerns the son of a mother who is ambitious yet socially frustrated, and who seeks a form of fulfilment by envisioning her son as her own private phallic property. Here, the father *may* insert himself between mother and son to encourage their separation – or he may not. This is the kind of psychological situation where I *would* see the father as an 'awakener from sleep'. As the foregoing remarks hopefully make clear, I generally do not see the father *primarily* as one who breaks up the mother–son relationship. Rather his role is in relation to the aggressive energy in his son. Aggression involves more than a separation from the mother.

To conclude the section on the father–son relationship, I should like to add a few words on homosexuality. Though we distinguish homosexual genital sex from homoerotic involvements, psychological life must always have something of a homosexual component in it. That enables us to talk of a 'homosexual Oedipus complex'; for a boy, there are feelings of love and attraction for his father and a desire to eliminate his mother. However, if a boy fantasizes his father as strong and admirable, *and* his mother as vastly inferior and unlovable, then the outcome may be an overvaluation or idealization of the father in general, and the father's penis in particular. This would not be 'penis' symbolizing the passionately spiritual father mentioned earlier, but more of a doughy, nutritional penis – indeed, a form of breast substitute for the absence of a desirable mother.

The father and his children

Towards the end of the previous section, there was a deliberate unravelling of the symmetry of the heterosexual matrix within which much of our thinking about these matters seemingly has to be grounded. Mothers do what fathers do, fathers what mothers do, there is a permanent homosexual presence, the father's penis stands for a breast on occasion.

Perhaps we have been tempted to ignore Freud's perception of an innate bisexuality and have taken heterosexuality as something so fundamental that it is beyond debate. If this is what has happened, then our imaginings of what a father is or could be will be truncated. Our clinical perceptions are interfered with if, out of a heterosexist consensus and an overliteral anatomy, we refer to the 'phallic mother' when what is going on in the transference–countertransference concerns the father. For female therapists, particularly at the outset of their practices, it is often difficult to accept that the patient's image of them is as 'father', with father's body, penis, and stubble. Perhaps male therapists have less of a problem here since, after thirty-five years of object relations and the focus on mother–infant interaction, male therapists know for sure that they also have female bodies, breasts, and womb.

Ogden (1987: 494) has commented independently on what he sees as an 'inability' on the part of some female therapists to manage countertransference difficulties with female patients. Ogden sees this as resulting from an overconflicted identification with her own father that makes it hard for her to accept a paternal transference because this makes her literal womanhood into something 'second best'. Indeed it would – if her definition of woman was unduly limited, perhaps to woman = mother. My suggestion is that optimal erotic playback from the father, as described above, is a crucial factor in a female's envisioning of herself in a sufficiently broad and nonliteral way so as to facilitate her assumption of the paternal role in the transference. My depiction of father–daughter interaction focuses precisely on this point: the range of psychological possibilities open to the daughter as woman is immense. When the daughter becomes a therapist, her therapeutic range reflects her own experience of erotic playback.

It feels important to reverse the poles within the two major arguments I have been developing about the father in personality development generally and in the formation of gender identity in particular. These concerned the erotically involved father in the enrichment of his daughter's personality, and the father who, by means of reverie, transforms the aggressive impulses and fantasies of his son. *The father's erotic playback is also required by his son and his transformation of aggression by his daughter.* If we do not make this acknowledgement, then, just like many of our patients, we are ensnared by the delusion of gender certainty.

6

Beyond the
feminine principle

In this chapter, I look at developments in analytical psychology
concerning gender identity, gender characteristics, and gender role.
This is set against the background of a general debate about
psychology of sex and gender and the question of sex-based
psychology. As in the previous chapters, the linkage between
gender certainty and gender confusion is a central concern, as is the
tracking of fluidity, flexibility, and a pluralistic ethos in connection
with gender.

The gender debate

Some questions: are men innately more aggressive than women?
Does that explain their social and political dominance? Is there
such a thing as innately 'masculine' or innately 'feminine'
psychology?

In his book *Archetype: a Natural History of the Self*, Anthony
Stevens drew on the work of the sociobiologists Wilson and
Goldberg to reach the conclusion that 'male dominance is a
manifestation of the "psychophysiological reality" of our species.
In addition [there is] genetic and neurophysiological evidence
relating to the biology of sexual differentiation.... Patriarchy, it
seems is the natural condition of mankind' (Stevens 1982:
188-92).

In *Jung and the Post-Jungians*, I drew on the work of Janet
Sayers to critique Stevens's position (Samuels 1985a: 220-2).
Sayers felt that those opposed to changes in women's role had
appropriated biology to their cause and she demolished the
sociobiological case in a witty and learned way. For instance,

92

Wilson quoted studies that showed that boys were consistently more able than girls at mathematics but that girls have a higher degree of verbal ability. And boys are, in Wilson's view, more aggressive in social play. From these bases, Wilson concluded that 'even with identical education and equal access to all professions men are likely to continue to play a disproportionate role in political life, business and science' (quoted in Sayers 1982: 77). She wryly remarks that it is hard to see how males' lesser verbal ability leads to their being better fitted for political life. Surely, if biology really does determine social role, it should be the other way round?

Recently I came across the work of another academic psychologist, Gerda Siann (1985). She comprehensively surveyed the various research findings that purport to link aggression to the male hormones. She concluded that 'no specific areas in the brain or nervous system have been pinpointed as controlling aggression' and that an overview of the repeated studies shows that androgenized girls do not seem more aggressive than their peers, siblings, or mothers. Overandrogenized males do not display noteworthy dominance, assertion, or aggression in spite of the fact that their greater size would guarantee victory (they seem to be rather gentle people). What is more, Siann's careful reading of the research findings shows that castration has no effect on the overall aggressive behaviour of sex offenders, save in relation to actual sexual behaviour. Finally, plasma testosterone levels do not seem to relate directly to aggressive behaviour. Siann's overall conclusion was:

> the evidence does not show any clear and unambiguous relationship between male hormones and the propensity to display violent behaviour or feel aggressive emotion. Indeed the likelihood of such a simple unidirectional relationship has been thrown into doubt by two additional lines of investigation. The first shows that the secretion of male hormones is itself directly affected by environmental and social variables, and the second is concerned with the speculation that female hormones may also be implicated in violent behaviour and aggressive emotion.
>
> (Siann 1985: 37)

Siann also investigated the published research linking genetic inheritance and aggression. Her findings, which make interesting reading when read in conjunction with the discussion in the next chapter on the hereditary factor in borderline disorder, was that there is no evidence for the genetic transmission of aggression or violence (Siann 1985: 39). *In sum, there is no corporeal innate factor in aggression.* The possibility remains that there is a noncorporeal innate factor – that aggression is linked to sex by invisible, psychological factors. We shall consider that possibility in a moment.

To sustain Stevens's sociobiological viewpoint, female aggression has to be overlooked or minimized. What is more, there is a confusion between 'aggression' and 'dominance'. Not all human dominance depends on aggression. We have to explain phenomena such as altruistic or self-sacrificing behaviour, conscience, the checks placed on the power of a leader, human capacity for collective decision-making, and so forth.

What follows is a discussion of the third question with which we started this section: are there such things as innate 'masculine' and, more pertinently perhaps, innate 'feminine' psychologies? If there are, then there could be a noncorporeal innate factor in aggression.

Beyond the feminine principle

It is hard to write flexibly and fluidly about what is flexible and fluid. The danger when trying to reflect on our current preoccupation with gender is that we might become too clear and too organized – a reaction formation to the inevitable anxiety (and guilt) we experience at finding that what we thought was solid and fixed is perforated and shifting. Humanity is not just divided into women and men but also into those who are certain about gender and those who are confused about gender. As we have seen, getting the balance between gender certainty and gender confusion is a hard task. Clinically, we see the negative effects of an excess of either position and working with individual patients in the area of gender identity is a kind of research work before moving on to the collective stage and a wider scale.

For gender confusions have as important a role to play as gender certainties. They contribute something imaginative to social and political reform and change. I refer to 'confusion' and not to something that sounds more laudable like 'flexibility' because, experientially, that is precisely what it is, no bones about it. Not for the first time in psychology, we can fashion the strengths out of an apparent weakness. To do this, I have found that I have had to learn from women about what they have been through.

Does use of the word confusion not imply the possibility of definition and clarity concerning gender? The way I use the word 'certainty' in relation to gender is intended to suggest that, while clear definition is theoretically possible, it is, for the most part, illusory and/or problematic.

In order to discuss the subject at all, the distinction between sex and gender should be noted, allowing for some overlap as well. *Sex* (male and female) refers to anatomy and the biological substrate to behaviour, to the extent that there is one. *Gender* (masculine and feminine) is a cultural or psychological term, arising in part from observations and identifications within the family, hence relative and flexible, and capable of sustaining change. Now, in some approaches, particularly in analytical psychology, what can happen is that a form of determinism creeps in and the invariant nature of gender is assumed, just as if gender characteristics and qualities were as fixed as sexual ones. The history of women shows that change is possible just because the social meaning of womanhood is malleable. But when this is ignored, as by Stevens, the possibilities of change, other than as part of ordinary maturation and individuation, are lost.

Is there such a thing as a 'feminine psychology'? I'll begin with a general discussion, then consider whether there is a feminine psychology that applies to women. In a moment, I'll look at the 'feminine' in relation to men, and, after that, at femininity and masculinity as metaphors.

Males and females do have experiences that vary markedly. But it is a huge step from that to a claim that they actually *function* sufficiently discrepantly psychologically for us to speak of two distinct psychologies. The evidence concerning this is muddled and hard to assess. For instance, the discovery that boys build towers and girls build enclosures when they are given bricks can be taken to show a *similarity* of functioning rather than difference (which is what is usually claimed). Both sexes are interested in their bodies and, possibly, in the differences between male and female bodies. Both sexes express that interest in the same way – *symbolically*, in play with bricks. Or, put in another form, *both sexes approach the difference between the sexes in the same way*. The differences that we see in gender role and gender identity can then be looked at as having arisen in the same manner. The psychological *processes* by which a male becomes an aggressive businessman and a female a

95

nurturing and submissive housewife are the *same* and one should not be deceived by the dissimilarity in the end product.

What I have been describing is not a woman's relation to an *innate* femininity or to an *innate* masculinity. Rather I am talking of her *relation to the phenomenon of difference*. Then we can consider the social or cultural structures erected on the basis of that difference. Each woman lives her life in interplay with such difference. This leads at once to questions of gender role (for example, how a woman can best express her aggression in our culture) but these questions need not be couched in terms of innate femininity or innate masculinity, nor in terms of a femi- nine–masculine spectrum. Rather, they might be expressed in terms of *difference*. In the example, the difference between aggression and submission needs to be seen as different from the difference between men and women! Or, put another way, whatever differences there might be between women and men are not illuminated or signified by the difference between submission and aggression. In the previous two chapters, we have been exploring how gender difference is formed in relations between parents and children and by cultural and social organization.

I am aware that *men* are said to have access to the 'feminine', or to the 'feminine principle' and I used to think that such an unremittingly interior view was the jewel in the Jungian crown. Now I am not so sure. If we're attempting to describe psychological performance, we have to be sure *why* terms with gendered associations and appellations are being used at all. Otherwise we end up with statements such as that 'masculine' aggression is available to women via their relation to the animus, or 'feminine' reflection in the man via his anima. But aggression is part of woman and reflection is part of man. What is more, there are so many kinds of aggression open to women that even current attempts to speak of a woman's aggression as 'feminine' rather than 'masculine' still bind her as tightly as ever. Let us begin to speak merely of aggression. Gender engenders confusion – and this is made worse when gender terms are used exclusively in an inner way. When we speak of 'inner' femininity in a man, we bring in all the unnecessary problems of reification and substantive abstraction that I have been describing. We still cannot assume that psychological *functioning* is different in men and women, *though we know that the creatures 'man' and 'woman' are different.*

The question of 'difference' brings us to a point where we can play back these ideas into analytical psychology. From Jung's overall theory of opposites, which hamstrings us by its insistence on contrasexuality ('masculine' assertion via the animus, etc.), we can extract the theme of *difference*. The notion of difference, I suggest, can help us in the discussion about gender. Not innate 'opposites', which lead us to create an unjustified psychological division expressed in lists of antithetical qualities, each list yearning for the other list so as to become 'whole'. A marriage made on paper. No, I am referring to the fact, image, and social reality of difference *itself*. Not what differences between women and men there are, or have always been; if we pursue that, we end up captured by our captivation and obsession with myth and with the eternal, part of the legacy from Jung. I am interested in *what difference is like*, what the experience of difference is like (and how that experience is distorted in the borderline disorders). Not what a woman *is*, but what being a woman is *like*. Not the archetypal structuring of woman's world but woman's personal experience in today's world. Not the *meaning* of a woman's life but her *experience* of her life. Each person remains a 'man' or a 'woman', but what that means to each becomes immediate and relative, and hence capable of generational expansion and cultural challenge. My suggestion has been that *paternal deficits constrict the expansion and truncate the challenge.*

In both the collective, external debate about gender characteristics and the personal, internal debate about gender identity, the question of 'masculine' and 'feminine' is best left in suspension – even, and the word is used advisedly, in some confusion. *'Gender confusion' is a necessary antidote to gender certainty* and has its own creative contribution to make. This is particularly true in the treatment of borderline disorders, as we shall see in the next chapter. For, when we consider gender and the borderline we will see how gender confusion and gender certainty can operate in isolation from each other. *Inadvertently, those who propound a 'feminine principle' play into and replicate the dynamics of unconscious gender certainty,* denying gender confusion.

It is probably fair to say that post-Jungian analytical psychology has become preoccupied with gender certainty and gender confusion in its concern with the 'feminine principle'. Here, I am not referring to the writings on women and 'feminine psychology' by Jung and his early circle of followers. The problems with that body of work are well known and often repeated. But in the 1970s and 1980s, mainly in the United States, women writers in analytical psychology have set out to revise, or revolutionize, the early work. Such writers are struggling to be 'post-Jungian' in their attempt to critique those of Jung's ideas that seem unsatisfactory or just plain wrong without dismissing Jung altogether.

The reason why there has been a concentration on the 'feminine principle' in recent Jungian writing is that it has provided a means to celebrate the specificity of women's identity, life, and experience. In addition, having the notion of a 'feminine principle' in mind helps to make a critique of culture out of personal confrontations with it. The basic desire of feminists who are involved in Jungian psychology has been to refuse and refute the denigration of women that is perceived in analytical psychology, to bring the feminine gender in from the condescending margins, and to promote an alternative philosophy of life to that expressed in the power institutions of a male-dominated society.

Taken as a whole, and I realize I am generalizing, feminism which draws on Jung's ideas stands out from other varieties, with which I feel more in sympathy, in two main ways. Both of these stem from Jung's approach, resist eradication, and cause great difficulties. It is assumed that there is something eternal about *femininity* and , hence, about *women*; that women therefore display certain essential transcultural and ahistorical characteristics; and that these can be described in psychological terms. What is omitted is the on-going role of the prevailing culture in the construction of the 'feminine' and a confusion develops between what is claimed to be eternal and what is currently observed to be the case. It is here that the deadweight of the heritage of archetypal theory is felt, but as the mirror image of Jung's problem. He assumed that there is something eternal about *women* and, hence, about *femininity*. As Young-Eisendrath (1987: 47) writes, 'certain beliefs about difference – for example, about gender and racial differences – have influenced our thinking about the meaning of symbolic representations, behaviours, style, and manner of people who are alien to the roots of our psychology in Switzerland'. She goes on to say that we need 'something more than maps and charts of our own design'.

I would like to say what I find problematic in the many attempts to locate eternal models or maps for the psychological activity of women in mythology and goddess imagery. When such imagery is used as a kind of role model or resource for a woman in her here-and-now pain and struggle, that is one thing. But when it is claimed that such endeavour is a reclamation of qualities and characteristics that once prevailed in human society only to be smashed by the patriarchy, then that is altogether more suspect. For it is a highly disputed point, to put it mildly, that such an era ever existed. Could this be a case of taking myth too literally? And isn't there a hidden danger here? For if men were to claim that they are in the direct line of psychic inheritance of the characteristics and qualities of gods and heroes, then we'd end up with the status quo, with things just as they are, for they couldn't be any other way. As far as role-modelling and resource provision goes, surely any woman, even or especially an analyst, can perform this task for another woman.

It could be argued that referring to a goddess as a role model or resource is to miss the point about what is special in a divine figure – the numinosity that attaches to such a figure and hence provides a special form of authority. I am not convinced by this argument, for any figure can constellate the kind of venerating transference that is exemplified in the mortal-divine relation. This is something well known to any and every analyst who has experienced an idealizing transference. If the numinosity is not what is specific to the goddess, then, as I suggested, it is her a-temporality, that which is claimed as eternal and absolute in her.

The search for hidden sources of authority is a project constellated by what is seen as a flawed cultural tradition. But there may also be a 'flaw' in the project itself, for such a search demonstrates the very sense of weakness and lack of authority which it seeks to overcome. Engaging in a rivalrous search for female archetypes could lead to a new set of restrictions on female experience, as several writers have observed (Lauter and Rupprecht 1985: 9 discuss this point in detail).

Could we try to play the feminine principle in a pragmatic and not an eternal or absolute key? If so, then its truth would be measured, in William James's words, 'by the extent to which it brings us into satisfactory relations with other parts of our experience' (1911: 157). We would have to start assembling material on the experience of difference as well as on the experience of womanhood and manhood. Sociologists and academic psychologists may have done this but depth psychologists have not – or not yet. Then, in Shorter's words, we would become less concerned with the 'image' of woman and more with 'likeness' to that image. She says: 'Likeness is consciousness of image and its embodiment.... It is not a question of imitation; each person becomes in part and to the measure that he (sic) is able "like to" the image' (Shorter 1987: 40). Or in Caroline Stevens's words: 'as a woman, anything I do is feminine' (personal communication, 1987).

The second point of disagreement between feminism in analytical psychology and feminism generally has to do with the impression that much Jungian discourse on the 'feminine' seems directed away from political and social action. Dwelling upon interiority and feeling becomes an end in itself. So, just as middle-class Victorian women were believed to be the repository of sensibility and confined to hearth and home, in the Jungian manner of it, women in the nuclear age are meant to be mainly private creatures.

My concern is that much thinking and writing around the 'feminine principle' has opened a secret door into analytical psychology for the return of what is, paradoxically and ironically, an overstructured approach to psyche, heavily dependent upon abstraction and decidedly moralistic. What I'm suggesting is that much contemporary Jungian work on feminine psychology may be seen as far more of an 'imitation of Jung' than was consciously intended. The intention of rectifying Jung's mistakes and prejudices has been perverted.

Trawling the recent literature, I have been struck by the massiveness of the feminine problematic, signified in numerous phrases such as: feminine elements of being, feminine modality of being, femininity of self, feminine ways of knowing, feminine authority, feminine assertion, feminine reflection, feminine dimensions of the soul, primal feminine energy pattern, feminine power, feminine response, feminine creativity, feminine mysteries, feminine body, feminine subjectivity, feminine transformation. I could have quadrupled the list; for ease of reference, I have subsumed all these terms under the general heading of the 'feminine principle'.

Something oppressive has come into being – not, repeat not, because what is claimed as the *content* of the 'feminine principle' is oppressive but because celebrating the feminine has raised it to the status of an ego-ideal, leading to a simple and pointless reversal of power positions. Further, perhaps it is the shadow of feminism generally to make women feel inadequate when they don't come up to its mark – or cannot emulate notable feminist figures.

Gender, metaphor, and the body

I would like to say a few words now about the literal and
metaphoric relationships between anatomy and psychology to draw
together the psychological and scientific aspects of the gender
debate, and because I will be talking again about this towards the
end of the chapter. A literal determinism has seduced those who
seek to make a simple equation between body and psyche. We do
not really know what the relationship between them is but it is
probably *indirect*. The fact that a penis penetrates and a womb
contains tells us absolutely nothing about the psychological
qualities of those who actually possess such organs. One does not
have to be a clinician to recognize penetrative women and receptive
men – nor to conclude that psychology has projected its fantasies
onto the body.

A claim is often made that a female's body contains in it certain
qualities and characteristics that lead to there being a quite specific
and innate female psychology, based on the female body and quite
divorced from male psychology, based on the male body. Now, as I
just mentioned, there seems to be no problem with the idea that
males and females have experiences of their bodies as different
from the other sex's body. But the argument that innate
psychological differences between the sexes are based on the body
has serious and insidious difficulties in it. It *sounds* so grounded, so
reasonable, so common-sensical, so different from social or
ideological styles of exploring gender issues. However, if
psychological activity is body-based then, as body is more or less a
constant over the entire history of humanity, body-based
psychological theory can only *support* the horrendous gender
situation with which we are faced just now. For, if it is body-based,
how can it be altered? It must be an inevitability and we would have
to agree with Stevens when he argues that 'patriarchy is the natural
condition of mankind' (Stevens 1982: 188).

Of course, psychology cannot be split off from the body. But the
link is on a deeper level even than that of anatomical or
endocrinological distinctiveness. The link between psyche and
body surely refers to the body *as a whole* – its moods and
movements, its pride and shame, its rigour and its messiness. On
this level, the body in question is already a psychological body, a
psychesoma, an imaginal body even – providing a whole range of
experiences. Sometimes, this imaginal body provides crossover
experiences, 'masculine' for women and 'feminine' for men. When

the link between psyche and body is envisioned in terms of the body as a whole, then whether that body is anatomically male or anatomically female is less significant. But I am not attempting to deny anyone's experience of their body, nor to dispute the value of paying attention to the body. Indeed, the descriptions in this book of the father's relations with his children are markedly oriented towards physical experience and activity.

Even on a literal, bodily level, recent advances in anatomical research show that things are not what they seem to be. This renders attempts to link bodily and psychological characteristics, even of a subtle and metaphorical kind, highly relative, mutable, and conditioned by the state of knowledge and belief at any one time. In her book *Eve's Secrets* (1987), Lowndes engages in a comparative study of women's and men's sex organs. It turns out that the results of such studies depend completely upon what is compared. For instance, we usually compare penis and vagina, or penis and clitoris. But what if we compare the penis to the sum of clitoris, urethra, and vagina (the so-called CUV)? Then, according to Lowndes, the fact that the clitoris does have a much longer and deeper structure under the skin that merely culminates in the visible crown means that the female possesses an organ equal in size to the penis and composed of the same erectile material. What is more, a woman has a glans – this is not to be found on her clitoris but close by the opening of her urethra, a raised area as yet possessing no consensual medical name. Looking at the man, Lowndes points out how little is known about the inside of the penis and suggests that in the *corpora cavernosa* there is an area, or spot, that is as sensitive as the clitoris and performs the same functions: a male clitoris.

Lowndes has also found that men and women both have erections, though the charging with blood is visible more markedly in the male. She has also established, by means of careful test measurement, that there is a female ejaculation, composed of fluid that is neither urine nor vaginal secretion.

Anatomical differences between sex organs of men and women are, on the basis of Lowndes's work, quite literally skin-deep. *However, the point is not whether she is right or wrong about it but rather to underline the problems with regarding the body as a fixed element in a body–psyche linkage.* Again, this is not to deny such a link, merely to point out the impossibility of dismissing fantasy and/or changing knowledge from our eventual conclusions.

A further instance of the psychological significance of such work is that it is not at all new. In 400 BC Hippocrates said that men and women both ejaculate. In AD 150 Galen said that the vagina and ovaries are penis and testicles 'inside out'. In 1561 Fallopio discovered, as well as his tubes, that the clitoris has deep structures. In 1672 Regnier de Graaf looked for and found evidence of female ejaculation. It seems that what we say is the case about the body is already psychological (e.g. Freud or, indeed, Kinsey).

Why is this issue of the body as a possible base for sex-specific psychology so critical? I can give two suggestions about this. First, the whole cultural versus innate gender debate is, or has become numinous. If I have taken one side rather than advancing a multifactorial theory, this is partly because it is what *I* think, partly because that's my personal style, and partly because a clash of doctrines is where the life in psychology is to be found. Again, though I think I'm right, it does not matter so much whether I am right or wrong, but whether what I am talking about can be recognized.

The second reason why the gender debate stirs us has to do with our ambivalence about our constitution, the psychological make-up that we bring into the world. On the one hand, how secure and fulfilling to know that one is quite definitely a man or a woman! I certainly feel a need for certainty and at no time do I suggest that there are no such entities as men or women. On the other hand, I am sure that anatomy is not destiny and am trying to work my resentment at the idea that it might be into a critique of those who tell me it is. There are no *direct* messages from the body.

Which leads back to the great problem with an overdependence in theory-making on the body's impact on psychology. If anatomy is destiny, then nothing can be done to change the position of women. So women who base their quest for a new and positive meaning for femininity on the body inadvertently undermine their own cause. On the contrary, we know how definitions of women and men change over time. Up until the end of the eighteenth century, for instance, representations of men in literature and drama quite often had them as crying – so different from this century, in which big boys don't cry. The body is not an icon in a vacuum.

It follows that animus and anima images are not of men and women because animus and anima qualities are 'masculine' and 'feminine'. No – here, for the individual woman or man, anatomy is a metaphor for the richness and potential of the 'other'. A man will imagine what is 'other' to him in the symbolic form of a woman – a being with another anatomy. A woman will symbolize what is foreign to her in terms of the kind of body she does not herself have. The so-called contrasexuality is more something 'contra-psychological'; anatomy is a metaphor for that . But anatomy is absolutely *not* a metaphor for any particular emotional charact-eristic or set of characteristics. That depends on the individual and on whatever is presently outside her or his conscious grasp and hence in need of being represented by a personification of the opposite sex. *The difference between you and your animus or anima is very different from the difference between you and a man or woman.* (I do realize that I am discussing animus and anima in their personified forms but I am bringing them in as illustrative of the indirect nature of the relation between body and psyche.)

What I am saying is that *'metaphor' can be as seductively misleading and one-sided as 'literalism'*. Sometimes, it is claimed that 'masculine' and 'feminine' are metaphors (you know, 'just' metaphors) for two distinct *Weltanschauungen* or the typical styles of operating of the two cerebral hemispheres. Why can't we just talk of *Weltanschauungen* or just of hemispheres? When we bring in either masculinity and femininity *or* maleness and femaleness we are projecting a dichotomy that certainly exists in human ideation and functioning onto convenient receptors for the projections. Then the argument that masculinity and femininity should be understood nonliterally, as really having nothing to do with bodily men and bodily women in a social context, may be taken as a recognition that a projection has been made, but falling far short of a successful recollection of it, certainly as far as our culture is concerned. All the other divisions that we know about – rational/irrational, Apollonian/Dionysian, classical/romantic, digital/analogic, and so forth – all these exist in every human being. They cannot conveniently be assigned by gender (or sex), save by the kind of bifurcated projection I have depicted. Why do we make such a projection? Surely it is more than a question of language? It could be because we find difficulty in living with both sides of our murky human natures. In our borderline way, we import a degree of certainty and clarity, and hence reduce anxiety, by making the projection. Summarizing my view: it is in this projection that we find the origins of dualist ambitions to construct distinct psychologies for the two sexes and of the attempt to use 'masculinity' and 'femininity' solely as metaphors.

The whole gender debate suggests that, as with the father's relations to his children, we need to question whether heterosexuality itself should be taken as innate and therefore as something fundamental and beyond discussion, or whether it, too, has a nonbiological dimension. Freud's perception was of an innate *bisexuality* followed later by heterosexuality. Jung's view was that man and woman are each incomplete without the other: heterosexuality is therefore a given. In this sense he differs from Freud's emphasis on bisexuality as the natural state of mankind. In Freud's approach, sexual identity arises from the enforced twin demands of reproduction and society. What I have been arguing shifts the concept of bisexuality from something undifferentiated (polymorphous or polyvalent) into a vision of *there being available to all a variety of positions in relation to gender role – without recourse to the illusion of androgyny.*

Feminist art critics have faced up to many of these problems concerning the body. In a critique of the relation between the biologic and the cultural, Parker and Pollock state that 'acknowledging the importance of events of the body ... is not reducible to biological essentialism, a facet of patriarchal ideology which supposes a primordial difference between the sexes determined by anatomical and specifically genital structures. How the body is lived and experienced is implicated at all levels in social or societally determined psychic processes' (Parker and Pollock 1987: 29). Parker and Pollock go on to describe an art work entitled 'Menstruation II' by Cate Elwes. During her period, dressed in white and seated in a white, glass-fronted box, she could be watched bleeding. Questions and her answers could be written on the walls of the box. Elwes wrote, 'The work reconstitutes menstruation as a metaphorical framework in which it becomes the medium for the expression of ideas and experience by giving it the authority of cultural form and placing it within an art context' (quoted in Parker and Pollock 1987: 30).

If discriminations like these are not made, then those analytical psychologists who espouse the idea of innate, body-based, sex-specific psychologies, find themselves lined up with those groupings often referred to as the 'New Right'. New Right assumptions about sex-specific psychology tend to be based on appeals to tradition and often have a romantic appeal but, as Statham has argued in her paper 'Women, the new right and social work' (1987), those working therapeutically need to be aware of the way in which the assumptions can be used to promote the notion of 'order' and of how women's activities, in particular, are decisively limited.

The same point is made, with a good deal of passion, by Anne

McManus in the August 1987 issue of the British feminist journal *Spare Rib*. She wrote:

> Feminism is flowing with the rightward tide, its critical radical spirit diluted beyond recognition ... A decisive shift came in the transformation of women's *liberation* from oppression, to today's *confirmation* of that oppression in a type of popular feminism which unashamedly embraces anything female. Never mind that this implies a conservative re-embracing of traditional women's roles that the original movement was all about denouncing. Now any old gullible gush practised by women is feminist, especially if it's emotive, and authentic (what isn't authentic anyway at this level?), and anti-male rationality. A false dichotomy between thinking men and feeling women evacuates reason to men while women's fates are sealed, trapped again in eternal emotionality which leaves male power safely intact. Thus women are immobilised and trivialised by their very softness and tenderness, voluntarily abdicating the dirty power struggle, and *thereby* the power, to those who have it.

7

Gender and the borderline

In borderline personality disorders, the rigid separation of gender certainty and gender confusion is exemplified. The parallel is with the way the borderline individual often keeps his/her neurotic and psychotic elements apart (in addition to their interpenetration). However, the possibility of healing the split between gender certainty and gender confusion in borderline patients like Penny (see Chapter 5) inspires us to think of healing the split in a culture that is divided in the same way.

Throughout this chapter there are numerous parallels to be drawn with the debate on gender discussed in the previous one. We can see how the balance of understanding concerning borderline psychology falls into a spectrum, with an oscillation between an emphasis on the innate disposition of the individual patient, transmitted by heredity, or emphasis on family dynamics, and an interactive perspective that couples both of these emphases. The two debates on gender and on the borderline are not about the same thing. But the parallels between them mean that the two can be played into one another: gender and the borderline; borderline and gender. Common to the two debates are issues concerning heredity, aggression, and tension between inborn and environmental factors. Though the two debates are intellectually unconnected, they have a similar *shape* and flavour. It may be interesting to let the two debates interact and see what one does to the other. Then an intellectually imaginative act – to look at one problematic (borderline) in terms of the other (gender). It is no accident that the figure of the father gradually forms out of the mists of this method for the father links up the hereditary factor, aggression, borderline personality organization, and the chimera of gender.

It may be felt that this approach, which is essentially *reflexive*, working on the psychology of psychology, somehow lacks heart, in that ideas are set in interactive motion rather than being adhered to with commitment. Certainly, if the main plank of the chapter were to be comparison, there would be a valid criticism. But it is not. Rather, the shifting and mutable nature of ideograms like 'gender' and 'borderline' is respected and responded to by letting them 'fix' each other. I do not neglect the central emotional experience of choice in relation to competing theories (as the last chapter certainly demonstrates). However, as mentioned in Chapter 1, in addition to finding a *numinosum* in what is chosen, I also find something numinous in the act of choice itself.

The fascination of the borderline

First, it is necessary to consider why the clinical concept of 'borderline' has exercised such a fascination for analytical theorists in recent years. Here, I want to make an introductory suggestion: the issue of aggression, which is a central one for most approaches to borderline disorders, may be a clue as to why borderline phenomenology is currently of such enormous interest – to the point where some have become fed up with the idea. We live in aggressive times and nuclear weapons heighten the dangers of the expression of aggression. Problems concerning aggression and the owning of aggressive fantasy are also central to depression and my 'take' on borderline disorder is that it masks serious depressive illness as well as psychosis. Thus, borderline conditions may be looked at as affective disorders, involving distortions in self-image and gender identity, as opposed to ambulant schizophrenia, defensively contained. What we see in borderline symptomatology may be *depression sine depressione*. None of the usual clinical features of depression are present: no retardation or delusional guilt. Instead, we see agitation, anxiety, massive despair, and nihilistic delusions – of the decay and destruction of the body.

Nosologically, depression in borderline conditions probably has to be seen as a form of depressive psychosis. Crucially, depressive psychosis differs from nonpsychotic depression in that the sufferer shows no signs of wanting to be rid of the condition, which is, instead, accepted. This acceptance is of the nature of a bowing to an authoritarian inner source that says, paternalistically, that it is wrong to get well.

Continuing to probe the many reasons for analysts' current interest in borderline conditions, it is possible to see that some of these are themselves reflexive; that is, they arise from the self-interested point of view of the analyst. For instance, there is a requirement to justify theoretically what is already happening clinically anyway and to make private and implicit theory public and official (see Samuels 1985a: 267-9). Analysis has always displayed an ambivalent face towards its patients. On the one hand, analysis always shows signs of wanting to be selective, to *vomit* out the unsuitable (symptom, patient, trainee), to be elitist. But, on the other hand, analysis also wants to include everyone in its therapy, the whole world even, in a gigantic act of *swallowing*. The obsessive attempts to define, list, and evaluate the characteristics of borderline conditions show this vomiting/swallowing ambiguity: who should be excluded from treatment, who might be included in it (see Gunderson and Singer 1975).

The borderline speaks to us so deeply because in it we test the *limits* of sanity and madness. Jung is supposed to have said, 'Show me a sane man and I will cure him for you', but I prefer Chico Marx: 'You can't fool me. There ain't no Sanity Clause.' We know from the anti-psychiatrists how impossible it is to define sanity and madness. Being sane means not being in hospital; sanity is in part the result of social learning, not least of cultural gender expectations. Yet we do know when someone is completely crazy. The whole idea of a borderline between sanity and madness, and particularly of a personality organization (that is, people) connected with that, may be seen as our attempt to settle our anxiety about madness. We are saying: we can talk of sanity and madness (neurosis and psychosis) *precisely because* we have allowed for a grey area between them. We are also saying: even a grey area is a defined area and, once we've defined an area, we can do something in/about it – 'treat' it.

Though the words are not used much, on account of our current subtlety and liberality in relation to them, the ideograms of sanity and madness have not vanished from collective consciousness. Instead, we have sought to defuse madness by evacuating its religious, daemonic, mysterious connotations and replacing them with the peculiar blend of Romantic nature-worship and scientism that constitutes modern psychiatry and depth psychology. When we study and treat borderline patients, our envious fascination is with their tricksterish capacity to be 'mad' without completely letting go of being sane. The borderline state is a way of going mad tactfully and without attracting too much attention. *The clever construction of the grey reinforces the secret presence of the black and white.*

The borderline person corralls the ecstasy of madness. That is, not completely crazy, not incapable of making a point or a decision, not dead. Some of the features of borderline personality organization in the lists referred to above do unwittingly show the ecstasy of the borderline: intense affect, sometimes with depersonalization; impulsive behaviour, sometimes directed against the self; brief psychotic experiences; disturbed personal relationships, sometimes exceedingly intimate and sometimes distant. This could be the profile of a saint.

Then there is the general fascination of the border as an image. Hermes was the god of borders and boundaries and the kind of creativity associated with liminality may be found in a state of madness that isn't lost in the fog of absolute craziness. The borderline patient is just sane enough to *see* the archetypes rather than live them out impulsively.

Of course, there is no border. Are there ever true borders (for example, between the sexes) in human psychology, or only border areas, no-man's lands, DMZs, joint sovereignties? At least border areas can be permeable, with room for inputs and outputs. The body comes to mind here for it is all border area. If border areas are permeable, then the element in psychic structure that they most closely resemble is the ego. Ego (and analyst, for that matter) need just the right amount of permeability. Too many perforations and the unconscious floods in; we lose personal and social cohesiveness. Too few, and there will be a brittle and unproductive divorce from creative libido; we lose religious sensibility and the artistic instinct. *Just as there needs to be movement between ego and unconscious, so there needs to be movement between the neurotic and psychotic parts of a personality* – hence the relevance of the gender certainty/gender confusion dichotomy mentioned at the start of the chapter.

Maybe the borderline is a protection. When analytical writers refer to it as a type of personality organization or as defensive, they have this in mind. But on which side of the borderline lies the enemy? To continue in too martial a vein is to become unable to conceive of neurosis and psychosis *together*, of primary and secondary process together, of fantasy and directed thinking together, of gender certainty and gender confusion together.

What does a border, or boundary, mean in interpersonal life? It is impossible to say with conviction that the border is 'between' people – i.e. that border is to do with 'separation'. Intense dyadic relationships have access to the *mundus imaginalis*, and then the border may be viewed as surrounding the couple, or linking them – or there may be no need to postulate a border at all (see Chapter 9).

The borderline debate

The remarkable thing about the psychoanalytic debate concerning borderline disorder is that it is taking place at all. For the whole enterprise is radically undermined by the sentiment that there is no such disease entity as the borderline, and that borderline phenomenology is best understood either in terms of narcissistic personality disorder or latent schizophrenia. Nevertheless, and because of some or all of the reasons for its fascination that have been suggested, the idea of borderline seems here to stay.

The debate referred to revolves, as readers will know, around the names of Kernberg and Kohut. As so often in vicious, personalized power struggles, the protagonists have much in common. Both are reacting against a fossilized usage of ego psychology, though Kernberg is keen to retain a place for structural metapsychology in his model. Both have tried to go beyond drive theory, particularly where that is used outside of a fabric of relationship. To the outsider, Kernbergian object relations and Kohut's formulation of the self/selfobject relationship seem to overlap.

But when it comes to the diagnosis, aetiology, and treatment of borderline disorder, disagreement sets in. Kernberg's (1967; 1975; 1984) emphasis is on an innate, or at least very early excess of aggression that, coupled with a low tolerance of anxiety and lack of impulse control, leads to a defensive division of the ego. The individual's problems with the intensity of his/her aggression are said to be constitutionally determined. Concerning psychosexual development, Kernberg observes in such patients: (1) a premature and complicated experience of the Oedipus complex; (2) inability to distinguish between father and mother; (3) a tendency for father to replace mother as the object of dependency; (4) either or both parents seen as dangerous to sexual fulfilment. In general, there is a muddle in the patient between what Kernberg sees as appropriate two-person psychological functioning and three-person psychological functioning. Treatment of borderline conditions is by 'expressive' psychotherapy, emphasizing the usual psychoanalytic desiderata: neutrality, transference interpretation, etc.

Kohut objects to Kernberg's reliance on the idea of conflict. Kohut regards all psychoanalytic endeavour previous to his own as marred by the emphasis on conflict (1971; 1977). Conflict, according to Kohut, rests on the old-fashioned biological bias of psychoanalysis, especially ego psychology. It is an external imposition onto the internal subjective world of meaning, an artificial drawing up of the lines of battle by an outsider, contradicting the felt experience of the person. The notion of conflict rests on some idea of a 'mental apparatus' within and through which the conflict takes place. Above all, conflict psychology refers to drive-related needs and wishes that may or may not be met. Kohut's replacement for this is a relational model, stressing developmental needs such as for mirroring and empathy. Interestingly, Kohut (1978) did call for conflict psychology and his self-psychology to be used in tandem, a call that was not taken up. Indeed, it was explicitly rejected by some (e.g. Wallerstein 1983). Elsewhere, I suggested that, in analytical psychology, there was evidence that this call has been heeded, albeit unknowingly (Samuels 1985a: 128, 161-2).

According to Kohut, borderline disorders may be seen as deficits in the fabric of an evolving self, caused by an insufficiently empathic and mirroring early environment. In the borderline patient, the self is in a state of permanent or protracted break-up, weakness, or distortion. It should be noted that Kohut has ceased to use a schema of subsystems, one of which might overwhelm the others. There may be different self-images or self-representations that do not fit harmoniously together, but then that is part of being human. They are all still 'self'.

Kohut's preferred treatment for borderline conditions is, like Kernberg's, psychoanalytic in orientation. But Kohut concentrates more on the facilitation of self–selfobject relations by mirroring and empathy and less on the interpretation of conflict. In spite of Kohut's express statement that empathy has not 'replaced' interpretation, Kernberg criticizes Kohut for merely enabling patients to 'rationalise' their anger against the parents who have let them down. Kohut is therefore charged with being supportive and educative, hence unpsychoanalytic. Kernberg also claims that Kohut has left no place for aggression in the analysis of the borderline patient; this is because of his underplaying of aggression in the aetiology of borderline conditions. In a nutshell, Kernberg's accusation is that Kohut, *qua* analyst, is a mother:

The misinterpretation and overgeneralisation of these findings imply that, for patients in regression, it is the therapist's empathic presence – rather than his interpretation – that is really helpful; that it is the patient's identification with this mothering function – rather than his coming to terms with his intrapsychic conflicts – that is important.... Empathy is a prerequisite for interpretive work, not its replacement.

(Kernberg 1979: 231-2)

If we look at this charge more closely, two questions come to mind. First, does Kernberg advocate analyst-as-father, or does he merely claim to have mother-and-father aspects of himself as analyst in balance? Second, is something revealed about Kernberg's fantasy of a mother: one who makes no place for aggression? In more sober vein, it seems that we do need to discuss the whole question of *the mirroring of aggressive impulses and fantasies* (as in Chapter 5, the section on the role of the father in transforming aggressive impulses and fantasies).

In terms of depth psychology's perennial quest to find out whether something 'really' happened or whether it was 'fantasy', Kohut and Kernberg hold opposite positions. Kernberg's perspective is markedly internal, Kohut's seems to be exceedingly external. Actually, Kohut has made a truly synthesizing contribution here. He says, in effect, that while the reported actual child abuse, for instance, may not have happened, this does not mean that we are dealing solely with fantasy or wish. It is possible to experience and refer to an *actual* atmosphere of child abuse, not just 'psychically real' for the child. The atmosphere is as 'real' as you like. As far as I am aware, Kohut was the first psychoanalyst explicitly to make this point (Kohut 1983).

Both Kernberg and Kohut describe borderline dynamics in terms of an avoided psychosis. The resultant connection to schizophrenia takes us back to the roots of the borderline concept, which are in biologically-based psychiatry (Stone 1986: 5-13). Though the history is important, there is also a fundamental contemporary challenge here. When we consider the possibility of innate excesses of aggression or constitutionally low levels of anxiety tolerance, we have, in the back of our minds, some form of innate delimiter of mental health and mental illness. As I suggested earlier, the borderline syndrome has an extraordinary capacity to bring such issues to the forefront of attention.

113

In the discussion about gender-based psychology, we met a similar theme: the extent to which psychological performance is delimited and limited by anatomical sex. We saw that it is questionable to link levels of aggression to biological factors and that raises the whole question of whether a person's actual sex predisposes them towards a certain kind of psychopathology.

The hereditary factor

One specific issue that is relevant to discussing borderline disorder and discussing gender is that of innate aggression. Psychoanalysis as a whole entertains several ideas about aggression: it is innate; later patterns of aggressive discharge and relating depend on earlier ones; if early experiences of aggression are unsatisfactory, aggression may take a predominantly malign form in later life. Now, I am not intending to discuss the death instinct here, nor the question of cumulative psychopathology over a lifetime. Rather, what concerns me is *the hereditary factor*. I have tried to be consistent in my use of the terms 'innate' and 'hereditary factor'. By innate, I mean something inborn, common to all. By the hereditary factor I mean, broadly speaking, the individual's dose or portion of some innate quality, conceived of as stemming from his or her family of origin.

When an idea arouses great anxiety, it is worth investigating. It is interesting to see how Kernberg's latest statement of his position (Kernberg 1984) downplays the innate nature of an excess of aggression in favour of aggression deriving from massive, very early frustration. The effect is to make aggression a *secondary* element and frustration the key dynamic. Sometimes, the hereditary factor is sidestepped and a multifactorial viewpoint advanced, usually with considerable finesse. For example, Stone suggests that, while the hereditary factor will push some people towards a borderline state in spite of the high quality of their parenting, there are also very destructive families that can do that all on their own without any help from genetic liability (Stone 1986: 421).

Of course, Stone is probably right but what shines out is the particular quality of anxiety produced by the hereditary factor, by the genes. Not what is *not* in our genes, but what *is* in them. When we discussed gender, we saw how the same kind of anxiety is present, so it may be worthwhile trying to anatomize it.

The hereditary factor stalks the nature–nurture divide – itself a false distinction, of course. Kohut's assumption, as he tries to go beyond drive theory, is that the body-based and the biologic are enemies to his kind of empathic–introspective understandings. It is as if the biological were not human. The anxiety, which I am affected by as well, is that we may lose our freedom of manoeuvre, even our freedom as persons and as analysts, if we try to ingest the hereditary factor. It is certainly the case that genetics is usually employed in a reactionary or conservative cause and therefore we are right to be worried.

Perhaps we can best get at the kind of anxiety the hereditary factor arouses by regarding our reaction as a form of moral panic. Innate aggression, *as an idea*, produces a whole variety of responses in us, ranging from scientific understanding, to wise acceptance, to idealistic rejections, to religious belief in perfectibility. We are frightened that we may find that *illness* is the fundament of the personality, that the archaic distortions in our complexes are, themselves, the grounds of our being, that we are constitutionally unable to cope with ourselves, that we are inherently deviant, born in sin. The moment the innate enters, even in an interactional, multifactorial approach, something comes in whose impact is massive and unpredictable.

Jung's views on the causation of schizophrenia shed light on both the innate–environment question and on what we might mean by sanity and insanity. The evolution of Jung's thought reveals his uncertainty. He is clear that schizophrenia is a psychosomatic disorder, that changes in body chemistry and personality distortions are somehow intertwined. Jung did not consider borderline disorders as such, of course, but the concern to establish whether chemistry or personality is primary is directly relevant to the contemporary problem.

Jung's superior, Bleuler, thought that some kind of toxin or poison was developed by the body that then led to psychological disturbance. Jung's crucial contribution was to establish that psyche was sufficiently important for us to reverse the elements: psychological activity may lead to somatic changes. Jung did attempt to combine his ideas with those of Bleuler, however, by means of an ingenious formula. While the mysterious toxin might well exist in all of us, it would only have its devastating effect if psychological circumstances were favourable to this. Alternatively, a person might be genetically predisposed to develop the toxin and this would 'invade' the complexes. That schizophrenia was

115

anything other than an innate, neurological abnormality was, in its time, revolutionary (see Samuels *et al.* 1986). That its causation was psychogenic within a psychosomatic framework (Jung's final position, *CW* 3: paras. 553f.) enabled him to propose that psychological treatment – psychotherapy – was appropriate. *Our position is different. We have trouble with the toxin!*

Admitting that the constitutional and the inherited play their part, even a determining part, in the formation of borderline personality or gender identity does not require us to give up on hopes of social change or on therapy or to throw out the texts of developmental psychology. Hailing *everything* as inborn or 'archetypal' is counterphobic, a reaction formation to the hereditary factor, a blind refusal to countenance individual *peculiarity* and the *specificity* of 'constitution'. Facing the hereditary factor in the level of aggression in each and every one of us of whichever sex makes it even more important to track the individual movement of a person *with and through their inborn characteristics*, with and through their fate, in and through their family and culture.

Historically, the earliest discussions about borderline patients involved the idea of a hereditary 'taint' (see Stone 1986: 1-5). Stone decided to investigate the psychiatric histories of the relatives of borderline patients, using (mainly) Kernberg's criteria for the diagnosis. His conclusion was that:

many patients called borderline – by most of the popular definitions – appear to have a pronounced hereditary predisposition to mental illness. Often this factor is sufficiently striking to permit the clinician to make an educated guess about the patient's vulnerability, his eventual course and the type of psychotherapy and medication that will prove most effective.

Stone then adopts a historical perspective and continues:

The importance of a hereditary factor in these conditions is no new discovery; it was taken for granted by the psychiatric and psychoanalytic communities until the second generation of psychoanalysts began to adopt a more linear and purely psychologic model of causation.

(Stone 1986: 493)

As noted earlier, Stone does slightly modify his findings by referring to families that are so destructive that they can bring about a borderline situation without any innate predisposition being present. But that surely begs the question: *Is there an effectual difference between inheritance in genetic and inheritance in familial terms?*

I must confess that I was surprised to find that 'inheritance' turned out to be at the heart of the borderline mystery because my own views (for example, on gender) usually tend towards the environment–cultural end of any explicatory spectrum. What I have discovered while working with borderline patients, and on these ideas, is the kind of anxiety in me about the hereditary factor that I have been depicting. If something *less* than total insanity can be inherited then maybe *everything* psychological can be. We have to entertain the idea of a 'soft heredity' as well as a 'hard' kind, meaning inheritance of a pattern and proportion of passions, especially aggression.

The mythos that speaks most directly to the conundrum of the innate is that of Sisyphus. His ultimate crime was to try to avoid the most innate factor of all – death – and his punishment as tricky as the means he used in his futile attempt. Just when we feel free of whom we always were, that aggressive inner runt, we have to go back to the beginning, to the beginnings. Which of us has not suddenly got much worse in the last segment of our personal analysis? Sisyphus becomes spokesman for our theme in other ways. His original crime was to inform on Zeus for having abducted the nymph Aegina. And the strategem by which he arranges his return from Hades involves the co-operation of his wife. Sisyphus' stone rolls together images of the father, the father's sexuality, and the perennial hope that other people, one's spouse in particular, will help one to avoid the unavoidable.

Aggression, gender, and borderline personality disorder

In spite of its concern with aggression, as Galenson (1986) has noted, depth psychology has contributed very little to our understanding of the 'normal' developmental sequence of aggression. One reason for this may be the way in which stimuli for aggression are different from those for hunger, say. They *seem* environmental rather than self-generated. Perhaps this is how we prefer to conceive of aggression, even when, intellectually, we concede its innate nature.

To illustrate the effects of parental deprivation upon aggressive development, Galenson presented an account of eight female infants in a therapeutic nursery, all from disadvantaged backgrounds and whose fathers were not readily available to them. Their very early development was unremarkable but, as they started to walk, they were abandoned by their mothers emotionally. They were often struck for being 'bad' and, eventually, the little girls developed the habit of striking their dolls and their mothers. When these children were around 18 months old, they showed an interesting pattern in relation to any adult men they encountered: 'a combination of teasing and flirtatiousness.... Unlike the usual pattern of sexual arousal, however, the strong admixture of aggression in these children made it difficult to decide whether they were loving or attacking these men' (Galenson 1986: 352). What is more, the way the girls related to their mothers strongly resembled the way the mothers related to men. Galenson's descriptions underscore the links between aggression and gender identity.

Stone (1981) saw things in reverse, as it were. Galenson's observations connect an aggressive mother with later gender problems, whereas his opinion was that, in many instances, actual incest contributes greatly to the formation of borderline personality organization:

> Women who have been victimized in this manner, particularly by older male relatives, often develop sharply polarized and ambivalent attitudes towards men, an image of themselves as both angel and prostitute, a reckless and impulsive lifestyle, and chaotic, turbulent relationships with men, oscillating between adoration and jealous mistrustfulness.
>
> (Stone 1986: 422)

We should be careful lest the borderline spectrum become a tag for women. Maybe this already happened; Stone opines that the diagnosis ratio is between 2:1 and 3:1 in favour of women. It is conceivable that aggression in women may look 'excessive' if women are regarded as 'normally' and 'naturally' unaggressive. Therefore, the diagnosis of borderline personality disorder on the ground of excess aggression would be erroneous. On the other hand, as women are *aware* that they are supposed to be unaggressive, and as this awareness is lifelong, a woman's subjective experience of her aggression, and the attitude of her parents to it, may contribute to a state of 'excess' in terms of psychic reality. Unfortunately, as so often, gender-role stereotyping has a way of becoming a self-fulfilling truth.

To conclude the chapter, let us now look at such gender-role stereotyping on a cultural level.

The imitation game (I)

The mathematician Alan Turing was interested in seeing whether machine intelligence would ever match that of humans. He proposed to do this by playing the 'Imitation Game' (Hofstadter and Dennett 1981: 70-3). Though Turing was going to use a computer, the game can be played by people. In the Imitation Game, two concealed persons are questioned. One is a man and the other a woman. The man attempts to imitate a woman and the woman answers as herself. The other participants have to decide, on the basis of their answers, which is the man and which the woman. The object is not to show that there are no gender differences but how elusive such differences are.

A colleague of mine, David Curry, thought that it would be interesting to play the Imitation Game. Curry was working with a suitable group of students and I am extremely grateful to him for providing me with an account of what happened.

A and B were sent to different rooms and a messenger appointed to relay the questions and answers. In all, eleven questions were asked. Here is a selection:

Q: If you have breast-fed your baby describe the sensation. If not, describe what feeding was like. A: It was a mixture of being at one with the baby, of getting to know the baby as a separate person and often a visceral attachment to the baby which made my stomach turn over when the baby cried. B: It was actually a very hard experience – ill after birth – not producing enough milk. Baby was separated most of time from me in an incubator – only saw him at feeding times and after a week my milk dried. It felt like getting blood from a stone.

Q: What differences do you see between men's and women's

intuition? A: A woman's intuition is allowed and has more chance to develop. B: On the whole women are far more intuitive and sensitive at reading between the lines.

Q: What do you fear most about women? A: Pretence – my mother used to pretend to be weak. I felt I had to mother her and protect her. B: My mother was a very stabilizing influence in my life and this has led me to be very much at ease with women.

Q: What do you fear most about men? A: Their pretence – my father used to pretend to be powerful. I felt he was too fragile. B: My father was a very powerful man who used to attack me mentally and physically and this has left 'scars' in one or two of my subsequent relationships.

Q: How was it for you? A: Lovely darling – and for you? B: It was pretty good.

Q: How do you feel if you are the one who doesn't have an orgasm? A: That's OK – but it does depend on the timing. B: The times when I do have an orgasm are so good I can cope with the rest.

The reader is invited to play the game. Which is the woman? The answer is at the end of the chapter.

The imitation game (II)

The Imitation Game is also the title of a play by Ian McEwan, who is well known in England. In his introduction to the piece, McEwan tells of its genesis. McEwan first became interested in the personality of Turing, a brilliant young scientist who was at the heart of the Ultra operation in World War II. This was the vast project to decipher the German Enigma codes by means of primitive electromagnetic computing machines. I do not know how well this story is known in the United States but the fact that the Allies were able to read German communications was absolutely central to the prosecution of the war effort (see Winterbotham 1974). In Britain, the name 'Bletchley' (the place where Ultra was located) sets off associations of ingenuity, secrecy, and treachery, for Russian agents passed its secrets to the Soviet Union. Even today, the full story has not been published.

McEwan abandoned this original idea but, in passing, he had

found out both about Turing's Imitation Game and the social organization of Bletchley:

> by the end of the war ten thousand people were working in and around Bletchley. The great majority of them were women doing vital but repetitive jobs working the machines. The 'need to know' rule meant that the women knew as much as was necessary to do their jobs, which was very little. As far as I could discover, there were no women at the centre of Ultra.
>
> (McEwan 1981: 16)

Gradually, McEwan came to think of Ultra as symbolizing, not only the war, but a whole culture: 'the closer you moved to the centre, the more men you found; the further to the periphery, the more women' (McEwan 1981: 17)

So McEwan made his protagonist a woman, Cathy, of lower-middle-class background, who goes to work at Bletchley. Cathy is a talented musician, but is prevented from doing a music course by her tyrannical, small-minded father. With a writer's sensibility, McEwan renders the father as implacably hostile to Cathy's sexuality, considering her evil and promiscuous (she isn't, she's a virgin). Cathy is presented almost as a typical 'borderline' character. She is prone to violent outbursts, has strange turns, struggles in her relationships, and is clearly deeply involved with this negative father of hers.

Cathy arrives at Bletchley and starts her job. She evinces curiosity about what is going on and is warned off. Cathy falls in love with one of the top scientists, Turner, and he invites her to his rooms for tea. They go to bed:

Turner: Are my hands cold?
Cathy: Yes.
Turner: Sorry.
Cathy: It's all right.
Turner: Cathy, are you... is this your first...
Cathy: Yes, it's my first time.
Turner: You don't mind me asking?
Cathy: No, of course not.

   Cathy smiles slightly mischievously.

   What about you?
Turner: What me? (*lying*) It's not...it isn't really my first time...

Cathy: That's good. You know exactly what to do then.
Turner: Well...

Cathy kisses him.

Cathy: You know all the secrets.

She cuddles against him.

But Turner is impotent and accuses Cathy of mocking him with her remark 'You know all the secrets'. He says that she has planned this humiliation, and then he storms off. After Turner has gone, Cathy gets up, washes, and dresses. She moves over to Turner's desk and starts reading the papers on it. A colleague of Turner's comes in, discovers her, and she is arrested and imprisoned for the rest of the war.

McEwan placed a sexual relationship, and its attendant misunderstandings, at the heart of the play. The relationship generates anxiety, confusions, and misunderstandings that both represent and underpin the dynamics of culture. At the end of the play, Cathy talks to the officer who tells her she must go to prison even though they know she is harmless. Finally, she speaks out haltingly against 'gender certainty':

If the girls fired the guns as well as the boys...if girls fired guns and women generals planned the battles...then the men would feel there was no...morality to war, they would have no one to fight for, nowhere to leave their consciences...war would appear to them as savage and as pointless as it really is. The men want the women to stay out of the fighting so they can give it meaning.

When we went to bed, it didn't matter that he couldn't...I didn't care. I liked him. He didn't have to be efficient and brilliant at everything...I liked him more...But he couldn't bear to appear weak before me. He just couldn't stand it. Isn't that the same thing? I mean...as the war.

A was the woman; B was the man.

8

The image of
the parents in bed:
from primal scene
to pluralism

In Chapter 3, when I was discussing parental imagery as a form of psyche's self-monitoring, I mentioned that primal-scene imagery would receive a chapter to itself. In this chapter on the primal scene, the interweave between what might be taken literally, what metaphorically, and what on both levels continues to occupy me. The question of plural interpretation in the clinical situation is also relevant again. The father's presence and image, together with those of the mother, form the raw material of the primal scene. So the chapter follows on from what has already been written.

But there is another sense in which this chapter draws together my previous thoughts, providing a caesura before the last parts of the book on clinical practice and moral process. This concerns the issue of pluralism in depth psychology. For the experience of primal scene imagery may be understood as an individual's emotional attempt to function pluralistically, coupling together his or her various psychic elements and agencies without losing their individual tone and functioning. As far as the emotional development of a depth psychologist is concerned, primal scene imagery refers to attempts to develop one's own ideas *within a tradition* for, as Winnicott recognized, 'there is no such thing as originality except on the basis of a tradition' (Winnicott 1974: 117). It is possible to acknowledge the previous generations' achievements without being devastatingly overawed by them. Similarly, from a theoretical angle, how the primal scene is apperceived and its imagery interpreted can scarcely avoid the competitive interplay of strongly held views.

Images and experiences of parental intercourse and the parental marriage hover between and connect inner and outer, personal and archetypal, destructive and creative. Images are the operant element in fantasy; it is they who permit talk of subjective reality. Because the primal scene has to do with origins and the mystery of a beginning it exerts a fascination; because it has to do with outcome and a tangible result it has a compulsive attraction. We know this from our own analyses, from our work with patients, and from the history of the early days of the psychoanalytic movement.

Why 'in bed'? Concepts (such as the primal scene) need and create contexts, thereby becoming images. Jung points out 'the term "image" is intended to express not only the form of the activity taking place, but the typical situation in which the activity is released' (*CW* 9i: para. 152). The image of the parents in bed is, quite literally, a matter of chicken and egg. The individual is created out of primal scene activity but the scene, *qua* scene, does not itself exist except as part of a combining of endowment with experience. As a colleague has said, it is hard to get the image of the parents in bed together. It is a creation and a symbol for life as it develops. Bringing things together is a précis of creativity.

The question of the role of parental images in the development of personality is an interesting one. Issues such as the balance between reality and fantasy in the formation of internal imagery, the degree of importance of sexuality, and the purposive uses to which inner conceptions and preconceptions may be put are as relevant now as they ever were. In this chapter I am concerned with imagery developing over a period of time, changing or not changing as the case may be. Imagery is seen as deriving from the synthesis of fantasy and fact, subjective with objective elements.

In the chapter I argue that imagery around the parents in bed can be seen as a conjunction of the divine and the grotesque. Not only are these linked, but what is divine is sometimes primitive and what is grotesque is sometimes sublime. In any event, there is a connection which, it is argued, is central to developing self- image, gender identity, and personal relationships.

The conjunction of the grotesque and the divine suggests the presence of a god, and the god who fits the bill, who most aptly could be described as a grotesque divine, is Hermes. Hermes' positive, transforming, connecting aspect is considered together with his tricksterism, his dishonesty, and his sexual perversity and obscenity. Two strands of argument emerge from this. First, that the function of apparently criminal or immoral impulses and behaviour needs reviewing as a developmental factor. The second strand is that Hermes' pluralistic encapsulation of adaptability and flexibility signifies something central for the resolution of neurotic conflicts generated by the primal scene. Jung says that 'Mercurius consists of all conceivable opposites ... is a unity in spite of the fact that his innumerable inner contradictions can dramatically fly apart into an equal number of disparate and apparently independent figures' (*CW* 13: para. 284). Hermes is 'many-sided' (*CW* 13: para. 267) and has 'a limitless number of names' (*CW* 13: para. 284). My interest in adaptability began first in relation to its opposite – uroboric omnipotence in which, for example, precise inner preconceptions as to the ideal partner controlled heterosexual activity (Samuels 1980).

The adaptation that is focused on is that which must occur between the world of two-person relationships and that of three-person relationships. As Jung puts it, Mercurius is 'called husband and wife, bridegroom and bride, or lover and beloved' (*CW* 13: para. 268). His hermaphroditism suggests not only early sexualized confusion, but also the possibility of psychic resolution. Jung connects Mercurius with the Trinity in particular and 'triune divinity in general' (*ibid.*: para. 271), and, while the chapter does not explore this, it can be said that threeness and triangles are of the essence of the Oedipus complex and, of course, the image of the parents in bed. Hermes is three-headed, but he is also a unity and therefore contains seeds of acceptance of the plurality of family and the emergence and integration of differentiated parental images.

The move from twoness to threeness takes place, on the one hand, in the outer world as the baby 'discovers' his father in reality and experiences differences from the mother. On the other hand, however, in the inner world of imagery, a move is also taking place in which images of twoness evolve into images of threeness as the father separates from the internal family matrix. There are two primary images of twoness – mother and baby, and then the baby's image of his parents – and in the chapter I attempt to describe the interactive processes between these images of twoness as the individual moves towards three-person operating. Similarities and differences in the style and tone of mother-infant imagery and parents-in-bed imagery are examined and it is hypothesized that a specific psychic activity is taking place in which these images of twoness create a climate in which images of threeness can exist and the paternal image emerge.

The antiquities of human development

Jung and Freud's argument over how literally to take analytical material concerning parental intercourse revolved around the question of whether an adult could produce what looked like actual memories but what were in fact subsequent fantasies. Jung's *ex post facto* explanations stimulated Freud to ask where the later fantasies came from. Freud's insistence that the fantasies must come from *somewhere* led him into man's prehistory. For example, in the *Introductory Lectures on Psychoanalysis* he writes:

> There can be no doubt that the sources [of primal scene phantasies] lie in the instincts; but it still has to be explained why the same phantasies with the same content are created on every occasion. I am prepared with an answer that I know will seem daring to you. I believe that these primal phantasies, and no doubt a few others as well, are a phylogenetic endowment. In them the individual reaches beyond his own experience into primeval experience at points where his own experience has been too rudimentary ... I have repeatedly been led to suggest that the psychology of the neuroses may have more stored up in it of the antiquities of human development than any other source.
>
> (Freud 1916-17: 370-1)

Freud suggests the existence of pre-subjective schemata that might even be strong enough to predominate over the experience of the individual: 'Wherever experiences fail to fit in with the hereditary schema they become remodelled in the imagination' (Freud 1918: 119).

We may not agree with Freud's Lamarckian overtones – the suggestion that primal fantasies are a residue of specific memories of prehistoric experiences – but there is less problem with the position that, in general terms, mental structures have a phylogenetic base. In *The Language of Psychoanalysis* Laplanche and Pontalis point out that all the so-called primal fantasies relate to the origins and that 'like collective myths they claim to provide a representation of and a "solution" to whatever constitutes an enigma for the child' (Laplanche and Pontalis 1980: 332). In many respects these views correspond to Jung's theory of archetypes (see Samuels 1985a: 42-4).

126

In *From the history of an infantile neurosis* (1918) Freud observed that, for the Wolf Man, the main determinants of the primal scene were that it constituted paternal aggression, that therefore the parental marriage was sado-masochistic, that by identifying with either partner in turn the child derived sado-masochistic sexual pleasure causing guilt and anxiety, and that the child fantasized what happened in intercourse as involving anal penetration with attendant imagery of dirt, mess, and power struggle. A key problem for the Wolf Man was caused by his feminine side. He conceived of the sexual opposites in terms of active and passive rather than male and female (Freud 1918: 46). In Jungian terms, the Wolf Man's archetypal images remain unmediated by experiences in the outer world. Summarizing Freud's findings, we can say that the child both projects inner contents and misunderstands on a cognitive level what is happening – his experience is too 'rudimentary'.

The 'parents' are not the parents at all

As we saw in Chapter 5, Jung disputed the solely sexual significance of incest fantasies, stressing, in addition, the role of incestuous sexuality in psychic growth. We have also seen (in Chapter 3) how images of parents function symbolically as psychological potentials within a person. What does the image of the copulating parents represent? Remember, 'in reality the whole drama takes place in the individual's own psyche, where the "parents" are not the parents at all but only their images' (*CW* 5: para. 507). The image of the parents in bed is a metaphor for a *coniunctio oppositorum*. Though this Latin tag can be understood literally as a coming together of *opposites*, a more satisfactory reading would refer us to an *integration* of all manner of psychological phenomena and characteristics, many of which appear to us as so unlikely to belong together as to be 'opposites'. That is, the opposites *seem* to be opposites and therefore the emotional task feels like one of bringing them together. But, as we saw in Chapter 1, there is no need to postulate a psyche entirely characterized by oppositional organization.

Thus the question of the image of the parents in bed as a coming together of opposites can be worked on in more detail, according to the degree and quality of differentiation a person makes between the images of mother and father. For a *coniunctio oppositorum* only becomes fertile when the elements are distinguishable. In plain language, it's not a *stuck* image of parental togetherness that we see in a fertile primal scene, but something divided and unstuck, hence vital – but also linked, hence imaginable. Image holds the linked division in momentary balance.

Differentiation of the parents facilitates looking beyond or through the real parents to membership of the human race and to issues of ontology, purpose, and meaning. 'Mankind has always instinctively added the pre-existent divine pair to the personal parents – the "god" father and "god" mother of the newborn child – so that from sheer unconsciousness or short-sighted rationalism, he should never forget himself so far as to invest his own parents with divinity' (*CW* 9i: para. 172). Differentiation within the image of the parents in bed connects directly with the numinous and with ideas regarding the purpose of life. This seems appropriate, for the primal scene is about genesis and you cannot split alpha from omega. Differentiation implies plurality and conflict; granted sufficient ego-strength, this can lead to conjunction.

However, just as 'the opposites' need to be understood nonliterally, so, too, does the notion of conjunction. One need not think of an annihilation of the initial separate entities, rather of a tripartite possibility: each of the two initial separate entities *and* whatever is implicated in their conjunction – a pluralistic formulation: unity and diversity.

The images of the two parents form the most appropriate raw material for what Jung termed the syzygy – meaning a pair of linked opposites but most often referring to masculine and feminine images (or a pairing of animus and anima). As we saw in Chapter 6 in relation to the question of why animus and anima images are of men and women, the differences between the personifications need to be understood as metaphor. If the psyche is trying to express its multifarious and variegated nature and the possibility of an integration of its plurality, then images of the parents in bed perform this job perfectly. Not because the parents are literally 'opposites'; not because all they do is 'conjoin'; but because they want to be together, have been together, in the individual's mind are still together – and want to be apart, have been apart, and are still apart.

The problem of differentiation remains – indeed, we have to differentiate different kinds of differentiation. For example, a patient referred to her parents' marriage as a 'great big circular jigsaw fuck-up'. She was referring to her incomprehension, her envy, and her feeling of exclusion. The word 'jigsaw' contains the seed of a puzzling experience of differentiation – but, for the moment, only an intellectual solution.

My view is that *personal experiences of primal scene imagery and their working through determine, to a considerable extent, a person's capacity to sustain conflict constructively.* This general point becomes more pertinent when applied to the field of depth psychology. Stuck parental imagery implies intolerance, fantasies of superiority, and difficulties with hearing the views of others. Primal scene imagery in vigorous motion suggests other possibilities – pluralistic possibilities – and other, variegated archetypal states of mind.

Merger and differentiation

Neumann took up the point about discrimination and worked on the differentiation of an early, merged parental imago. My idea is that a process of separating an image of each parent out of an image in which they are merged goes on at the same time as (i.e. is synchronous with) attachment and separation processes with regard to the mother. The distinction between separation *of* the parents and separation *from* mother is not primarily a chronological one.

It can be argued that the image of merged parents arises from a relatively undifferentiated state of mother–infant relations. As Newton points out, there is a problem here of point of view, both with regard to mother–infant and parent-in-bed imagery, because the lack of twoness in both images is what is experienced psychically even if we, the observers, can see that twoness is 'objectively' the case (Newton 1981: 73). If the merged parental image persists beyond an age-appropriate point then it becomes psychopathological and hence an example of the 'stuckness' that is not, and cannot be, a true *coniunctio*. The transition on which we are focusing is from images of mergedness and stuckness towards images of true union of separate entities with attendant conflict.

For the 'unsticking' to take place, Neumann ascribed to the infant affect and behaviour of a vigorous, instinctual, and hence guilt-inducing kind:

This destruction [of the merged parents] is closely associated with the act of eating and assimilation ... The formation of consciousness goes hand in hand with a fragmentation of the world continuum into separate objects, parts, figures, which can only then be assimilated, taken in, integrated, made conscious ... in a word, eaten ... Aggression, destruction, dismemberment and killing are intimately associated with the corresponding bodily functions of eating, chewing, biting and particularly with the symbolism of the teeth as instruments of these activities, all of which are essential for the formation of an independent ego.

(Neumann 1954: 124)

Neumann is arguing that the act of biting and its accompanying fantasies constitute an attempt to differentiate the stuck parental image, to comprehend imaginatively a primal scene in which two distinct parents may have intercourse. 'Not only do ... male and female grow out of this development of opposites ... but opposites like "sacred" and "profane", "good" and "evil" are now assigned their place in the world' (Neumann 1954: 109). (See Chapter 11 for a discussion of the psychological value of aggression.)

Neumann goes on to make an interesting point. He refers to the image of the merged parents as a 'primal deity' in the inner life of the child. It follows that the differentiation of the merged parents into the opposites of mother and father clears the way for the emergence of a type of polytheism – 'God is now experienced and revealed under as many aspects as there are Gods. This means that the ego's powers of expression and understanding have increased enormously' (Neumann 1954: 325). I would add that one facet of this increase in range is the capacity to tolerate the presence of the father. Polytheism is a way of describing the move from paranoid–schizoid mechanisms of control towards variegated two-person exchange and the depressive position. It also stands for the positive aspects of polymorphousness, namely fertility and creative potency. Polytheism rejects idealized fantasies of unitary fusion states (monotheism, if you like). But pluralism, as an expression of psychic vitality, embraces both polytheism and monotheism (see Chapter 1). Its capacity to do this is a primal-scene capacity: parents joined (monotheism) and parents apart but related (polytheism) and a linkage of parents-joined and parents-apart (pluralism).

Projection, introjection, and the image of the parents in bed

Klein approached the problem from a different direction. She stated that the infant conceives of his parents in an almost continuous state of intercourse and is thus able to project any bodily impulse whatsoever on to the image of the parental couple (or, to be more precise, the image of the parents coupling). As Segal says, 'The infant will phantasy his parents as exchanging gratifications, oral, urethral, anal or genital, according to the prevalence of his own impulses ... This gives rise to feelings of the most acute deprivation, jealousy and envy, since the parents are perceived as giving each other precisely those gratifications which the infant wishes for himself' (Segal 1973: 103). The infant then internalizes this heavily coloured image of parental intercourse and the image is now ready for reprojecting, for example, when the individual contemplates a marriage of his own.

One interesting overlap between Klein and Jung and involving the figure of Hermes might be mentioned. Jung shows that Mercurius represents 'continuous cohabitation' and comments on the numerous obscene representations of the *coniunctio*. He adds to this 'pictures in old manuscripts of excretory acts including vomiting' (*CW* 13: para. 278).

It is noticeable that Klein's source of positive connotation within the infant concerning the parents in bed is confined to projections of the infant's own real or fantasized gratifications and wishes leading to envy of the parents in coitus (Klein 1929: 111). Jung's stress on the images of the parents in bed symbolizing an innate potential for integration and individuation is foreign to Klein's theory. She argues that:

...the Oedipus conflict begins under the complete dominance of sadism...the attack launched [upon the objects] with all the weapons of sadism rouses the subject's dread of an analogous attack upon himself from the external and the internalized objects...a special intensity is imparted by the fact that a union of the two parents is in question...these united parents are extremely cruel and much dreaded assailants.

(Klein 1929: 212-13)

Earlier she noted with regard to case material that 'aggressive motor discharges' are provoked by the primal scene (Klein 1929:

122). Riviere demonstrated the extremity of the position in her remark that a patient's unconscious feeling that he has good parents inside him means that the parents are 'idealized...and he is filled with a sense of omnipotence, perfection, grandeur and so on' (Riviere 1952: 21). In essence, Klein is taking what is happening at the breast or anus and, as it were, 'applying' it to the primal scene. There is therefore some interplay between feeding fantasies and primal scene fantasies. One might speculate about the extent to which the interplay in the adult psyche is *two-way*. We can ask, what is the influence of primal scene fantasies on feeding fantasies?

For instance, a patient is deeply involved in the animal welfare movement. While making love, she fantasizes that she is a cow being experimented on by scientists, being cut open and so on. She also fantasizes that within her vagina are teeth-like syringes that emit fluids that 'neutralize' her husband's sperm. Her oral aggression is projected into her primal scene imagery, but she also reports her father as supercilious and sadistic towards a less well-educated mother. The two sets of imagery influence each other and follow a similar pattern in their movement from states of identity and subjective merging to the formation of positive and negative attachments involving some differentiation and finally to full differentiation and creative or destructive intercourse.

As we saw in Chapter 2, there is a sense in which it is only after the recognition of the primal scene as involving two people, and the emergence of the father, that a full two-person relationship between mother and infant may be said to be constellated. When the infant becomes aware of the existence of a third person, he or she is forced to give up any identification with the mother, or fantasies of being fused with her. We found that chronology is not always the most satisfactory perspective from which to view psychic events; threeness may precede twoness, psychologically speaking.

Emergence of the father image

At this point it might be useful to consider the emergence and development of the infant's image of his or her father and his or her relationship to him. There would seem to be three strands in this. First, the infant experiences his or her real father as different from the mother – for example, by discovering a different sort of chest, or smell, or voice. Second, the image of the father has always been there for the infant as potentiality requiring fleshing out through experience. Finally, there is a sense in which the image of the father can be looked at as constructed or synthesized out of the interaction of images of mother and infant with images of the parents in bed. The image of the father and the infant's relation to him is predicated in part on their common relation to the mother. This last factor is of great significance, as we saw in Chapter 4.

What we can see is image creating image, the transitivity of imagery (see Chapter 2). The separation of the infant out of an intense feeding dyad and his or her differentiation of his or her parents are interactive processes. In the case of the mother–infant relationship the sequence is togetherness–separation–rapprochement. The infant experiences and develops an image of a relationship *he or she is in*. In the case of the image of the parents the sequence for the infant is stuckness–differentiation–conjunction; the infant is confronted by a relationship and an image of a relationship *he or she is not in*. The image of mother and infant and the image of the parents are themselves linked. Their transitive interaction and mutual mediation lead to the image of the father.

Parthenogenetic delusion

Money-Kyrle's remarks concerning parental intercourse in his paper 'The aims of psychoanalysis' are helpful in bringing out the subtle interweave between the developing relationship of mother and infant and the infant's perception and experience of the parental marriage. He says, 'All you can do is to allow your internal parents to come together and they will beget and conceive the child' and 'remember that, in the inner world, parthenogenetic creativity is a megalomanic delusion' (Money-Kyrle 1971: 103). Money-Kyrle's bringing in of parthenogenesis is significant for two reasons. First, because accepting that one has been created is the foundation of a religious attitude and second, because a teleological factor is implied in parental intercourse from the point of view of the child. Differentiating the parents gives the individual a chance to create something. But, as the following example shows, this does not always happen.

A successful entrepreneur felt his parents always closed ranks against him in family arguments. He could not see their togetherness as anything other than a ploy used against him, a fake trick. His image was of the parents arm-in-arm like an overposed early photograph – static and unreal. A feeling of togetherness with a woman was beyond him because it felt like the nothingness he fantasized in his parents' marriage. Mutuality had to be eliminated and was replaced by hypercriticism of his partner and competitiveness.

The grotesque and the divine

To conclude this section of the chapter I want to note Redfearn's comment that experiences of the primal scene antedate the emergence of the human self-image. Thus, one gets 'bizarre and monstrous forms on the one hand or god-like forms on the other' (Redfearn 1978: 235). I think that the bizarre and the monstrous, and the divine and the sublime, may be involved in another important *coniunctio oppositorum*. The linking of grotesque and divine would then take its place alongside the linked human and divine parents of Jung's theory. As we shall see, grotesque, divine, and human dance a figure round the image of the parents in bed.

Recapitulation

I should like to recapitulate the themes that I shall develop further. From Freud, the need to look at man's prehistory and also to learn how grotesque fantasy about sexuality fills the gaps in rudimentary knowledge. From Jung, valuing of the image of parental intercourse as containing seeds of psychic integration for the individual and also the paramount need for conscious discrimination. Neumann, taking the problem of differentiation further, allocating to the baby's bite the function of separating the merged parental image and also pointing out the increase in experiential variety and flexibility that follows the emergence of masculine and feminine – polytheism. Klein, showing how mother–infant fantasy and primal scene fantasy interact. Money-Kyrle, stating how vital it is to allow the parents their creativity and warning against parthenogenetic inflation. Finally, Redfearn, underlining the enormous range of imagery involved in the primal scene from the most sublime to the most horrendous.

In many people there is a movement between an undifferentiated image of the parents and an image of union involving conflict as well as harmony. Psychopathologically there are two main possibilities: either a failure of the image of merged parents to differentiate or the creation of extreme images representing only one of the opposites. Each of these would lead to a negative and destructive archetypal state of mind.

It might be useful to list some of the conjunctions:

conjunction of human and divine;
conjunction of masculine and feminine;
conjunction of grotesque and divine;

and some of the undifferentiated images:

image of the parents in bed 'stuck' together;
image of the parents in bed fused with mother–infant imagery;

and some of the extremities:

grotesque sexual fantasy (Wolf Man);
idealization – confusion with divine parents.

In the next section of the chapter I go more deeply into some of the connecting factors between these ideas.

Hermes and his family

As I have been trying to demonstrate, thoughts about and reactions to the image of the parents in bed tend to polarize around the divine and the grotesque ends of a spectrum. Freud, Klein, Neumann, and others, while not regarding the process as unhealthy, tend to see and to stress images of a violent, perverted, animal kind. Jung and Money-Kyrle on the other hand, tend to see harmony and conjunction first and then the darker side. It occurs to me that this swinging, which is apparent in the theoreticians when perceived as a group, may tell us something about the way in which a child (and later the child in the adult) develops and experiences primal scene imagery. Psychological theory reflects psyche itself (see the last chapter).

The individual needs some sort of thematic organizer around the polarities of grotesque and divine – which is where Hermes comes in. The god is used as a way of describing the ego's attempts to come to terms with what is involved in the primal scene. I am saying that it is all very well for Money-Kyrle to identify a 'direct line' connecting 'favourable development', 'the first good object', the recognition of parental coitus as a 'supremely creative act', and a good subsequent sexual and marital relationship (Money-Kyrle

1971: 105). This is a healthy sounding description of a healthy process and of course Money-Kyrle in no way avoids issues of psychopathology; but his unfolding seems more redolent of a hierarchy of (ideal) goals than of journey or process. Although what I detect in the figure of Hermes may ultimately move towards such goals, there is much twisting and turning through which the individual must live. Hermes' multifaceted nature permits him to link what sometimes seems unlinkable even to the theorist – and how much more difficult to bring together for the infant. My contention is that, although the hermetic strand in the working through of primal-scene emotions may appear to leave us stranded on the darker side of things, in reality this is not the case.

Meltzer, writing of metapsychology, states that 'every person has to have what you might describe as a religion in which his internal objects perform the functions of gods' (Meltzer 1981: 179). He argues that this religion derives its power, not from belief, but because these gods do actually perform functions in the mind. Meltzer stresses the godlike functions of internal objects such as parental figures, but does not rule out the idea that part-selves ('the child parts of the personality') with archetypal potentials have a similar divine role. Hermes would then stand as a representation of a part-self.

In the literature, Hermes is seen as an agent and as a principle of transformation and connection; he is also a psychopomp or soul guide. As such he is much involved with change and development. Called Mercurius (quicksilver) he is elusive, always on the move, which is why he has to be contained in the alchemical vessel or consulting room. In alchemy Mercurius acts as a catalytic or linking element. As well as linking 'masculine' and 'feminine' he also links highest and lowest: Holy Ghost and Devil, wisdom and matter. Like any god he is two-faced – for Hermes the other side is his trickster nature. He is inventive in both senses of the word.

This two-facedness causes problems for commentators. In informal discussions with colleagues the introduction of the word 'Hermes' produced two radically different responses. Either all the 'good' aspects were listed (transformation, psychopomp, etc.) or all the 'bad' ones (trickster, thief, liar). It is hard to hold both sides together and of course there is overlap between Hermes/Mercury the classical god and the alchemical Mercurius. Hermes is part of what Jung calls 'the psychology...of the Mercurius duplex who on the one hand is Hermes the mystagogue and psychopomp and on the other hand is the poisonous dragon, the evil spirit and "trickster"'

(*CW* 9i: para. 689, Jung's quotation marks). Jung says this in connection with an artistically gifted patient who produced a 'typical tetradic mandala' and stuck it on a sheet of thick paper. On the other side there was a matching circle packed with drawings of sexual perversions. Jung connects that with the 'chaos' (again, for some reason, the quotation marks) that hides behind the self.

Elsewhere, Jung insists that the trickster myth is actively sustained and promoted by consciousness as a sort of reference point for human origins and indicates that, in the cycle, the trickster does become more civilized and even 'useful and sensible' (*CW* 9i: para. 474). I hope to expand these points in connection with Hermes and primal scene imagery.

Let us now look at the myth in more detail. In the Hermes story he is the son of Zeus and the nymph Maia, who is the daughter of Atlas. On the day of his birth he sees a tortoise near the cave and is overcome by delight. He kills the tortoise and discovers that he can make a musical instrument from the shell, a lyre. He returns to the cave and sings a song to his mother and father referring to their love affair and telling, in the words of *The Homeric Hymn to Hermes*, 'all the glorious tale of his own begetting'. The next thing Hermes experiences is hunger and he wants very much to eat meat. He steals a herd of cattle from his brother Apollo and drives the cattle backwards to the cave, thus cleverly creating confusing tracks. He makes a sacrifice. He manages to fool Apollo and Zeus for a while about what he has done but eventually Apollo finds out and tries to bind Hermes but cannot. A peace deal is made in which each brother imparts or donates certain of his skills to his brother-god. Hermes teaches Apollo music and Apollo becomes the god of music. Apollo hands the role of psychopomp to Hermes. The crowning event of Hermes' first day is his audience with Zeus where he is made one of the Olympiads, the messenger of the gods.

Hermes is portrayed as a highly social god, interested in trade and commerce and exchange, befriending men on numerous occasions – for example, he gives Odysseus a magic plant to help him resist Circe and also accompanies Herakles on his descent into Hades. He befriends the gods too – most notably when he rescues his father Zeus in a war with the giants. Interestingly, in the myth Hera consents to suckle Hermes, though she is usually represented as being extremely jealous of Zeus' affairs and the results of them. Apart from being helpful, Hermes plays numerous practical jokes on mortals and immortals alike. He contributes deceit and lies to the contents of Pandora's box. He is intelligent, flexible, and creative;

he can make fires for cooking and heating, for example. On the other hand, he can take the form of a sudden silence. His altars seem to have been phallic as were many of his representations. His role as the guide of souls to Hades overlaps with his functions as the god of travellers and of the crossroads.

Hermes is often depicted as chasing and/or raping some nymph or other – he is sexually rampant. Two of his offspring express this graphically. Priapus, who is sometimes stated to be Hermes' father as well as his son, is highly promiscuous, doubly phallic, front and rear, grotesque, obscene, pornographic, transsexual, transvestite, horrendous. The other son, Pan, is, *inter alia*, the god of masturbation and of nightmares.

Discussion of the myth

Let us look more closely at this archetypal metaphor for a developmental phase. Lopez-Pedraza points out that Hermes does not seem to have a complex about the primal scene, though his genogram would make interesting reading (Lopez-Pedraza 1977: 28). His father, Zeus, is a well-known tyrant, highly insecure and moody. His mother's father feels he carries the world on his shoulders, and so on. In fact Hermes *celebrates* his begetting in a song. One thinks here of Money-Kyrle's word 'allow' in connection with creative parental intercourse. Hermes does not indulge in parthenogenetic inflated fantasy; he sings of the act that brought him into being, specifically acknowledging the participation of both parents. Music-making connects with the idea that differentiating the parents is a creative act. Does Hermes deny primal scene envy here? Apparently not, but there is a humorous or even mocking tone to some of his song. And his later actions concerning the cattle theft need to be considered. He takes the meat he craves from the one who has it – his brother Apollo. That is, he makes an envious onslaught on Apollo's wealth. The *envy* can be twinned with the *celebration* mentioned earlier – is not this what we often feel at someone else's good fortune? Then Hermes is deceitful about his theft... .

What does his thieving or taking mean? Why is a god a thief? Jung, following Schopenhauer and Buddhism, points out that it is individuation that lies behind such evils as stealing. In Christianity, similarly, human nature has to be tainted by original sin in order to be redeemed by Christ's self-sacrifice. This is because man in a completely natural state would be like an animal, neither good nor pure. Instinctuality and total unconsciousness would prevail if a distinction between good and evil was not drawn. Jung puts it like this:

> Since without guilt there is no moral consciousness and without awareness of differences no consciousness at all, we must concede that the strange intervention [of God introducing the distinction between good and evil to the world] was absolutely necessary for the development of any kind of consciousness and in this sense was for the good.
>
> (*CW* 13: para. 244)

Hermes' many good acts and his 'good' development (for example the way in which he and Apollo sort things out) come out of and after the evil act of stealing.

Perhaps the words 'stealing' and 'thieving' have connotations that make them invariably negative. Do they rule out the possibility of the freely offered gift, for instance, the mother's devoted offer of her breast? Hermes does get this from Hera, who is able to control any impulse to transfer her hostility towards Zeus onto the baby. So that *is* present in the story; the thieving is something else. I think that taking or stealing are words for what we call today introjection and internalization. Following Laplanche and Pontalis (1980: 229), introjection means that 'in phantasy the subject transposes objects and their inherent qualities from the "outside" to the "inside" of himself'. Internalization can be said to mean much the same but with one important difference. In the case of internalization what is transposed is the image of a *relationship* or interpersonal process (*ibid.*: 226). Hermes' thieving has much in common with this transposition, which is central to the idea of internalization.

This throws a different light on Hermes' mendacity and stealing. These features would then be part of a developmental process that would make considerations of morality and approval or disapproval irrelevant. Pre-morality (and even immorality) is fundamental to being human. The anthropologist Edmund Leach was reported in *The Times* of 3 September 1981 as saying, 'Nature cannot tell lies, but human beings can and do...Human beings engage in wilful deception on a massive scale. The ability to tell lies is perhaps our most striking human characteristic.' (In Chapter 11, moral issues such as these are explored in depth.)

Hermes and sexuality

Hermes is not a conventionally heroic figure; he is basic, down to earth, vital. Nowhere does this vitality show more than in his sexuality. Hermes and his sons Priapus and Pan bring together rape, sado-masochism, posterior intercourse, and all manner of obscenities. These are not completely divorced from genital sexuality – Hermes does have intercourse with his nymphs. But, remembering our search for the god of the primal scene, consider the following. Freud saw paternal aggression, sado-masochism, and posterior intercourse as the main grotesque fantasies occasioned by the primal scene. He wondered where they 'came from'. This archetypal metaphor is a partial answer to Freud's archetypal question.

Pan is the god of masturbation and masturbation fantasies and hence closely connected with the signs and symbols of infantile sexuality. He is also the god of nightmares from which we awake or are awoken sweating and frightened. If the primal scene, as a real event, has impact on a child then it will be mainly in the middle of the night. Parents report how often the baby cries or the child intrudes during love-making. The other son Priapus is both homo- and heteroerotic, truly polymorphous in both Freud's and Meltzer's (1973) sense.

Hermes is more than pervert or trickster; like any god he is something less than individuated. In his lack of a settled relationship with a female partner his is not an image of maturity either. His naughtiness is babylike and appealing, it is part of his eternal youth. Part, too, of youth and of growing up is, as Lopez-Pedraza says, 'to be initiated into sexual fantasies...Hermes is the god of sexuality, including cheap sexuality and love by chance' (Lopez-Pedraza 1977: 99). My feeling about Hermes' trickster side is that it is enacted in mocking the parents, denying and envying their separateness and creativeness, and in grandiose, parthenogenetic fantasy – sometimes he is described as his own parents and sometimes as parentless.

Case illustration

A patient of mine, aged forty, is a social worker (all details have been disguised). He is a large, bulky, hunched man with a gruff, abrupt manner, superficially masculine. In his inner world he sees himself as a teenage girl. His background involved a home dominated by women, a classic description of a weak father, and a fantasy of parental intercourse in which mother initiated, was on top, and brought about father's early death by sexual voraciousness. A major theme of the therapy has been a work conflict with his dynamic, quick-thinking, and tricky boss who belittles him and interferes with his areas of responsibility. However, in his dreams the boss, far from being an enemy, is seen as a helpful figure – for instance giving him a rifle in a war, saving him because of knowing a foreign language. The boss appears as a tour guide and as an emissary from the Pope. The Hermetic overtones of all this are clear. To complete the picture, on the shady side, my patient and his boss have to hide some stolen goods and when the boss gives my patient some money there is some missing.

It has become clear to me that I, too, adopted a Hermetic stance. I felt tempted to become my patient's discussant and devise plans or even tricks with which to fight back. Gradually, the work situation improved as my patient won the respect of his boss and in dreams a more male self-image slowly appeared. Two dreams (nearly three years apart) concerning the death of his father show this. In the first there is to be a lawsuit against him, concerning a society lady, that he must be educated to contest. In the second, the dream emphasizes that he is not to blame for his father's death. A further dream on this theme involves him berating an uncle for backing out of a border crossing somewhere in Europe. The uncle *always* backs out. My patient advances into no man's land (!) alone and crosses into the new country (in his association, Poland – this was dreamt at the time of a Soviet–Polish crisis).

The emergent masculinity produced changes in primal scene imagery. These two dreams are also separated by approximately three years:

I am in the river floating downstream. There are sleeping people in all the houses. I don't have keys so I smash a hole in the window to get in. I am afraid. I come across a rat and a space monster copulating. They are lying on a ramp like a crucifix. Small monkeylike creatures dance around and in a box there is a sort of insect that reproduces by splitting itself. I know it has no sex life.

The second, later, dream:

I am watching a man diving under the water. I tell my wife's brother that *this* is how to dive. On the sea-bed the diver meets his wife who is an animal of some sort but also human. She gives the man an oxygen tube and they have beautiful intercourse buoyed up by the water. As they continue their love-making, a glass dome fills with beads of many colours in regular and soothing patterns. Then the couple sit in armchairs like we had at home.

Recently his wife dreamt that they were getting married again.

This example naturally leaves out much analytic interaction, interpretation of homosexual transference, and aggression towards me. The adoption of a Hermetic criminality did lead to the psychic developments outlined above. I cannot say that I remained uninvolved or in control of what was happening.

The patient produced a blending of images of the relation to his mother with images of his parents in bed. By tolerating considerable acting-out on his part in the form of flirtations with other types of therapy and growth activity, I fostered a mother–son differentiation and that, in turn, permitted the emergence of differentiated parental imagery. Our Hermetic activity also contributed to producing an impetus that put the primal scene into motion as an act that unites two separate entities.

9

Countertransference
and the *mundus imaginalis*

This chapter and the one that follows are primarily clinical in orientation with a focus on the experience of the analyst as he or she encounters the patient. However, the evolution of the idea of countertransference evokes the entire history of analysis itself. For I think it is true to say that there has been a move away from a biological, scientific vision of the psyche to one that accentuates the human and also the imaginal factors. The enormous shifts in attitude to countertransference exemplify these moves.

In the chapter I explore some links between current understandings of countertransference and the *mundus imaginalis*, the imaginal world, a term deriving from a different discipline but useful and suggestive in a variety of ways. To effect the link between a clinical concept such as countertransference and the *mundus imaginalis*, I will be making use of a research project I have conducted in which the countertransference experiences of nearly thirty psychotherapists have been collected, collated, and evaluated. I think this is one of the earliest projects of its kind and the empirical approach gives a firm base to my overall intent. This is to propose a theory that will, in pluralistic vein, harness together the functional realities of the analyst's profession and its implicit value system or ideology – an interplay of technique and soul, data and emotion, questionnaire and rhetoric, process and content, relationship and image, left and right hemispheric activity. If I speak of the analyst's use of him/herself, I am concerned with his or her ethos, his or her attitude towards his or her behaviour, his or her self-conception.

Here is a brief illustration of the phenomena with which I am dealing. The words are those of one of the therapists who collaborated in the project:

Veronica is 20 and single. She is depressed and lives at home with her parents; she works for a bank. At school she was a model pupil and head girl. She started drinking heavily in her late teens and turned down several offers of university places at the last moment. After my third session with her, as I was getting into my car, I experienced a sharp moment of anxiety, an image of a car crash came to me and I found myself thinking, 'What'll happen to Veronica if I have a car crash?'

The therapist knew she was not going mad and that what had happened related to her patient. She was an experienced worker and able to manage her shaken feelings. Her conclusion was that she was being affected by her patient's massive feelings of destructiveness towards her and that her worry about the patient's well-being was representative of the patient's own guilt. The therapist regarded her countertransference reactions as having been stimulated by communications from the patient. Though such reactions are by no means the only source of information about the patient, they play a special part because of the depth and intensity of their impact upon the therapist. My concern is with this type of countertransference experience, to try to understand it and explain how such things can happen at all.

Countertransference in psychoanalysis

In his discussions of psychoanalytic technique, Freud felt that countertransference obscured the analyst's capacity to function effectively, to use his mind as an 'instrument' (Freud 1913). By countertransference, Freud meant something more than the analyst's having feelings towards his patient of which he was aware. Freud was referring to the analyst's 'own complexes and internal resistances', hence to parts of the analyst's unconscious brought into active functioning by contact with a patient (Freud 1910a). Freud scarcely revised this essentially negative view of countertransference (as he did with the concept of transference, also seen initially as a handicap).

Although I am focusing on an attitude much more positive than Freud's, it should not be forgotten that there *is* such a thing as neurotic countertransference. This needs to be considered in parallel with the general claim that *some countertransference reactions in the analyst are best seen as resulting from unconscious communications from the patient* and hence of use in the analysis, as in the opening illustration.

There seem to have been three strands in post-Freudian psychoanalytic thinking about countertransference. The first, associated with the names of Heimann and Little, stresses the analyst's emotionality, his or her total involvement in the analytical process. From this, it is then felt that the analyst's unconscious 'understands' that of the patient on a feeling level. Psychoanalysts who have developed this view stress that such countertransference feelings should not be discharged or expressed but rather lived with, reflected upon, used to help the work along (Heimann 1950; Little 1960). As far as the patient is concerned, it is his regression that is being facilitated and valued, an innovation in itself and best encapsulated in Kris' phrase, 'regression of ego in the service of ego' (Kris 1952). 'Token care' may be offered on occasion; for instance, small objects to which the patient has become attached may be taken home to bridge the gap between sessions, a glass of water or milk may be brought, cushions and blankets will be available. Such offerings may be seen as natural extensions of an emotionally based approach.

The second reconstruction of psychoanalytic thinking about countertransference is to be found in Langs's work on the therapeutic process, utilizing a form of communication theory (Langs 1978). Everything that happens in a session, whether originating in patient or analyst, may be regarded as a *symbolic communication*, and psychoanalysis is conceived as an interactional field. In this approach, the psychoanalyst's contribution becomes as analysable as that of the patient. Langs points out that each participant is attempting to place parts of his or her own inner mental state inside the other. The analyst is trying to reach into his or her patient with, perhaps, an understanding of what makes him or her tick. One reason why the patient places what is troublesome to him or her inside the analyst is so that it might, perhaps, be understood. This placement will have a profound and unsettling effect on the analyst. But, precisely because the analyst cannot ignore such an upheaval within him/herself, he or she gains an entrance to the difficult areas of his or her patient's psyche, the access route being through his or her own disturbance. In other words, an analyst *hopes* that he or she will have a countertransference reaction to his or her patient because, in that way, he or she can be an analyst. The logical outcome of this is that the patient must be regarded as the analyst's ally. Langs feels that, even now, many Freudian analysts do not see the patient in a positive light. He writes: 'The patient as enemy and as resisting dominates the analyst's unconscious images, while the patient as ally and as curative is far less appreciated' (Langs 1979: 100). This image of the patient as ally crops up in the more specifically Jungian contribution to countertransference developments that we shall discuss in a moment.

Searles, though by no means using the same conceptual vocabulary as Langs, strikes a similar chord when he suggests that an analyst should allow a more severely damaged or regressed patient to see how the work has affected him. Searles includes in this both the analyst's childlike feelings and his more adult emotions. For example, when the theme of the work is oedipal, Searles is most concerned not to repeat 'an unconscious denial of the child's importance to the parent' (Searles 1959: 302).

The third way in which contemporary psychoanalysts, such as Racker, have modified Freud's negativity about counter-transference makes explicit use of projective and introjective processes (and, above all, of projective identification) to explain how it is that parts of the patient's psyche turn up in the analyst's emotions and behaviour (Racker 1968). Those ideas will be examined in a concluding section but, for now, it should be noted that the concept of projective identification refers to much more than an infantile defence or something pathological in an adult.

To summarize: post-Freudian evolution of the idea of countertransference as communication embraces the themes of involvement, emotion, containment, symbolism, self-revelation, and projection. One outcome has been that a wider range of patients may be treated than previously (cf. Gorkin 1987: 85). This has been both caused and promoted by the acceptance of visible warmth as part of a psychoanalyst's professional behaviour. Though the psychoanalyst may at times behave *like* a mirror, he or she is not a mirror.

This general loosening in psychoanalysis has led to the emergence of one quality above all others as crucial to the practice of psychoanalysis. That quality is *empathy*.

Kohut has left us a mysterious definition of empathy (Kohut 1982). This, he says, may be defined as 'vicarious introspection'. The poetic phrase is quite stunning in the range of possibilities offered: examining the psyche of another in one's own psyche, examining one's own psyche in the psyche of another, using one's psyche to see what it is like to be another, letting another's psyche

146

into one's own so as to look at it – and so forth. In the same way that there is a form of observation that is suited to the outer world, empathy is 'a mode of observation attuned to the inner life of man'. But empathy is more than a way of gathering emotional information; it also suggests an immensely powerful relationship between people. So Kohut has forged a stout connection between, first, understanding the inner life of a person and, then, an intense personal relationship between people. It is on that note that I want to end this review of what has happened in psychoanalysis: analysis as a relationship between people that helps in an inner exploration.

Countertransference in analytical psychology

The contribution of analytical psychology to the general area of countertransference is more that of an extension to the founder's work than an alteration of it, for, as in many other instances, Jung's sensings of what was central to psychological treatment have proved more prescient than Freud's. As early as 1929, Jung was saying that 'You can exert no influence if you are not susceptible to influence... The patient influences [the analyst] unconsciously... One of the best-known symptoms of this kind is *the countertransference evoked by the transference*' (*CW* 16: para. 163, my italics). And, in the same paper, Jung refers to counter-transference as a 'highly important organ of information'.

It is against this sympathetic background that we should view Fordham's introduction in 1957 of the term 'syntonic counter-transference'. The word 'syntonic' is used in radio commun-ications to describe the accurate tuning of a receiver so that transmissions from one particular transmitter may be received. In Fordham's usage, the unconscious of the analyst is tuned into what emanates from the patient's transmitter. The analyst may find himself feeling something or behaving in a way that relates to, or is expressing, the patient's inner world, again as in my opening illustration.

It is through introjection that an analyst perceives a patient's unconscious processes in him/herself, and Fordham realized that it was necessary to *use* this syntonic countertransference to understand the patient better. But to reach this position Fordham had to move far beyond the orthodoxy of his time. Up to then, for the analyst to have a fantasy about his or her patient, or to experience impulses to behave strangely, had been regarded as cardinal sins, evidence of neurotic blind spots in the analyst – and nothing more. Of course, Fordham does not neglect the neurotic aspect of countertransference, referring to this as 'illusory countertransference'.

More recently, Fordham posed the following question: if the analyst's countertransference is a normal part of analysis, then why continue to refer to it as countertransference, with implications of pathological fantasy or delusion? Fordham suggested that we might talk simply of interaction (or dialectical interaction) and reserve countertransference for something neurotic. Though this amazing return to Freud's position is a logical outcrop of Fordham's whole approach to the analytical process, the idea has not been taken up (Fordham 1979; personal communication 1985).

It should not be thought that this psychoanalytically influenced approach of the Developmental School is the only relevant move in analytical psychology. There has also been an attempt by more classically inclined analytical psychologists to use the image of the Wounded Healer to further an understanding of counter-transference (though the word 'countertransference' may not actually be used).

Meier (1949) drew parallels between the ancient healing practices of the temples of Asclepius and modern analysis. Though this was primarily an attempt to show historical continuity within the collective psyche, two points stand out for the clinician. The *temenos*, or temple precinct, in which healing took place, is the predecessor of the enclosed analytical setting. The teacher of the healing arts, Chiron the centaur, is depicted as suffering from an incurable wound – the modern analyst is also such a Wounded Healer.

Guggenbühl-Craig (1971) continued to explore the image of the Wounded Healer. His idea was that we tend to split this archetypal image so that the analyst becomes all-powerful, strong, healthy, and able. The patient remains nothing but a patient: passive, dependent, and prone to compliance. Now, there is really a split *within* both patient and analyst. If it is the case that analysts have inner wounds, then to present oneself as totally healthy is to cut off from part of one's inner world. Likewise, if the patient is only seen as ill, then he or she is cut off from his or her own inner healer or capacity to heal him/herself (see also Chapter 3).

When a person becomes sick, the 'healer-wounded' image comes into operation. The outer person is sick but there is also his or her inner healer to consider. Initially, and to get the treatment moving, this will be projected onto the analyst. But Guggenbühl-Craig's point is that his projection must be taken back so that the patient can utilize his or her own healthy attributes. The analyst, too, must make an initial projection. This is of his or her wounded part onto the patient; thus he or she is helped to feel sympathetic, understanding, and disposed to help. He or she, too, must withdraw this projection in due course so as to release his or her patient's capacity to be healthy. This implies the analyst staying in touch with his or her inner wounds. The process may be repeated over and over in an analysis.

Guggenbühl-Craig's descriptions may be compared to Langs's catchphrase of the 'patient as ally'. Similarly, Money-Kyrle wrote that 'The aim of psychoanalysis is to help the patient understand, and so overcome, emotional impediments to his discovering what he innately already knows' (Money-Kyrle, 1971: 104). And Sterba (1934) saw as fundamental to the analytical process that the patient must split his or her ego, identifying one part with the analyst, so observing and reflecting on the material he or she produces as patient. The patient's material constitutes the other part of his or her ego. The patient's reflecting ego may be regarded as an activation of his or her inner healer.

Continuing to look at what analytical psychology has to say about countertransference, a research project was carried out in Germany in the early 1970s. Four analytical psychologists met to study their various countertransferences and, in particular, to record their associations to the material of the patients at the same time as they recorded the patient's comments. Here is what the report of that project has to say about associations to dream imagery:

> The most astonishing result for us was the psychological connection between the analysts' chains of associations and the patients'. For the psychotherapist it is, of course, self-evident that the chain of associations should be connected together in a psychologically meaningful way. So it was to be expected that this connection would be found not only in the patient's chain of associations but in the analyst's as well; what we had not expected was that the two chains would again be connected with each other so that they again correspond meaningfully all along the line. Perhaps the situation may best be characterised by the spontaneous exclamation of one of our members: 'The patients continually

say what I am thinking and feeling at the moment!'
(Dieckmann 1974: 111)

The proposal of that research group was that such events are caused by the existence in man of a separate and more archaic perceptual system than the one of which he is aware.

To recapitulate: in analytical psychology, attention has been paid to the way projection and introjection combine to make an analyst function as if part of his or her patient's inner world. It has also been regarded as vital that excessive healer-wounded splits in both analyst and patient be brought together so that the patient's inner healer be released. Finally, a wholly different perceptual system is proposed to explain how it is that analysts get so comprehensively in touch with their patients.

Putting the Jungian and Freudian ideas together, we may, dare I say it, even speak of an analytical consensus and one that may be used as an assumption: that some countertransference reactions in the analyst stem from, and may be regarded as communications from the patient, and that the analyst's inner world, as it appears to him or her, is the *via regia* into the inner world of the patient.

Research project: hypothesis

Before introducing more of the research material, I want to state the hypothesis on which the project was based. My thinking is that there are two rather different sorts of usable countertransference – though both may be seen as communications from the patient. The difference between the two is shown in this simple example. Suppose, after a session with a particular patient, I feel depressed (this may be a single occurrence or part of a series). Now I may know from my own reading of myself that I am not actually depressed, and certainly not seriously depressed. I may conclude that the depressed state I am in is a result of my close contact with this particular patient. It may be that the patient is feeling depressed right now and that neither of us is aware of that. In this instance, my depression is a reflection of his depression. So I would call this a example of *reflective countertransference*. In time, I may be able to make use of this knowledge, particularly if I had not realized the existence (or extent) of the patient's depression. But there is another possibility. My experience of becoming a depressed person may stem from the presence and operation of such a 'person' in the patient's psyche. The patient may have experienced a parent as depressed and my reaction precisely embodies the patient's emotionally experienced parent. I have also become a part of the patient's inner world. I stress 'inner world' rather than the patient's actual infancy or history to make the point that I am not attempting any kind of factual reconstruction. That 'person' will inevitably also be symbolic of a theme active in the patient's psyche or of a part of his personality. This entire state of affairs I have come to call *embodied countertransference* and it is to be distinguished from the former category of reflective countertransference. There is a considerable difference between, on the one hand, my reflecting of the here-and-now state of my patient, feeling just what he or she is unconscious of at the moment, and, on the other, my embodiment of an entity, theme, or person of a longstanding, intrapsychic, inner-world nature. One problem for the analyst is that, experientially, the two states may seem similar. Perhaps some countertransferences are both reflective and embodied.

'Embodied' is intended to suggest a physical, actual, material, sensual expression in the analyst of something in the patient's inner world, a drawing together and solidification of this, an incarnation by the analyst of a part of the patient's psyche and, as the *Shorter Oxford English Dictionary* defines it, a 'clothing' by the analyst of the patient's soul. If our psyche tends to personify, as Jung suggests, then embodiment speaks of the way the person/analyst plays his or her part in that.

I am grateful to Symington (personal communication, 1986) for suggesting that it is important to distinguish between countertransference states in the analyst that refer to the patient's ego and countertransference states that refer more to the patient's objects. Reflective countertransferences would, I think, refer more to the patient's ego position whereas embodied countertransferences could refer to either the patient's ego or to his or her objects, according to the specific context. The main point is that the problem that the analyst and patient are working on can become embodied in the analyst.

Now any analyst who proposes new terms must explain why he or she does so in order not to be charged with word-mongering. This is particularly the case when, as in this instance, the new terms overlap with those already in use. Fordham's concept of syntonic countertransference is one for which I, in common with many analytical psychologists, am extremely grateful. His achievement was to drag analysts out of their ivory towers, help them truly to listen to what their patients were trying to tell them, and make a reality out of pious commitments to 'the dialectical approach'. But gradually I began to feel that the term 'syntonic' was distant from my experience; often one does not feel in tune with the patient in these countertransferences and there may be dissonance inside oneself. Later, it may be clear that one was in tune. So 'syntonic' leans too much towards an Olympian standpoint, intellectual, even technical or technological, and, hence, to radiate commitment to a mode of observation more suited to the outer world than to the empathic processes we are talking about. Embodiment, on the other hand, does imply a becoming, with its consequent involvements, and also a suggestion of a medium for countertransference communications from the patient; this, it will turn out, is often the analyst's body. Again, many of these countertransference states are nonverbal or pre-verbal – and embodiment speaks to that.

The unease with the notion of syntonic countertransference was a particular problem for me, as I was deliberately trying to keep my theorizing on the 'low road', 'experience-near', in Kohut's phrases, using the empirical stance and data collection together with an empathic attitude (Kohut 1982). So I chose the terms 'embodied' and 'reflective' quite deliberately, to be of help in the task of bracketing countertransference (specific to the practice of analysis) and the *mundus imaginalis*, a more general, cultural term employed in archetypal psychology. It may turn out that these ideas particularize and extend Fordham's theory – paradoxically by invoking an approach with which he is in total disagreement (numerous personal communications 1976-88).

The term 'incarnate', which was one of the associations to which embodiment led, has a history in analytical psychology. It was first used in 1956 by Plaut to describe how an analyst may have to let himself become what the patient's imagery dictates he be. However, Plaut's pioneering paper referred to the analyst's reactions to transference projections of which he was aware, and to his control (or lack of it) of his response. For example, what to do when a woman patient saw him as a remarkable teacher; should he contradict this, teach her about wise old men, or 'incarnate' the image so as to develop a knowledge of how to use it? Plaut's concern was not with states in the analyst that are apparently devoid of any causation outside of the analytic relationship.

It should be reiterated that not all countertransference reactions are usable communications from the patient. We need to bear neurotic countertransference in mind – identifying with the patient, idealizing the patient, the analyst's retaliation to the patient's aggression, his or her destruction of his or her own work, his or her attempt to satisfy his or her own infantile needs through the relationship with the patient. Nor is it always immediately clear what the patient's communications mean. As Jung said, the analyst may have to stay in a muddled, bewildered state for a period, allowing an understanding to germinate, if it will. An ability to rest with the anxiety and maintain an attitude of affective involvement becomes crucial.

Research project: results

I will turn now to the material that I gathered through the research project in 1983. I embarked on it because I felt a need to check hypotheses like the reflective/embodied countertransference model and did not trust myself to use my own case material in isolation. Since 1976 I had been giving seminars to psychotherapy trainees in which I suggested that there were these two sorts of countertransference. I contacted thirty-two qualified psychotherapists who had been in supervision with me during this period and asked them for a few examples of countertransference reactions of theirs that they considered to result from the unconscious communications of their patients (see note at end of chapter). The hypothesis that there are two different kinds of countertransference was restated, and the participants were reminded of the existence of neurotic countertransference. The countertransference reaction was to be reported in detail and I asked which kind of countertransference this was thought to be and how this experience had affected the work. The final question, which summarizes the intent of the whole project, was: 'Can you say how the patient may have provoked or evoked these feelings in you?'

Readers may wonder why the research hypothesis was made plain to the participants. This was no secret for they all knew of it anyway, having heard me expatiate on the subject. The transference to me could be managed by avoiding asking whether the hypothesis was 'true' and focusing enquiry on the way the participants were or were not using the concepts. The clinical validity of the hypothesis is expressed in its possession or lack of clinical usefulness.

Methodological justification came from Popper (Popper 1963). Using falsifiability as a yardstick, the classification of countertransference is offered as a predictive theory whose hypotheses may then be tested. There is a cumulative quality about this undertaking (and Popper regards such a quality as crucial to scientific enquiry). An attempt is made to preserve as much as possible of preceding theories. After all, we are dealing with nothing more than successive provisional approximations to the truth. There are further observations that might be made about this kind of theorizing, all deriving from Popper. It does not matter how I arrived at the hypothesis; this has no bearing on its standing. What is more, there is no value in having an open (in the sense of empty) mind; the inductive method, in which data is surveyed and generalizations about it formulated, is in no sense 'objective'. From that, we must affirm that it is perfectly in order that the research material is partially derived from the hypothesis it is intended to test; it always is.

As it turned out, the results of the project were of sufficiently manageable proportions for me also to be able to use the currently discredited but traditionally admired inductive approach. The results could be surveyed to see if a pattern emerged that might be generalizable into a theory. That is, if the theory had been in existence, the results obtained could have been explained by it. As we have seen, my interests and expectations meant that the survey was by no means a random one. Still, its outcome was that another, quite different, categorization of countertransference emerged to be set alongside the reflective/embodied distinction. I shall return to this later in the chapter.

It may also be necessary to justify such empiricism to those who see it as opposed to poetic, rhetorical, imaginal explorations. An empirical base does not necessarily lead to prosaic conclusions. The findings of the project are quite the opposite. Empiricism, as expressed in this research venture, supports a poetic, metaphorical, imaginal explanation for the mysterious workings of counter-transference.

The 26 completed replies covered a total of 57 cases. Because some cases involved more than one example of a countertrans-ference communication and because some countertransferences could be said to be both reflective and embodied, the total of such examples came to 76. Of these, 35 (46 per cent) were held by the respondents to be of embodied countertransference and 41 (54 per cent) of reflective countertransference.

It was abundantly clear that the participants could see how to use such a classification of countertransference. Here is an example said to be of embodied countertransference. The patient was a young, unmarried woman who had presented originally with a mixture of intolerable guilt accompanied by a sense of responsibility for the spiritual and moral welfare of others. She had also had a depressive breakdown. She had had several traumatic religious experiences in childhood. This is the therapist's account:

> This event happened after three years of work when we were thinking of adding a second session. She was always extremely controlled, with periods in every session which felt almost autistic. She said nothing which had not already been minutely examined 'inside'. She watched my face for the slightest move, flicker of an eye, for instance, and would interpret what she thought she saw there – to herself – as me laughing at her, getting fed up with her, getting irritated by her. I suggested that perhaps one day she might feel able to entrust a bit more of what was inside to me, with the feeling that I would not change it or take it away, that I could just hold it. As I was speaking I had a very strong impression or image of a large black open-mouthed pot which was strong yet open – like a big belly. The pot was huge and black and also like a witch's cauldron (I later realised). I said to her that it would be rather like having a pot which she could safely leave things in. Her immediate reaction was that it would be like a wall which something had been hurled at violently. My instantaneous image was of a violent expelling-type vomit, running down the wall, uncontained and wasted. We were both quite staggered by the strength and opposite nature of the two images we had had.

The therapist felt that the pot image demonstrated that the patient's mother had longed to be of use to her. But the witch's cauldron and the image of vomiting suggest something else besides. The cauldron was described as big enough to swallow up a human being – and hence a sinister and dangerous part-self or splinter psyche within the patient. Thus there were two aspects to this embodied countertransference: her mother's longing on the one hand and, on the other, an embodiment by the therapist of a split-off part of the patient's psyche.

The next illustration is an example of a reflective counter-transference. This therapist found herself coming to supervision with me in clothes very like those worn by her patient at their most recent session. This was something she realized during the supervision, but, in fact, I had been struck by the clothes she was wearing the moment I met her at the door, a little-boy presentation, school sweater, crooked tie and collar, muddied, practical shoes. And, though I did not know it, she was wearing a coat of the same colour as her patient's, a coat she had not worn for years until that day. As we talked, it became clear that the patient had never felt able to relate closely to her mother. She was the middle of three daughters and had been 'assigned' to her father – memories of being placed, unwillingly, on his knee. She had never felt 'at one' with her mother. And she certainly could not let herself feel *like* her mother, like a woman. The way she had resolved this was to let herself be 'Daddy's girl' but in a way that ruled out incestuous involvement (the little-boy strategy).

The therapist's behaviour, in which she became merged with her patient, might have been considered neurotic. But the notion that it reflects her patient's desire to be at one with her therapist, and, indeed, her whole life struggle to obtain mothering, is equally plausible. For instance, the therapist writes: 'In some ways she had been treating me like a man although she had sought out a woman therapist. I found myself being more active and penetrating than my usual style and generally more assertive'. Mattinson (1975) has written of the way in which the dynamics of one situation (therapy) are reflected in those of an adjacent situation (supervision); this is also well illustrated in the workshop transcript that follows.

What I have been describing was, for me, a confirmation of a hypothesis. As I mentioned earlier, in addition to that, it was also possible to detect an overall pattern in the seventy-six counter-transference responses and, moreover, one about which I had had no hypothesis. The countertransference responses described fell into distinct groups or categories, as follows.

First, *bodily and behavioural responses*. For example: wearing the same clothes as the patient, walking into a lamp-post, forgetting to discuss something important, a strange sensation in the solar plexus, a pain in a particular part of the body, sexual arousal, sleep.

Second, *feeling responses*. For example: anger, impatience, powerfulness, powerlessness, envy, irritation, depression, manipulation, redundancy, being flooded, bored.

Finally, *fantasy responses*. For example: this is the wrong patient, there's something wrong with my feet, a large black pot, I killed her mother, I'm a prostitute, I feel reverence for her serious, private place, *he* has God on *his* side, all colour has gone out of the world, a car crash, he'll rummage through my desk and books if I leave the room, the patient is getting bigger and bigger and is filling the room.

Exposing myself to these accounts, this time without the protection of the reflective/embodied theory, made me aware that all these instances of countertransference may be said to be images, and this is true even of the bodily or feeling responses. They are images because they are active in the psyche in the absence of a direct stimulus that could be said to have caused them to exist. That is, nothing has been done to the analyst that would, in the usual way of things, explain the presence of such a reaction in him or her. A person may be conscious or unconscious of an image but, either way, the image may be regarded as promoting feelings and behaviour and not as secondary, a coded message about them (cf. Newton 1965; Kugler's (1982) use of a term such as 'acoustic image'; Chapters 2 and 8, this book).

In the questionnaire, I also asked the participants what was the presenting problem of their patients. One finding is particularly interesting. It would seem that patients with instinctual (sex, aggression, food) problems are more likely to evoke reflective and embodied countertransference than other patients. What is highlighted, therefore, is the special part that may be played by the body in the patient's evocation of countertransference in the analyst. This bodily proposition will have to be looked at alongside the earlier idea that it is the image that is the decisive factor. Here, the *mundus imaginalis* turned out to be relevant.

In both the 'pot' example of embodied countertransference and the 'clothes' example of reflective countertransference, imagery and bodily perceptions played intermingled roles. In sum: the hope is that these findings justify a classification of usable countertransference responses into reflective and embodied, and that both terms accurately depict what happens. Further, the additional grouping of countertransferences under the headings of bodily and behavioural, feeling, and fantasy responses may also be justified.

Implications for technique

A central technical issue is constellated by a vision of countertransference as a possible communication from the patient: what is the analyst to do with the knowledge he or she may gain from an analysis of his or her countertransference experiences? Should he or she disclose them to the patient? If so, how? Should the analyst weld his or her understanding of the countertransference into his or her interpretations? If so, how? Should he or she do little more than stay in touch with what is being discovered?

When I first began to think about these matters, I expected to find a sharp divide between Freudians and Jungians, with the latter group being more willing, even eager, to disclose counter-transference material. True, a few Jungian analysts (e.g. R. Stein 1987) are strong advocates of disclosure, particularly of feelings about the patient generated in the analyst. But even such an extreme viewpoint is also represented in psychoanalysis, for example by Winnicott in 'Hate in the countertransference' (1949). The comprehensive literature review in Gorkin (1987) suggests strongly that there are numerous psychoanalysts who can see occasions on which it is advisable and justifiable to disclose countertransference. In psychoanalysis much more has been written about the *kind* of patient with whom this is appropriate than in analytical psychology.

Perhaps because of the Freudian/Jungian consensus referred to above, most analysts seem to agree with Segal's position, summarized by Casement (1986a: 548):

> the analyst is in no position to interpret if the interpretation is based only upon what the analyst is feeling in the session. Unless it is possible to identify how the patient is contributing to what the analyst is feeling, and in such a way that the patient could recognise this, then it is better to remain silent.

Casement notes the twin dangers of gratifying patients who want a magician for an analyst and of persecuting others with omniscience. Precisely because of dangers like these, I felt it necessary to go on with my investigations of countertransference, so as to find an ideological basis for the careful use of the tacit knowledge of the patient that the countertransference can provide for the analyst. In other words, I think more is needed than an understanding of the dynamics of any one patient. What is required is an understanding of how these phenomena generally tend to function. I do not mean a tight theory or categorization, because that would defeat the purpose of utilizing countertransference, but I do mean something more than clinical pragmatics. My working out of the theme of the *mundus imaginalis* is intended to be that kind of ideological project.

Succinctly, an understanding of what it is that the analyst reflects or/and embodies can serve as a kind of resource out of which he or she fashions the actual words and images of the interpretation, rendering them fresh and, above all, related to the patient – hence not 'cliché interpretations' (Casement 1986b).

What I aim at is summarized thrillingly in this note sent by Bion to Meltzer (who quotes it in 1978: 126):

> Now I would use as a model: the diamond cutter's method of cutting a stone so that a ray of light entering the stone is reflected back *by the same path* in such a way that the light is augmented – the same 'free association' is reflected back by the same path, but with augmented 'brilliance'. So the patient is able to see his 'reflection', only more clearly than he can see his personality as expressed by himself alone (i.e. without an analyst).

At this point, I should like to introduce a transcription of an audio-tape recording of a workshop I conducted on counter-transference. As with the transcripts in Chapter 3, the reader should be aware that group-associative and other processes and the natural focusing instigated by having a theme sometimes give a peculiar cast to the material.

Analyst A (male): This is a new person that I'm working with. About four sessions. My image is of her sitting on the couch in the office and she typically takes her shoes off and puts her feet up on the couch. She makes herself seem very comfortable though I don't think she is. She wears very dramatic clothes: white attractive, striking. One of the issues in the therapy is that she has had or managed to have therapists abuse her, including sexually, as did her father. And now she has a desire to get vengeance on men. She also wants to protect other people from therapists' abuse so she is pursuing a legal action. I have this image of her as a *rather striking bird*. This complicates trying to sort out what is already a very difficult therapeutic interaction.

AS: My first reaction is to say don't try bioenergetics with this patient.

(Pause. Laughter.)

AS: I wonder why I said that disrespectful thing in relation to your patient – that's a countertransference on my part for sure. Have you thought of her as a sexual person; obviously, I was....

Analyst A: I have. But not of doing bioenergetics.

AS: This is the countertransference really because one doesn't make love to a bird draped in white. I expect you know about the self-protective aspects of the image for you?

Analyst A: Sure.

AS: But there's more to it. Here is a woman whose talk is all about sex but who produces an image in you of spirituality, virginity, something soaring, whiteness. The whole thing is the embodied countertransference, associations, and image. What you are embodying is a conflict *in her* – a split if you like, between sexuality and spirituality. No doubt it's something that it might be possible to work on with her. It's a terrific incongruity. Jung had an idea about the relationship between sex and spirit. He was on about the conversion of sexual libido into spirituality. Being a boy, he did it from the perspective of a boy with mother! For the girl, it's probably what the father does with her. When the symbolic aspects of incest are swept away by its actuality, then the father has failed in helping with that conversion. Then your patient has to live superficially, sexually for sure, but without spiritual depth.

Analyst A: Yes, that's the problem, sex is something physical only, without much significance. I'm trying to follow, I'm not a Jungian, I'm a psychoanalyst. I did feel that this is an image she projects and it's also a defensive posture on my part. I can see now that it is perhaps a communication from her to me that I must help her with the transition you've been describing which has been impossible for her. Maybe then she could let herself be really sexual instead of projecting it into therapists.

AS: In simple language, she's never been taken seriously. That gives a prospective aspect to her sleeping with previous therapists because that certainly gets her taken seriously and as special and you end up in court.

Participant (female): Could this image be the analyst's anima, or feminine side?

(Long pause.)

AS: I think the group dynamic is important here because he already said he isn't a Jungian and now you suddenly hit him with 'anima' and he doesn't know what to say! I think what's happening is this: you (as daughter) feel he (as father) said he didn't want to know you when he said he wasn't a Jungian. So you offer him your Jungian self once again, hoping for a better response. It's a father–daughter rejection/retaliation dynamic and it is dead relevant to this case.

Analyst A: I'm sitting on my hands here because I want to come in and say that anima is one Jungian concept I do know...

(Laughter.)

AS: So actually when she said 'anima' you were perfectly comfortable until I came lumbering in?

Analyst A: Well, no, I *was* uncomfortable when she said 'anima' but when you came in I started to feel protective towards her. Are you saying that this feeling of protectiveness is also one of these countertransferences?

AS: Probably. But I think still that what she said is the most important thing. She was saying (provocatively): 'I have a world view and depth that you as father are not taking seriously. I'm not being taken seriously.' What is tragic is that the father does want to take her seriously – he does know about anima but he couldn't say anything when she brought it up. He ends up 'sitting on his hands' in frustration. The whole episode is an embodiment of her problem. Going back to her own father: they couldn't meet because of the actualizing of the incest link and so the mutual understanding on a deep level got left out. What gets into people in a group is connected to the patient.

Participant (male): *I* saw her more as a bird of prey, dangerous to therapists, so I understood your bioenergetics joke. But she chose another male therapist. Why?

AS: There's probably lots of reasons but I'm saying she needs to be noticed by the father in a very special way and she is in search of that. It's profound, not mere attention-seeking. She needs acknowledgement as a sexual being who can also have depths – that's the issue we're embodying. The incestuous father didn't give her that acknowledgement and she felt massively deprived as well as abused and attacked.

It is now the time to explore the underlying ideology, the idea of the *mundus imaginalis*.

The *mundus imaginalis*

The *mundus imaginalis*, the imaginal world, is a term employed by Henry Corbin, the French philosopher and scholar (Corbin 1972;

1978; 1983). To use this term in an analytic context is not in itself original. Hillman's suggestion that we practise 'Jung's technique with Corbin's vision' is a precursor (Hillman 1980). This enables us to include inside the *mundus imaginalis* those images that Corbin regarded as a 'secularisation of the imaginal': grotesque, painful, pathological – analytical material. The *mundus imaginalis* refers to a precise order or level of reality, located somewhere between primary sense impressions and more developed cognition or spirituality.

The *mundus imaginalis* (Hillman adds) enables us to speak of the location of the archetypal. So we begin to regard the psyche as structured by its images alone rather than by unknowable, irrepresentable, theoretical, archetypes (see Samuels 1985a: 31-2 and Chapters 1 and 2, this book). Fordham also in a sense joined Hillman when he wondered whether the conventional archetypal structure/archetypal image split in analytical psychology has any meaning. Fordham's point was that the word 'image' in the term 'archetypal image' is redundant because no archetype can be discussed or have any being without an image; hence, 'archetype' includes and implies an image (Fordham 1970: 297). Hillman's version of the same argument was that, as we cannot even conceive of the so-called noumenal, hypothetical, archetype without an image, it is the image that is primary (Hillman 1980: 33n)

As Corbin sees it, the *mundus imaginalis* is an in-between state, an intermediate dimension, in his original French *entre-deux*, which may even have the meaning: 'neither one thing nor another' (Corbin 1983: 1). It is possible to see, therefore, how the *mundus imaginalis* acquired a relevance for the countertransference phenomena we have been discussing. They, too, are intermediate; in between patient and analyst, and also in between the analyst's conscious and unconscious. My use of Corbin's idea involves the suggestion that *two persons, in a certain kind of relationship, may constitute, or gain access to, or be linked by, that level of reality known as the mundus imaginalis.* For the patient, the analyst him/herself *is* an in-between, a real person and also a transference projection. For the analyst, the world he or she shares with the patient is also the patient's own imaginal world.

When the analyst experiences his or her countertransference on a personal level and yet knows its roots are in the patient, it is an in-between state. To be sure, it is *his or her* body, *his or her* imagery, *his or her* feelings or fantasies. But these things also belong to the patient, and have been squeezed into being and given substance by the analytical relationship. It would be a great mistake for the analyst to remain enmeshed in subjectivity (actually in possessiveness) or compulsive introspection or self-blame. What appeared to have happened to him or her and in him or her is truly in between the analyst and the patient, imaginally real not subjectively real.

My suggestion is that there is a two-person or shared *mundus imaginalis* that is constellated in analysis. To justify this, it is necessary to take the parallels further, and deeper, though bearing in mind what a further, literal translation of *entre-deux* as 'between two people' might suggest to us.

Corbin refers to the *mundus imaginalis* as having a 'central mediating function' so that all levels of reality may 'symbolise with each other' (Corbin 1972: 9). The parallel is with the way the analyst symbolizes something for the patient. The analyst's ego is a special kind of ego, highly permeable and flexible and having as its central mediating function the operation of the sluice gates between image and understanding. Again, Corbin writes of the way 'inner and hidden reality turns out to envelop, surround or contain that which at first was outer and visible' (Corbin 1972: 5). The analyst's countertransference response is outer and visible; what is inner and hidden is the patient's psychic reality that certainly envelops the analyst. For Corbin, the *mundus imaginalis* is a 'fully objective and real world with equivalents for everything existing in the sensible world without being perceptible by the senses' (Corbin 1972: 7). In the analyst's countertransference we see equivalents of the patient's internal reality, even though the sensory data for the analyst's experience is missing. Hence, the rationale for referring generally to these countertransferences as images (see p. 157, above).

Of all the suggestive possibilities for analysis to be found in Corbin's work, it is his equation of the *mundus imaginalis* with visionary states that I should like to develop (Corbin 1972: 4). The experiences of countertransference, as described in this chapter, may be regarded as visions. No direct sensory stimulus is involved in a vision and also the experience is not of an intellectual nature. Jung made the additional point that no deliberate act of imagination is involved either (Jung 1963: 327). All these facts are relevant to countertransference.

Many of the extraordinarily powerful experiences and images I have been discussing are also described by Jung when he refers to visions as 'disturbing spectacles of some tremendous process that

163

in every way transcend our human feeling and understanding' (*CW* 15: para. 141). Jung goes on to ask: 'Is it a vision of other worlds, or of the darknesses of the spirit, or of the primal beginnings of the human psyche?' We may add to the list: visions of another's psyche, empathic visions, analytical visions. Corbin's reference (Corbin 1983: 1) is to 'the organ of visionary knowledge'; for an analyst, when he is doing analysis, that organ is his counter-transference.

The argument so far is that the *mundus imaginalis* functions as a linking factor between patient and analyst and that some of the analyst's countertransference may be regarded as visions and hence part of this imaginal world. What I want to do now is to relate the proposed connection between countertransference and the *mundus imaginalis* to what emerged from the research project; in particular, to explore what the analyst's body and the *mundus imaginalis* have in common.

Using Corbin's metaphor, the analyst's body becomes less literal, a 'subtle body', a 'being in suspense', a link between soul and corporeality (Corbin 1972: 9). What I am trying to convey is that, in analysis, the analyst's body is not entirely his or her own and what it says to him or her is not a message for him or her alone. In pursuance of this healing of the body/soul dichotomy, I may add to the term 'analytical visions' another: bodily visions – 'not-me possessions' of the analyst.

It is not just Corbin who has explored this area; Jung, too, wrote of the in-between world, referring to it as *esse in anima*. And Jung also had something to say about these connections between body, sense-impressions, fantasy, and the subjective/objective dynamic. He wrote:

> a third, mediating standpoint is needed. *Esse in intellectu* lacks tangible reality, *esse in re* lacks mind.... Living reality is the product neither of the actual behaviour of things, nor of the formulated idea exclusively, but rather of the combination of both.
>
> (Jung *CW* 6: para. 77)

Jung went on to refer to this combination as fantasy, adding that fantasy 'fashions the bridge between the *irreconcilable claims of subject and object*' (my italics).

Capturing what is meant by bodily visions takes me once more back to Corbin. He was interested in studying what he described as 'the organ which perceives' the *mundus imaginalis*; this he refers to as 'imaginative consciousness' (Corbin 1972: 2). The analyst's imaginative consciousness and his perception of his bodily visions, apparently so disparate, may more accurately be seen as two different ways of approaching the same goal. For bodily perception is quite different from other kinds of perception because there is no *specific* organ that comes to mind in connection with it. As the philosopher Armstrong puts it:

> When I feel the heat of my hand, the motion of my limbs, the beating of my heart or the distension of my stomach, and do not feel these things by exploring my body with another portion of my body, there is no natural answer to the question 'What do you feel these states of your body *with*?'
>
> (Armstrong 1962: 10)

It was this argument that led Armstrong to propose that notion of 'bodily perception' and, as I hinted just now, his use of it and Corbin's of 'imaginative consciousness' are rather similar. Whichever of these terms are used, the issue that then emerges concerns the fate of the *mundus imaginalis* in analysis. Corbin writes that the *mundus imaginalis* can be useful and productive in linking intellect and sense impressions (Corbin 1983: 1). Or it can remain subservient to sense impressions and not serve the intellect. If this occurs, there is a resemblance to the analyst's remaining unaware of the implications of his or her countertransference; his or her bodily vision will not have a use.

The link between body and image is waiting to be further verbalized. In *A Midsummer Night's Dream*, Shakespeare wrote that 'imagination bodies forth the forms of things unknown' (Act 5, Scene 1). If countertransference communications are both images and bodily visions, then body and image shimmer together almost to the point of fusion. Here we may find quite another message in the word 'incarnate', that outgrowth of 'embodied'. When Plaut explained in 1970 what he had meant in 1956, he was worried that the religious association to 'incarnate' (spirit made flesh) had been troublesome. It seems to me, however, that his intuition was reliable. In the countertransference experience, the image is being made flesh. Where that means that the Other (the patient's psyche) is becoming personal (in the analyst's body), I would conclude that an analyst's countertransference may be further understood by regarding it as a religious or mystical experience.

Before this is dismissed as fanciful, parallels might be drawn between countertransference and a well-known list of the characteristics of the mystical experience (Happold 1963: 45-7). First, mystical states are ineffable; that is, they cannot be fully described to one who has not experienced something similar. Second, mystical states lead to knowledge and insight, often delivered with a tremendous sense of authority. Third, mystical states are transient. Fourth, mystical states *happen* to a person; even if he or she prepared him/herself, he or she is gripped by a power that feels quite foreign. Fifth, there is a sense that everything is connected to everything else, an intimation of purpose. Sixth, the mystical experience is timeless. Finally, the familiar ego is sensed not to be the real 'I' (see Powell 1985).

These points can be compared to the countertransferences described in this paper. It is difficult to explain them to one who has not experienced them. The analyst does gain insights from them, often in a shattering way. Countertransference states are momentary. Even analytical training cannot fully anticipate or prepare for the countertransference experience. One does feel connected to one's patient, in an intimacy at once beautiful and unbearable. Countertransference reactions have no sense of history; past and present are jumbled. Finally, the analyst knows his or her ego is not responsible for what is happening to him or her.

Koss (1986) also suggested that states of possession entered into by spirit healers may be compared to typical countertransference experiences. Similarly, in Chassidic mysticism, reference is made to a quality known as *Hitlahabut*, or ecstasy. Buber held that this quality transforms ordinary knowledge into a knowledge of the meaning of life. For the Chassids, *Hitlahabut* expresses itself bodily, in dance. As Buber says, in dance 'the whole body becomes subservient to the ecstatic soul' (Buber 1931: 35). Analysis, too, is a form of dance, and ecstasy is not an inappropriate word to describe some of the emotions generated (and reported in the research project).

Corbin regards the *mundus imaginalis* as 'indispensable for placing the visions of prophets and mystics, this is because it is there that they "take place" and deprived of the imaginal world they no longer "take place"' (Corbin 1978: 4). Both reflective and embodied countertransference have their location in the *mundus imaginalis*, which is also the medium for their transmission. These connections between mysticism and analysis need not seem surprising. Psychology and religion cannot simply let go of each other. It is not enough to say that one explores depths and the other heights, that one is about soul and the other about spirit, one about dreams and the other about miracles, that one is concerned with immanence and the other with transcendence. It is not the case that this analytical mysticism is a mysticism of the one true God. Far from it. Analysis is a mysticism of persons – and hence polyvalent, pluralistic, many-headed, many-bodied.

The idea of a mysticism of (or between) persons is one by which contemporary theology is captivated (and this in addition to Buber's work). For example, a theologian writes: 'There is no point at all in blinking at the fact that the raptures of the theistic mystic are closely akin to the transports of sexual union' (Zaehner 1957: 151). The erotic dimension is introduced purposefully: transference, incest, sexuality form one spine of analysis. This is how D.H. Lawrence describes love-making in *Sons and Lovers*: 'His hands were like creatures, living; his limbs, his body, were all life and consciousness, subject to no will of his, but living in themselves.'

Throwing out an idea for a future discussion, and leaning heavily on Bion (1970), may not the analyst also function as a mystic for the wider group of society as a whole, or some analysts so function within their own milieux? That is why it is so important to keep avenues of communication open to psychoanalysts and the psychodynamic mainstream to make sure that analytical mysticism has a context and does not expend itself onanistically and nihilistically.

So I will return to that mainstream for a while. In the way I have been writing about it, the *mundus imaginalis* has similar properties to what Winnicott called 'the third area', sometimes 'the area of experience', sometimes 'the area of illusion' (Winnicott 1974). This area of the psyche lies in between external life and internal reality but both contribute to it. Of course, there are differences between Winnicott and Corbin. Corbin writes of a pre-existing intermediate dimension, Winnicott of the intermediate as a joint creation of both poles. Corbin's metaphor struck me more forcibly than Winnicott's as far as countertransference is concerned. But Winnicott evolved his ideas out of his study of what two people experience in a very special relationship. This means he had interpersonal activity in mind as well as his concern for the internal world. This helps flesh out my suggestion that we can speak of a two-person *mundus imaginalis* or of a mysticism of persons. What Winnicott writes of the third area repays attention:

It is an area that is not challenged, because no claims are made
on its behalf except that it shall exist as a resting place for the
individual engaged in the perpetual human task of keeping
inner and outer reality separate yet interrelated.

(Winnicott 1974: 3)

I will try to anticipate a few objections to what has been
proposed. These could be on the traditional ground that anything to
do with the archetypal must consist of the products of the collective
unconscious. Mother, the analyst's anger, walking into a lamppost
– what have these to do with the objective psyche? I do not
anticipate such an objection from those who have worked more
deeply on what is to be understood as archetypal. Hillman, for
instance, writes that 'archetypal psychology cannot separate the
personal and the collective unconscious, for within every complex,
fantasy, and image of the personal psyche is an archetypal power'
(Hillman 1975b: 179-180). There, and in numerous other passages,
Hillman has reached the same place as those who, from the
developmental perspective, regard the personal and the collective
as indivisible. The distinction is that whereas Hillman searches for
an archetypal perspective on the personal, writers such as Williams
are committed to a personal perspective on the archetypal
(Williams 1963).

A further possible objection would be that the *mundus
imaginalis* is too precise an explanation for reflective and embodied
countertransference. These, it would be argued, are merely
manifestations of the self in its transpersonal guise or the result of
our common heritage. I would agree that it is our joint and mutual
connection to these factors that permits us even to discuss
countertransference as communication. But this is insufficient as
either description or explanation and may rest upon an idealization
of the self.

However, perhaps the *mundus imaginalis* hypothesis refers to
the alternate, archetypal perceptual system posited by the German
countertransference researchers? Although it *could* be said that
archetypal images have a power that enables them to be
experienced as shared, I would prefer to say that images that turn
out to be shared generate an archetypal power.

For another group of objectors, the concept of projective
identification may be sufficient to explain the aspects of
countertransference phenomena I have been discussing. However,
projective identification, while undoubtedly playing a part in the

formation of transference and countertransference, lacks something as an explanatory theory. In fact, as Meltzer points out, 'we are still in the process of discovering what projective identification "means"'. Meltzer's suggestion is that projective identification is an 'empty' concept, the result of an intuition of Klein's, and requiring clinical substantiation which, in the nature of things, will in fact be based on the use of the concept itself, for analysts cannot ignore it (Meltzer 1978: 38-9). The *mundus imaginalis* hypothesis can be used alongside the concept of projective identification by postulating on what projective identification is based, and then what it is that enables its operation to take place. Using words from other disciplines, the search is, respectively, for the 'rhizome' that nurtures projective identification and for the 'ether' that facilitates its transmission. Such factors would, by definition, be 'objective' (that is, collective or nonpersonal) and also require distinguishing from projective identification as a defence mechanism for an individual, even with an extension of its meaning to include normal, lifelong mental functioning.

By bringing in the images of the ether and a rhizome, I am trying to challenge the notion of empty space. We don't need to ask why projections travel, because they don't travel – the individuals concerned are already linked. It seems that the *mundus imaginalis* hypothesis fits in well with theories of personality development that postulate an initial togetherness, with *fantasies* of oneness. The baby in a state of being and the baby's objects are one (cf. Winnicott 1974: 80).

Meltzer speaks to this last point when, discussing Bion's work, he makes a fundamental distinction between, on the one hand, an analyst's response to his patient's productions via an examination of the structure of his own mind and, on the other, his scrutiny of its emotive and fantasy content (Meltzer 1978: 23). Meltzer goes on to pose a question that was a spur to the writing of the present chapter. When Klein first introduced the concept of projective identification, she did so in terms of *external* rather than internal objects. Later writers, such as Meltzer himself, applied the idea to internal objects. In the latter case, there is less difficulty in understanding how the process operates. For, in the internal world, psychic processes such as substitution and symbolization play the major part. But, Meltzer goes on:

If [projective identification] operated with external objects, serious questions arose regarding the means by which it was brought about, the actual impact on other people, including the analyst, and the ultimate fate of split-off and projected parts of the personality.

(Meltzer 1978: 23)

The *mundus imaginalis* hypothesis is an attempt to answer these questions. For it is a pre-existing environment for images that are produced relevantly and spontaneously. Images pertaining to one person crop up in the experience of another person because, on the imaginal level of reality, all images pertain to both.

The need to establish the phylogenetic background to projective identification was also explored by Gordon when she suggested that its role in the construction of countertransference reactions was based on the psychoid unconscious in which distinctions between psyche and soma do not apply. The relevance of projective identification is that its main occurrence is at a time in early development before soma and psyche have been truly differentiated (Gordon 1965: 129).

In the same way that a relationship requires a facilitating environment, a psychological process (such as projective identification) requires its own 'environment'; that can be expressed by the postulation of a certain realm or level of experience in the background. The *mundus imaginalis* meets the particular need because, by implication, it is to be regarded as a pre-existent, ready, as it were, to facilitate psychological processes. I have already mentioned this as the main difference between Corbin's and Winnicott's ideas. A similar point was made by Hamilton in relation to projective identification when she criticized the concept for its lack of reference to any pre-existing 'primary mutuality' between mother and child (Hamilton 1982: 60). The *mundus imaginalis* is an attempt to express the psychological basis of that mutuality at least as it appears in analysis.

Winnicott's contribution to the discussion is found in the distinction he makes between talking about 'mental mechanisms' and an 'experience of communication'. Winnicott's view is that an analyst cannot explore the latter without 'peddling in the intermediate area' (Winnicott 1963: 184). Davis and Wallbridge expand the point as follows:

Although a two-way exchange can be explained in terms of projection and introjection, and though these terms can cover the source of our feeling for other people, and how we are able to identify with them, something is still left unsaid about the vehicle of inter-communication.

(Davis and Wallbridge 1981: 124)

Similarly, the *mundus imaginalis* idea places less stress on movement and interaction, whether ——>, or <——, or <——>. It is an attempt to describe a 'vehicle' that encompasses the whole analytic field – interpersonal, interactive, intrapsychic, and intersubjective.

A further contrast between the *mundus imaginalis* hypothesis and projective identification is to be found in their relation to the idea of psychic reality. Meltzer points out that one of Klein's main contributions to psychoanalysis was her stress on 'the concreteness of psychic reality, (Meltzer 1978: 69). Jung's reference was to the necessity for his critics to recognize that 'a psychic process is something that really exists, and a psychic content is as real as a plant or an animal' (*CW* 14: para. 651). A problem with projective identification, however, is that it is usually described in terms of fantasy, which is the exact opposite of what is required. Several attempts have been made to remedy this. For example, Gordon suggested that identification is the psychic equivalent of ingestion, projection of excretion, and projective identification of fusion fantasies at the breast or adult coitus (Gordon 1965: 129). The fact that such an attempt is undertaken at all, coupled with Meltzer's observation, led me to consider the *mundus imaginalis* as a place where the concrete and the imagistic are intermingled; 'subtle body' being the best term to describe this.

There is little doubt that projective identification forms a part of empathy (the putting of oneself in the shoes of another). But a logical problem arises when an attempt is made to apply the projective identification/empathy link to countertransference. For the analyst is making use of the patient's projective identification to fashion his or her own empathic response. It is not usually a case of the patient using his or her transference projection to empathize with the analyst. What may be seen in analysis is the conversion of the *patient's projection* into the *analyst's empathy*. The problem can be stated another way: projective identification refers to the blurring of boundaries to the point of fantasies of fusion. At the same time, as Gordon points out, projective identification also involves the clarification or disentanglement of an internal muddle by the engagement of an external object (Gordon 1965: 143). The apparent contradiction may be resolved by postulating an area in the psyche wherein 'blurring' leads to 'disentanglement'.

Projective identifications are composed of images or imagos (cf. Racker 1968: 57, 73, 96, 119-120). This sense of the centrality of image is reinforced by Jung's definition of it. We are not dealing with parts of the personality but with a 'condensed expression of the psychic situation as a whole' (*CW* 6: para. 745). Jung goes on to discuss images in terms strikingly similar to those used by Corbin in relation to the *mundus imaginalis*: as mediators between undifferentiated emotion and more developed ideas (*CW* 6: para. 749).

Recent developments in this field

Since first communicating these ideas in 1983, I have become aware of others working along similar lines. For instance, Goodheart writes of 'the marriage of *imaginatio* and interaction', the former term referring to the portrayal of inner facts in the form of images and the latter to the protection of this development within the analytical relationship (Goodheart 1984: 101). Similarly, Schwartz-Salant writes of a 'mutually and imaginally experienced *coniunctio*' underpinning 'a Self structure between two people'. The attempt is to capture 'experiences that happen in a realm that is felt to be outside normal time sense and in a space felt to have substance. This space, long known as the subtle body, exists because of imagination, yet it also has autonomy' (Schwartz-Salant 1984: 10-11).

Schwartz-Salant has also proposed that we conceive of a series of unconscious couples that are always present in analysis: within each participant and as a counterpart to the analysing pair. Becoming aware of the interaction within and between these unconscious couples calls for a form of 'imaginal sight' on the part of the analyst (Schwartz-Salant 1986). Although I am in agreement with the main tenor of his thought, on these two points I am not in agreement. Schwartz-Salant suggests that the analyst be active in a quest for imaginal sight (1986: 33-4) whereas, in my approach, the analyst does nothing but wait for the countertransference experience to happen. I am not sure that the conceptualization (or image) of the unconscious couple is helpful for I would prefer to envision such phenomena as a normal part of either couple or individual functioning. The realms or levels of experience through which the couple(s) move are indeed radically different (and one of them is the imaginal realm), but the couple is still just a couple. By introducing a plethora of couples, there is a risk that what couples do could become idealized to the point that only material connected to the *coniunctio oppositorum* will be adequately analysed.

The interpersonal and the intrapsychic: on persons and images

In this chapter I set out to act as matchmaker for two world views, one empirical and the other poetic, one in which counter-transference becomes the root of the analyst's technique of interpretation and one in which such a clinical confine is anathema. Fordham's technique with Hillman's vision? Let me conclude by saying that the offspring of this particular marriage confronts us with a fascinating problem: do we gain anything from our habitual division between the interpersonal (that is, relationship) and the intrapsychic (that is, image)? What the project showed is that the interaction of patient and analyst and their relationship can be placed firmly *within* the imaginal realm without forgetting that there are two people present. An analyst can think, feel, or behave as if he or she were the patient, and also he or she can function as a part of the patient's psyche so that the *mundus imaginalis* becomes a shared dimension of experience. When we consider or reconsider our attitude to the division between the interpersonal and the intrapsychic, there is no need to fear an abandonment of the human element. In fact, I would suggest that, in the same way that our notion of the intrapsychic, internal world includes the part played by relations with other persons, our definition of what is interpersonal may also be enriched and expanded. Then internal imagery becomes seen as linking two people, the patient and analyst, and as fostering their relationship. It follows that to divorce work on the apparently imaginal and work on the apparently interpersonal is conceptually in error and practically limiting.

For it is no longer a question of opposing an examination of interpersonal communication to an examination of the imaginal world. If the idea of a two-person *mundus imaginalis* is taken seriously, then we must regard the interpersonal in terms of psyche speaking, and the imaginal in terms of an avenue of communication between two people, a relationship. Persons may carry imagery; imagery may originate in persons. It is necessary to see our field of reference in analysis as seamless and continuous so that ostensible 'images' and ostensible 'interpersonal communications' do not get separated, nor one gain ascendancy over the other on the basis of a preconceived hierarchy of importance. The coin is three-sided: to body and image can be added relationship.

This overlay between an interpersonal relationship and the intrapsychic image is addressed by Jung when he writes of alchemy, particularly in *The Psychology of the Transference* (*CW* 16). Looking at the woodcuts of the *Rosarium* (in the next chapter), one finds it quite impossible to say with conviction that this is solely about a two-person process. Equally, what is being depicted is not just one person's individuation. The focus of enquiry includes both – the seamless field of reference mentioned just now. This led Jung to say in a letter that 'the living mystery of life is *always* hidden between Two' (Jaffé 1979). Or, put another way, the soul (says Jung) 'is the very essence of relationship' (*CW* 16: para. 504).

With these thoughts in mind, we now turn our attention to alchemy.

Note

These were the questions I asked the participants in the research project:

1. Age of client.
2. Your age.
3. Marital status of client.
4. Your marital status.
5. Presenting problem(s).
6. Brief history of client.
7. Countertransference experience in detail.
8. Is this reflective or embodied?
9. How did this affect the future of the work?
10. How did this affect your understanding of the history?
11. Can you say how the client may have provoked or evoked these feelings in you? What did they say or do?
12. Any other comments?

10

The alchemical metaphor

This chapter draws together the following themes that have been explored in the book so far: a pluralistic perspective on what is to be taken as literal and what as metaphorical in psychology (Chapters 2 and 3); the necessity of erotic playback in psychological development (Chapter 5); the whole issue of 'masculine' and 'feminine' psychology (Chapter 6); and how bodily experiences of the analyst might be construed (the previous chapter).

In addition, though, the chapter is a throw-back to an earlier concern of mine: an attempt to present Jung as more in the mainstream of analytical thinking than is usually considered to be the case. A reason for this attempt was to establish Jung's credibility as a reliable base or core for further endeavour. Thus any lingering worries that he was a 'charlatan' or 'mystical' (in a pejorative sense) could be regarded as irreducible (cf. Hudson 1983).

Psychological life – personal relatedness and internal processes working in harness – seems to call for description and illumination by alchemical metaphor. 'Personality is a specific combination of dense depressive lead with inflammable aggressive sulphur with bitterly wise salt with volatile evasive mercury' (Hillman 1975b: 186). We speak of the 'chemistry' between people, of an 'atmosphere' in a room, of dialogues being 'fluid', of the analytical 'container'. Cooking sometimes seems like alchemy, and winemaking, supreme marriage of nature and culture.

When non-Jungians or beginning analytical psychologists dip into Jung for the purpose of finding out what he has to say about transference and countertransference, they are surprised to find that his main paper on the subject takes the form of a discussion of a

175

sixteenth-century alchemical tract (*CW* 16). What on earth can the *Rosarium philosophorum* and the discredited occult art of alchemy have to do with contemporary analysis and therapy? And, as transference–countertransference interaction has by now taken its place at the heart of analytic methodology, this alchemical concern of Jung's has meant that, even after four decades of hard work by members of the Society of Analytical Psychology and others, a suspicion remains that analytical psychologists do not work with transference phenomena. In fact, for a good proportion of the psychoanalytic community, Jung's preoccupation with alchemy may be summed up, in Glover's words, as 'absurd' (1950: 50) and obsessed with a religiose version of 'redemption' (1950: 145).

From within analytical psychology, the apparent absurdity has been counteracted in two ways. First, by demonstrating that Jung did have an additional conception of transference, that this did involve personal factors, and that he placed transference at the heart of the analytical process (e.g., *CW* 16: paras. 283-4). Fordham (1974) pointed out that Jung was actually writing in these terms at a time (1921) when psychoanalysis still tended to regard making the unconscious conscious as the central issue. And there may be reasons behind Jung's dismissal of transference in the Tavistock lectures in 1935 – perhaps he was offended by his audience's reluctance to discuss the collective unconscious and retaliated by dismissing *their* special interest (transference) as a 'hindrance', 'never an advantage' and generally as an obstacle to cure (*CW* 18).

Another way to overcome the alchemy credibility problem is to borrow and then, hopefully, integrate concepts from contemporary psychoanalysis, particularly those that reflect an aspect of Jung's thought. As Lambert, among others, has shown, there is nowadays a far greater affinity between psychoanalysis and analytical psychology than existed previously. So any lack of a focus upon transference has been remedied (Lambert 1981).

A third path, and the one I intend to follow, is to accept that alchemy provides metaphors for psychological activity generally and for analysis in particular – but without the qualification that it would be 'just' metaphor. The first task, then, is to praise metaphor to the point where its own centrality in psyche has to be admitted. The thesis is that alchemical imagery is very well suited indeed to capture the almost impossible essence of analysis or any other deep, human connection: the play between interpersonal relatedness on the one hand and imaginal, intrapsychic activity on the other.

Alchemical imagery not only permits the paradoxical nature of the interpersonal/intrapsychic seesaw to be grasped but does so in a way that acknowledges simultaneity, doing away with distracting substructure/superstructure division. The interpersonal and the imaginal are equal partners and the technical implication is that content analysis and process analysis can, must coexist. Alchemy helps us to bear this in mind, as we shall see.

Metaphor

There is an overlap between 'metaphor' and what Jung called 'symbol'. For Jung, the crucial function of a symbol was to express in a unique way a psychological fact incapable of being grasped at once by consciousness (*CW* 6: paras. 814-829). Perhaps two apparently contradictory elements will be held together and this will have a meaning for a person, suggesting all sorts of possibilities. For instance, a patient dreamt of skyscrapers which when elucidated, referred to a linkage of spiritual aspiration (reaching for the heights) and concrete achievement (bricks and mortar, technical knowledge). Jung distinguished between his use of symbol and what he called 'signs'; these connect things that are already known. For instance, the stylized bodies on the doors of public lavatories are signs. Jung's charge against psychoanalysis was that psychoanalytic symbol interpretation made signs of symbols and hence lost the possibility of understanding their fuller meaning. My opinion is that Jung made too rigid a divide here and that the problem for both psychoanalysis and analytical psychology is to avoid interpreting symbols by use of some kind of lexicon.

There are several differences between metaphor and symbol. Metaphor sits midway between sign and symbol for one half of metaphor is known to consciousness. One cannot *use* a symbol in the way a metaphor is used and it seems typical of metaphor that its function is *communication with another*, whereas symbols may more easily be seen as addressed to oneself. Finally, we can use another person's metaphor (alchemy, for example); this is not the case with a symbol. Nevertheless, both metaphor and symbol are constructed of *images* – hence the link to the *mundus imaginalis*.

There are two kinds of metaphor that I would differentiate (Aristotle identified four). The first we could call *direct metaphor* in which two entities or images are linked by virtue of a perceived closeness or similarity in functioning. Thus to compare the human brain to a computer is to effect a direct metaphor; both carry out complex calculations and other cognitive processes at enormous speed. Such a direct metaphor is like a simile in that the comparison is proclaimed as such. (Similes have an aesthetic function whereas metaphors have didactic or moralistic intent, according to Fowler's *Modern English Usage*.) The second kind of metaphor, which we could call *indirect metaphor*, requires reflection for its appreciation. In indirect metaphor, the image may touch one's depths before the conscious surface is affected. For instance: old age is the twilight of life. Or: love is the psychosis of the normal person. It is necessary to work harder with indirect metaphor and, in order to gain something from it at an emotional level, both elements require equal attention even though it is one that it is sought to illuminate. The alchemical metaphor for transference–countertransference is clearly of the second, indirect kind with the subsequent requirements of reflection and emotional involvement. If we are to utilize the metaphor, alchemy has to be considered *as if* it were as important as analysis.

It has been argued that metaphor is not only a way of perceiving the world but, rather, the only way we perceive. This conclusion may be seen in the writings of physicists such as Bohm (1980) and Capra (1975). Making models is how we construct reality. Be that as it may, metaphorical perception is in tune with our psyches. For metaphorical perception implies constant change, even reversibility of emotion, fluidity of values, ambivalence, and so forth. These are the characteristics of psyche even if we postulate a self to organize and contain them. Would humans need the organizing capacity of self if they were not also constantly in motion? (Cf. Lacan's ideas on metaphor and the structure of the unconscious.)

In passing, we may observe that metaphor also has an intellectual function, as philosophers of science such as Popper have noted. There is a place in science for terms whose meaning is changeable. Actually, said Popper, even definitions are relative for they exist by virtue of what is undefined. Popper's expression was that 'all definitions must ultimately go back to undefined terms' (quoted in Hillman 1975a: 153). Metaphor, like analogy, is an unconscious form of *thinking* (cf. Hubback 1973).

Metaphor is also built into our theory and practice as analysts. Consider a theoretical concept such as projective identification. Someone, not just an infant, unconsciously projects or places him/herself (or a part of him/herself) in another person. This may be to evacuate some unwelcome part of the personality or to control

178

the other person from within that other or to communicate something to that other. These goals are achieved by an unconscious identification of the other, or part of the other, with the projected content. Sometimes, the outcome is that the two persons change places psychologically speaking and the one into whom there has been a projection experiences a foreign body in him or her, trying to take him or her over. Written out like this, a theoretical concept like projective identification is revealed as metaphor. Similarly, from a clinical point of view, we use metaphor all the time. For metaphors are a way of talking about experience. When a patient comes for help with his or her problems, he or she is also bringing a unique model or metaphor of the world. Our first task as analysts and therapists is to understand the metaphor. We therefore acknowledge its power and then we start to break it down into smaller and more manageable metaphors, elucidating symbols and thus facilitating development.

One additional point: metaphor is itself a metaphor of the indirect kind. Therein lies its strength and capacity to permit multiple perspectives, even contradictory trends in the psyche. Once again, there is no base: one thing is not necessarily more important than another. Psychological plurality and a tolerance of ambivalence are fostered.

Jung's understanding of alchemy

Following the remarks about metaphor, we need to explore what Jung saw in alchemy, what he thought he was doing when he devoted much of the last twenty-five years of his life to its study. At one point, it is alchemy's demonstration of 'the remarkable capacity of the human psyche for change' that appeals (*CW* 7: para. 360). Alchemy, according to Jung, must not be regarded as misconceived chemistry because there is also a spiritual side of great psychological value to be considered. Jung's focus in 1935 was on:

> the transformation of personality through the blending and fusion of the noble with the base components, of the differentiated with the inferior functions, of the conscious with the unconscious.
>
> (*CW* 7: para. 360)

Therefore Jung saw in alchemy something of a precursor of his own analytical psychology and particularly his concept of the individuation process. Jung's thinking is also shown in a letter written in 1945 in which alchemy is said to be a 'grand projected image of unconscious thought-processes' (quoted in Jaffé 1979: 97). In *Memories, Dreams, Reflections* Jung stated that alchemy possessed a concept that 'corresponded to the transference – namely the *coniunctio*' (1963: 239); we shall have to look at Jung's claim in detail in a later section. Jung felt that the alchemists had intuitively discovered and imaginatively projected what has been verified in modern times. The lively imagery of alchemy differed markedly from the stylized and sexless expressions of medieval Christianity. Jung drew the parallel with the way psychoanalysis and analytical psychology contrasted with complacent and rational Victorian views of man.

Jung was attempting to imagine or work out what the psychological experiences of the alchemists might have been like. He was able to use his own experiences in self-analysis and as an analyst to achieve this; one gets an impression of a fraternity spanning the centuries. Perhaps Isaac Newton felt the same urge, for we know now that much of his work proceeded along alchemical lines and this material has at last seen the light of day despite 'accidents' that might have prevented its publication (Dobbs 1975).

Having touched on Jung's ideas, we also need to explore what alchemists actually did and what *they* thought they were doing. In one sense, it was all rather simple. The alchemists were trying to produce a new substance that would have extraordinary powers; this was the elixir of life, or a universal panacea, or the 'philosopher's stone' (the *lapis*). First, the alchemist had to gather suitable raw materials and, then, work on them to achieve his goal of transforming them into the stone. Not all alchemists were trying to change base materials into gold; the emphasis in their writing is equally upon the transformation of all that is dark and evil into something spiritually enriching (Tuby 1982: 8-9). As they worked, the alchemists were deeply affected by what was happening and, in concert with their practical functioning, enjoyed deep, passionate, enlightening psychological experiences. And, like analysts, they did not attempt to split the experience of the work from the work itself. Their visions and their procedures become one. As Kugler puts it, the alchemist worked simultaneously on the soul in matter and the matters in his soul (1982: 108). The assumption is that the soul may be set free from the material prison in which nature has locked it; the whole procedure is subversive, a work against nature, *opus contra naturam*, a release of *meaning* from out of the material and bodily world.

Anticipating the clinical application of the metaphor, this corresponds to what an analyst or therapist does when he or she goes to work with the patient to discover the source and purpose of the latter's neurosis and how to release the growth or soul imprisoned therein. What the modern therapist sees in man, the alchemists saw in metallic form.

The alchemical metaphor

Let's now look in more detail at how the alchemical metaphor may be applied to therapy and analysis (not, it should be noted, at alchemical-type imagery in clinical material). The term *coniunctio* was mentioned just now. For the alchemists this referred to the mating and mixing in the *vas* or alchemical vessel of the various disparate elements. There elements, the *prima materia* or *massa confusa* were carefully chosen for their propensity to combine and were envisioned as opposites whose mingling would produce a third, new product (something like chemical combination): this is the *coniunctio*. These elements were often represented by male and female figures. The fact that humans are used to represent chemical elements showed Jung that, far from being a strictly chemical investigation, alchemy was concerned with creative fantasy and thus with unconscious projection. In analysis, the *coniunctio*, the union of opposites, symbolizes five themes that can be differentiated to some extent.

First, the personal interaction of the analyst and his analytical 'opposite', the patient. Next, patterns of separation and combination of conflicted and warring elements within the patient's psyche (and a similar process within the analyst). Third, the *coniunctio* of these two *coniunctios*: personal relatedness and intrapsychic processes. Fourth, *coniunctio* in analysis speaks of the ego's integration of unconscious parts of the patient's psyche (and, again, the same process will be taking place within the analyst). All this is going on within the container provided by the analytic setting and relationship; this is the *vas*. Finally there is a *coniunctio* between the sensual or material world and the spiritual dimension – Jung's psychoid unconscious (*CW* 8: paras. 343–442).

Another relevant term is *hierosgamos*, translated literally as 'sacred marriage'. Many forms of this motif, signifying the conjunction of opposites, may be found. For instance, in Augustinian Christianity the sacred marriage is between Christ and his church and is consummated on the marriage-bed of the cross. In alchemy the sacred marriage is often referred to as a 'chemical marriage', in which the opposite elements, having been designated male and female, unite in a kind of intercourse to produce a third, unsullied, 'incorruptible' substance. As such a substance does not seem to exist in the physical world, alchemy became less important as natural science claimed primacy of place and attention in the Renaissance. From the psychological point of view, the *hierosgamos* refers to the way in which opposing or conflicting trends in the psyche, experienced as chaos and confusion, are transformed into a relative coherence. In analysis it is also hoped that such a transformation will take place so that neurotic conflicts and splits become more manageable, perhaps useful, or, sometimes, removed.

The idea of the *transmutability of elements* is central to alchemy because it affirms that transformation can occur. Similarly, there would be little point in analysis without an image of the possibility of psychological movement. This remains true even when the goal of analysis is said to be the deepening of experience or the widening of awareness rather than the removal of symptoms. For deepening itself represents a change or translation.

The alchemical adept worked in relation to another, usually an inner figure but sometimes a real person, referred to as his *soror mystica*, mystical sister (cf. *CW* 14: para. 161). Again, an analyst is not an analyst without his or her counterpart, the patient. The part played by the Other (with a capital 'o') in psychological processes has been noted by contemporary analysts; it is a subject to which we shall return (see pp. 185-7 for a fuller discussion).

The various stages of the alchemical process are given their own names. *Nigredo* implies a darkening of the *prima materia* and a sign that something of significance is about to happen. *Fermentatio* suggests a brewing, a mingling of elements that will produce a new substance, different in kind to the original components. *Mortificatio* is the stage when the original elements have ceased to exist in their initial form. *Putrefactio* sees a decay of the dead or dying original elements and the giving off of a vapour that is the harbinger of transformation.

From the clinical standpoint, these terms symbolize what

happens in analysis. *Nigredo* may take the form of an important dream that signals change, or an onset of the depression that often precedes movement. Sometimes, *nigredo* refers to the end of the honeymoon period of an analysis. *Fermentatio* is an apt term for the mingling of personalities that takes place in the transference–countertransference and also for events in the inner worlds of analyst and patient. *Mortificatio* and *putrefactio* describe the ways in which symptoms alter as the analytical relationship develops and intrapsychic changes come about (in object relations, for instance).

Finally, hovering over all, we find the figure of Mercurius, derived from Hermes and hence the god of transformation and transition, of discovery (Eureka!), the guider of souls, the messenger of the gods, the guardian of boundaries, the spirit of the crossroads, and hence of initiation, and the arch-trickster who can appear in innumerable forms and yet still be unmistakably himself. Mercurius speaks both of the renewal of old values *and* of revolution.

Analysis as process

Jung's view of analysis, expressed in many of his writings, is that of an interactive process. Analyst and patient are equally 'in' the treatment. The analyst's personality and development are as important as theory or technique and, above all, both participants may be affected, even transformed by what happens between them.

Figure 10.1

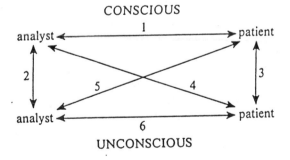

Figure 10.1 is based on a diagram of Jung's in *The Psychology of the Transference* (*CW* 16: 221). The double-headed arrows

indicate two-way relatedness. (1) indicates the conscious relationship between analyst and patient, the level of their rapport and, ultimately, the therapeutic alliance. (2) indicates the analyst's connection to his or her own unconscious, aided by his or her training analysis and, it should be added, containing whatever it is that makes him or her a Wounded Healer. (3) indicates the patient's relation to his or her unconscious, his or her resistance, conflicts, compulsions, obsessions, needs, shadow, etc. (4) indicates the analyst's attempt to understand the patient's unconscious situation and also the influence of the patient on the analyst's ego – what he or she knows he or she is learning from the patient. (5) indicates the analyst's use of empathy and intuition to deepen the relation to the patient and also what the analyst has unconsciously gained or lost from his or her contact with the patient. (6) indicates connection between the two unconscious systems of patient and analyst. There are two additional relations that should not be forgotten, though they would complicate the diagram (much as they cause complications in a real analysis): the relation to the apparent outer world (family, friends, job) of each participant.

How does a relationship between two people lead to internal change in one or both? How does internal change affect relationships? To answer these questions requires a deeper understanding of Jung's alchemical metaphor. Persons who appear in analytical material have a symbolic dimension that is often the crucial factor. That is why it is necessary to challenge our habitual distinction between the interpersonal and the intrapsychic and why the interaction of patient and analyst may be understood as placed firmly within an *imaginal* realm. As we saw in the previous chapter, our delineation of what is interpersonal may also be expanded so that internal imagery becomes the link between patient and analyst (two persons), fostering their relationship and mediating their exchange.

If we consider (4) in *Figure 10.1*, we can see that the patient's inner world, his or her unconscious, will appear in projected form in the bodily person of the analyst. What is required is a relation to an exterior person to facilitate its emergence as transference. When the alchemists use personages such as the king and queen in the *Rosarium* they, too, are making use of the human body to symbolize their technical procedures and their psychological life (*Figure 10.2*). The king and queen are sexual opposites but linked by their intercourse, marriage, and the court hierarchy (*CW* 16: 249). Analyst and patient are opposites within the frame of analysis; they

Figure 10.2

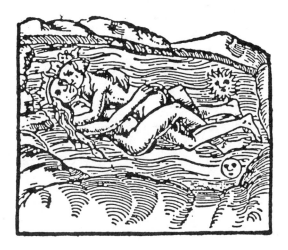

are analytically married, whatever their anatomical sex. They may
not be opposites in temperament and of course they are not actually
married; that is not the point. But sexuality is vital for its symbolic
aptness in suggesting at one and the same time difference
(conflicting opposites) and its resolution (intercourse). This is
shown in the illustrations in the form of the king and queen making
love, forming into a hermaphrodite, dying, and then experiencing a
renaissance. The bodies engaged in intercourse do refer us to a
mingling of two personalities in analysis. What is also evoked is a
cross-breeding of elements within the individual psyches of both
patient and analyst. It is *the symbolism of the sex act* that is crucial
and later we will look at other aspects of sexuality in analysis. The
biological outcome of sex is something new, and this, too, has a
marked symbolic relevance for a growth process – the baby as an
image of a new beginning, a new person, a new soul.

So, in addition to using the figures to represent what is
happening to the *prima materia* in the *vas*, the alchemist is also
transferring his own internal processes onto the king and queen. In
analysis it is the relationship with another that leads to internal
movement and growth. And the influence is reciprocal – movement
and growth enculture relationship.

The alchemical stress on the other, on relatedness and on
relationship with the *soror*, suggests a parallel with one of the
central themes of contemporary psychoanalysis: the experience of

Figure 10.3

oneself in a relationship with another person. Lacan noted this in
connection with mother and infant and referred to the mirror phase
of development (1949). Winnicott also wrote of the same
phenomena (1967). It is not always recognized that Neumann was
on the same track with his assertion (written in 1959) that the
mother 'carries' the infant's self (Neumann 1973). There is always
an other, even an Other, in the sense of a significant other. This can
be the unconscious itself, the analyst, the patient, the *soror*, the
blank page for the writer, his audience for the lecturer, God for the
mystic. The alchemists anticipate Lacan who writes of the Other in
analysis as 'the locus in which is constituted the I who speaks with
him who hears' (Lemaire 1977: 157). In a sense, the analytic
dialogue is itself the Other, at the point where the internal worlds
of patient and analyst overlap. Or one may imagine an Other in
relation to the entire analysis, a sort of guarantor of good faith; in
Lemaire's phrase, a 'third-party witness' (Lemaire 1977: 157). A
subsequent illustration to the *Rosarium* leads to a similar point
(*Figure 10.3*). It is called *the ascent of the soul* and shows the soul,
a baby or child, rising up to heaven before returning to breathe life

into the dead, two-headed body (*CW* 16: 285). The soul is the one (that is, integrated personality) born of the two (patient and analyst). Jung comments that 'only *one* soul departs from the two, for the two have indeed become one' (CW 16: para. 475). Death is not to be taken literally here, more as a symbolic precondition for new life, part of a cycle of decay and regeneration. The two-headedness indicates the thorough intermingling of the elements, for this body is both male and female. The analytical parallels are with the gradual move from neurotic symptomatology towards engagement with life and, furthermore, with the establishment at depth of the transference–countertransference relationship.

Eros in analysis

We have established the appropriateness of the explicitly sexual nature of the *Rosarium*. Sexuality, intercourse, anatomy are metaphors for aspects of psychological development; *hetero*sexuality reminds us of the importance of the Other. The variety of human sexual experience, which is one of the distinguishing characteristics of our species, both symbolizes and sets in motion human psychological variety. However, the proposition that sexuality has its symbolic meaning may have to be expanded: *sexuality has to be present for its symbolic meaning to be interpreted*. In order for psychological transformation to result from analytical interaction, that interaction must acquire and radiate something of an erotic nature. The interpersonal *coniunctio* inspires and ignites the internal *coniunctio*. The term *eros* includes such states in analysis as arousal, excitement, passion, love, and that most sexual of all experiences, frustration. There is always a level at which eros is a presence in analysis and psychological change in the patient implies and requires an erotic involvement on the part of the analyst, though not a physical enactment of this undeniably real experience. Before discussing this claim, it might help to review the conceptual background.

The use of 'eros' is deliberate even though confusion may be engendered by the imprecise relation of eros to genital sexuality. This is an imprecision that runs through both psychoanalysis and analytical psychology. In a sense, we can make a strength out of this apparent weakness. References to eros do, or do not, conjure up images of genitality depending on outlook, context, associations and ideology. We can therefore work with a spectrum of suggestive possibilities and eros stands as one of those terms without a fixed meaning whose value Popper emphasized.

For example, Freud's conception of eros underwent numerous modifications. Laplanche and Pontalis point out that the place of sexuality in Freud's thinking changed radically (Laplanche and Pontalis 1980: 242). First, it was seen as a subversive and problematic force. Then, when Freud developed his idea of the life and death instincts (1940), it was the death instinct that was 'the problem' and, strangely, sexuality that which helped to overcome it. In fact, Freud did not always equate sexuality and genital activity; he wrote of his concept of libido as identical to 'the Eros of the poets and philosophers which holds all living things together' (1920: 50). Eros is also referred to in terms of a 'more and more far-reaching combination of the particles into which living substance is dispersed' (1923: 40). This suggests that Freud's evolving concept of eros, even prior to the dual instinct theory, was rather broad. In 1910, he stated that 'libido' not only refers to genital sexual drives but also to everything covered by *lieben* (to love) (Freud 1910b). Could it be that, in his choice of a term with sexual connotations to encapsulate the life instincts, Freud struck essentially the same stratum of unconscious imagery as Jung and his alchemists? Jung felt that Freud took bodily sexuality too literally but Jung's Freud was often quite out of date and wide of the mark in other respects. Jung's view (*CW* 16: para. 533) was that, unless a certain degree of consciousness was attained, growth and change in the psyche would have to be expressed by sexual symbolism *faute de mieux* and that there was always a risk that things would get stuck there, either taken too literally (Freud) or not applied within a human frame (alchemy).

Briefly, we might add that even the so-called sexual revolution has done nothing to remove the numinous aspects of sexuality nor hunger for authentic relationship.

Jung, too, used 'eros' in a variety of ways. Sometimes he equates eros with sexuality or eroticism (*CW* 7: paras. 16- 34, written as late as 1943). More often, he writes of eros as an archetypal principle of psychological functioning – connectedness, relatedness, harmony, and named for Eros the lover of Psyche and son of Aphrodite. Sometimes the principle eros is referred to as a 'feminine' principle. This implies a complementary relationship with a 'masculine' principle (logos, 'the word', rationality, logic, intellect, achievement). We saw in Chapter 6 that the relativity of gender qualities makes Jung's use of 'masculine' and 'feminine' problematic and this becomes marked when he claims that men operate under logos and women under eros (*CW* 10: paras. 158, 255). There is a confusion between references to qualities that anyone might possess (which *might* be named masculine or feminine for whatever reason) and real men and women.

On the other hand, Jung was also of the opinion that eros and logos coexist and balance each other within an individual's psyche and irrespective of anatomical sex: 'it is the function of Eros to unite what Logos has sundered' (*CW* 10: para. 275).

Sometimes Jung moves beyond sex and gender qualities and even beyond complementarity: 'Eros is a *kosmogonos*, a creator and a father–mother of all higher consciousness' (1963: 386).

The earlier claim that erotic feelings are necessary for analysis should be considered alongside a more detailed examination of what is meant by 'erotic' in terms of a personal relationship. We can identify five aspects of this. First there is eroticism as an adjunct to reproduction. Then there is the possibility of lust. Thirdly, the partners perceive each other as individuals; hence caring, romantic, and aesthetic factors come into play. This occurs alongside projective and introjective processes. Next, we can speak of a spiritual dimension and each partner is deeply enhanced by the presence and impact of the other. Finally, an awareness dawns of a relationship quality that is very difficult to define. Jung's word for this was *sapientia* or wisdom and he reminds us that this is what Solomon chose when he could have had anything he wanted (*CW* 16: para. 361). We can now find other meanings in Jung's gnomic utterance about the mystery of life being hidden between two (see the previous chapter). One cannot pick and choose which of these aspects of eros will occur in analysis; nor will they appear in any given order – indeed, they may all be working in parallel having been present in potential form from the outset. The need is to unpack what is meant by *erotic*, giving each nuance its due and hence moving beyond fear or inhibition.

These remarks about the centrality of eros in therapy can be compared with Searles's observation of the inevitability of erotic feelings and fantasies in both patient and analyst in the clinical situation (1959). Briefly, Searles distinguishes the analyst's reciprocal response to erotic transference from his or her neurotic countertransference. The latter springs from a source *other* than the analytical relationship. Then there is the analyst's narcissistic pleasure in his or her patient's growth. Finally, the analyst has to explore the essential loveableness of the patient as a person who matters to him or her. Given this range of possibilities, we may even say 'no eros, no analysis'. Searles is pointing out that romantic and erotic fantasies and feelings towards the patient figure prominently in an analyst's experience. This remains true when the patient and analyst are of the same sex. Aside from homosexual desire, homoerotic feelings may take the form of identification with the patient, intense feelings of friendship or of rivalry, or voyeuristic fantasy. Again, such involvement is inevitable. It should be noted that Searles does not advocate 'confession' save in certain circumstances. And we know that failure to recall the symbolic dimension leads to sexual acting out with its damaging consequences. But the movement from sensual and concrete to symbolic cannot simply be wished into being; the 'lower' state and the 'higher' each has its place.

The argument suggests why the question of sexual activity between patient and analyst remains of perennial interest. Provided we interpret what looks like prurience as an involvement at an unconscious level with symbols of growth, cultural preoccupation with patient/therapist sex is not far off the mark (cf. Carotenuto 1982; Malcolm 1982; Taylor 1982; Ulanov 1979). The present aim is to revalue eros in analytical therapy, moving beyond a reductive perspective, which concentrates on infantile eroticization of feeling or behaviour, to a more positive estimation.

Eros and agape

There has been considerable interest in analytical psychology in *agape*, defined as nonerotic, disinterested love. According to Lambert, it is agape that enables an analyst to control his or her retaliatory fantasies *vis-à-vis* his or her patient (Lambert 1981: 40-1). Yet, as we have seen, in the absence of a connection that is truly erotic, transformation may not take place. Can eros ever be divorced from agape? Does not the act of helping bring its own pleasure and gratification (cf. Lambert 1981: 42)? The risk in leaving eros out or not specifying its presence is that the therapist's power shadow or the reparative fantasies accompanying his or her choice of profession are avoided. He or she is cut off from his or her own unconscious and hence unable to use his or her countertransference at all. In fact, there was a time when eros and agape were not regarded as truly separate. It is not my intention to set up a new either/or polarity; *sapientia* may represent the ultimate integration of agape and eros. Agape, and qualities such as survival, reliability, flexibility, understanding, do remain of the utmost importance for sexuality is not the only force in analysis, nor constantly present in the analysis of any one patient.

In contrast to Lambert, other post-Jungian writers such as Plaut (1977) and R. Stein (1974) have continued to develop Jung's thesis that incestuous regression is a necessity for psychological growth (*CW* 5). The erotic involvement of patient and analyst, hopefully understood in the terms just outlined and therefore not acted upon, is the analytical version of this psychological theme. The principle must be 'as much eros in analysis as necessary, not as much as possible'. The incest impulse and the incest taboo are as natural as each other. To stress the taboo but ignore the impulse may well provide a frustration-based boost to consciousness but this will be spurious, desiccated, intellectual. To stress the impulse but not the taboo leads to short-lived pleasure and the risk of exploitation of the patient's vulnerability by the analyst or, conversely, to the patient's capitalizing on his or her more than special connection to a powerful authority figure. We might add to this that it is one function of the incest prohibition to force an individual to consider with whom he or she may or may not mate. He or she has, therefore, to regard a potential partner *as an individual*; this stems from the limiting of his or her choices by the taboo. In addition, the prohibition forces libido out of its exclusively sexual channel into a deeper venture. This is demonstrated by *Figure 10.4* which precedes *Figure 10.3* in the *Rosarium* illustrations: the queen is preventing intercourse with her hand. However, the implication is that such deepening also requires an integration of its own carnal foundation. It would be interesting to discuss whether there are differences that require stating between the experiences in this area of male and female workers. I take it as an assumption that a male may appear as female in the transference and vice versa, and that age differences may not impinge as they would in ordinary social circumstances.

I am working towards the idea that eros in analysis may be seen as *normative*: we should expect eros and speculate on its absence in terms of psychopathology. This would be a different conceptualization from those that express surprise or concern at the *presence* of eros. The yardstick is passion, so that states of anger, hatred, and envy may also be considered from an eros (or negative eros) standpoint: is there warmth of feeling there? Or a more

Figure 10.4

schizoid coldness – even when love is being expressed, perhaps? The idea has use in initial interviews, for example. The analyst would be concerned to note that he was not stirred by the prospective patient. Though the capacity to move others has its sociopathic variants, it is also a sign of a level of emotional development

The dark body

In the previous chapter, I claimed that the analyst's body, functioning as an organ of perception, provides him or her with information about his or her patient. The nature and quality of the erotic involvement – the theme of this chapter – may then be seen as an important specific instance of a general phenomenon. Though it is the analyst's body that is involved and the sensation is quite real (literal), that body is also an imaginal or subtle body (metaphorical).

However, a focus on the healing aspects of eros in analysis should not obscure an additional impression of a darker side. Immersion in alchemical imagery has reinforced the picture of analysis as a 'dark' and difficult process (the *nigredo* of the alchemists). It has been remarked how the so-called 'treasures of the unconscious' involve incest, sado-masochism, and all the abhorred parts of personality that are only available 'behind Mother's back' (Redfearn 1979: 190).

Alchemy does not possess a sickness-health schema. Or, rather, everything is regarded as being in a state of disease, dissolution, decay. It is a dark way of looking at life and one that gives a generous place to psychic pain. The search for the *lapis*, the stone, is a search for a breakthrough into the light. Alchemical metaphors therefore support a nonquantitative approach to growth; it is the quality of the personal equation that counts. Winnicott put it like this:

> We are not only concerned with individual maturity and with the freedom of individuals from mental disorder or psychoneurosis; we are concerned with the richness of individuals in terms not of money but of inner psychic reality...Richness of quality rather than health is at the top of the ladder of human progress.
>
> (Winnicott 1962: 65-6)

What we seek in therapy and analysis is a concentration, deepening, distilling of personality. The minutiae of therapy and the therapeutic relationship help us to keep our feet on the ground. The trivial, the absurd, the ordinary remain the therapist's province. He or she potters away at his or her work, part doctor, part artist, part craftsman, part priest. He or she knows, for all the sophisticated theory and technique, how much is hit and miss. He or she hardly dares to say what it is that heals and has certainly ceased to speak in terms of cure (cf. Paolino 1981: 87). He or she works on the earthy and the concrete with metaphor and his or her metaphor is challenged by literal, bodily, and sensual realities. His or her body and images blur so that he or she cannot always say which it is that is active or to whom it belongs. The alchemists did their work in a *laboratorium* but they prayed for its success in an *oratorium*. And written above the door the words: *Deo concedente* – God willing.

11
Original morality
in a depressed culture

The last two chapters of the book explore moral and political aspects of psychological pluralism.

This chapter is about morality, imagination, depression, and aggression and I introduce the nuclear situation as a kind of case illustration. The chapter is written in a mixture of familiar and unfamiliar language. This is because unmediated psychodynamics seem to me an unsatisfactory basis for an analysis of culture unless a wider orientation is added, one that embraces the collective features in a cultural situation. So a link is made with a particular approach to moral process that I have developed. Links of that kind, and what we do with them, constitute the beginnings of working out a methodology to aid the integration of psyche's dynamics, the institutions of depth psychology, and the public sphere. Such an integration reflects the preoccupations of the first chapter and anticipates the content of the final chapter.

Women and men are moral creatures. Psychology, ethology, and the arts all attest to this. Yet, as confrontation with the problem of nuclear weapons shows, our fundamental sense of morality does not guarantee ethical behaviour either in relationship to ourselves, to others, or to the general environment. On its own this moral sense is inadequate; there has to be some dialogue and interplay with a different kind of morality. This second morality – equally inborn, easy to recognize but hard to define accurately – generates tolerance, forgiveness, openness, and an ingenious approach to problems. I want to call it *moral imagination* and to distinguish it from the first, fundamental, ineluctable morality that, in its certitude, I would like to designate *original morality*. The reference to original sin is deliberate.

194

In the chapter, I suggest that, while these two moralities differ, there is a crucial link and articulation between them. Original morality employed on its own has a tragic outcome. Yet it is the home base to which prodigal moral imagination constantly returns. Without the grounding in certitude that original morality supplies, moral imagination is too evasive by far.

We need not judge between the two moralities, branding one as schizoid and the other as mature and concerned, for original morality is not all blood and bone. Nor does one kind of morality adhere to the ego and the other to soul, for both subsist in each of these. Original morality does not *develop* into moral imagination, so I shall not be talking of the need to make individual a collective moral code or render personal an archetypal superego. Original morality ('sense') and moral imagination ('sensibility') are equally 'archetypal'. Hence, both have to become personal and express themselves in human relationships at all stages of life. Original morality and moral imagination are 'equals'; neither is superior to the other, nor divine.

Throughout the chapter, a personal matrix for moral process is assumed, in particular that provided by the infant–mother relationship that would, at any one time, display a mix of original morality and moral imagination in some proportion. However, as previously remarked, the argument is not primarily concerned with moral development as such; it is claimed that a baby can demonstrate moral imagination (e.g. when experiencing frustration) and an adult, original morality (e.g. when judging the behaviour of others). Similarly, in the paranoid–schizoid position, we may see moral imagination and, in the depressive position, original morality (see below, for further discussion of this point). Original morality and moral imagination are not stages of moral development in Kohlberg's sense (1968), nor is the former 'masculine' and the latter 'feminine' in Gilligan's (1982) usage (and see Sayers 1986: 19-20 for a convincing refutation of Gilligan's thesis).

What will emerge, I hope, is an anatomy of morality in its own terms rather than in the languages of myth or of the psychology of the individual. Then some communication among all of these may be fostered. The intention is to do more than aim towards a synthesis that would simply set two moral viewpoints side by side and then transcend their differences in a calm and superior manner. The pluralistic tension within morality between certainty and improvisation cannot be resolved as easily as that.

195

Positing these two moralities may illuminate some of those perennial conundrums about destructiveness, wickedness, and the shadow with special reference to the nuclear situation. These may be recast so that such dark riddles are seen as reflecting a clash of moralities rather than a struggle between morality and immorality or between conscience and evil or between ego and shadow. Morality itself contains a paradox and is a conflicted ideogram; the split resides in our moral perception, not between our moral side and our baser aspects.

If we could allow original morality its dialogue with moral imagination, maintaining the contact between them, and do this easily and reliably, there would be no need for the chapter. But what often happens is that we get hooked up on one or the other of original morality and moral imagination. If the former, then our approach to problems that cry out for choices to be made will be 'by the book', correct, stolid and safe, reliable – but missing out on the nuances of the situation. If we are hooked on moral imagination, our one-sidedness will have a different tone: bags of ingenuity and so-called 'flexibility', responsiveness to the uniqueness of the situation – but without any real grounding, conviction, or moral muscle. To make any headway at all when things are tough and complicated, we need the blend of certainty and improvisation that I have been describing. Moral imagination enables us effectively to use original morality; original morality guarantees the depth and authenticity of moral imagination. I will show how it is *depression*, functioning on a personal basis and on a cultural level, that is one of the main obstacles to the development of morality in its fullest sense. Depressive dynamics align with and support those of original morality and I will present depression as a kind of philosophy whose ideological stance is set against the reciprocity of original morality and moral imagination.

But first we should look at what is involved in a term such as original morality.

Original morality

Jung pointed out that morality emanates from within; it is a daimon, a voice that we have in us from the start. He was referring to our 'moral nature', of course, and not to precise moral formulations (*CW* 7: para. 30). At times, according to Jung, the moral aspect of man constitutes one of the primal pathways or canals along which, in metaphorical terms, libido may flow, equal in its fundamental status to biology and the spirit (*CW* 8: paras. 100-13). Conscience, then, is not a product of education or parental instruction; if it comes from anywhere, it comes from God. Jung's focus was on the split that may develop between personal ethics and the collective moral code. Jung's use of 'moral' and 'ethical' in relation to conscience is idiosyncratic and confusing (*CW* 10: paras. 825-57). Given that ethics, as a branch of philosophy, concerns itself with justification, codification, and assessment of moral principle, an 'ethical' conscience would suggest one more in tune with the values and norms of the day, the exact opposite of Jung's usage. Morality, viewed philosophically, is a term that defines a broad but well-known area of human behaviour and ideation. However, Jung writes as a psychologist not a philosopher and it is clear what he is getting at; we shall return to this later. What I'd like to add to Jung's recognition that morality has its own force and drive is an attempt to go further into its dynamics, without presupposing the kind of conflict he described as being at the heart of the formation of conscience (cf. Jacoby 1985: 165-9).

In contemporary psychoanalysis, we see similar claims being made for some kind of innate moral sense. One of Klein's contributions was to raise the possibility of the superego's being an innate factor. This idea then forms a theoretical base for Winnicott's insistence that children have an innate sense of guilt and hence are not born amoral (Davis and Wallbridge 1981: 72). Milner also suggests that we stop seeing morality solely as something implanted in children by parents and society (Milner 1977: 67). These psychoanalysts are not overlooking either the key role of parents and family in superego development, or the fact that what is rewarded by the cultural collective as moral, and hence what is punished as criminal, changes over time (nowadays one is not even hung for a sheep). What they *are* doing is pointing up the existence of a primal moral sense – original morality, in my phrase.

To my mind, Freud foreshadowed this view. One reading of his thinking about the superego suggests that he, too, was interested in seeing morality as a part of human make-up. All depends on what might be meant by words like 'archaic' when used in relation to the superego. Sometimes (e.g. Freud 1916-17: 370-1) such a word implies 'phylogenetic' and not merely 'traditional', and inhibitions upon instinctual activity are seen as 'organic' (Freud 1905: 176). Then there is an innate disposition for the self-preservative instincts to become more 'social'. The superego itself may be thought of as a vehicle for the transmission of culture, hence an omnipresent factor, neutral in itself – an archetypal structure, in the language of analytical psychology (Freud 1933: 232-3). To say that the superego is an archetypal structure, even a complex, is to do more than score a Jungian point. What is involved is the realization that morality, conscience, and so forth cannot even be conceived of, let alone discussed, outside of a context of morality and conscience.

As far as post-Jungian analytical psychology is concerned, there is Hillman's distinction between prohibition and inhibition (1975b). The former is external, situational, and mutable; the latter archetypal, internal, and present in many human motivations where it may lead to a psychological deepening. In this conception of inhibition, we can further see why it is important not to write off original morality as primitive or as holding a person back.

An adversary might argue that these depth psychologists have missed something. Man, as a part of nature, is red in tooth and claw. It is Freud's vision of *that* that ought to be stressed. Though morality is valuable, helping us to live together in peace for much of the time, it is secondary, a cultural product, even a fulfilled wish. Such a thinker might go on to talk about humans as animals, male dominance and authority, natural selection, the selfish gene, competition, and even the archetypes (e.g. Stevens 1982). These arguments require replies.

To begin with, authority is not necessarily authoritarian. As Dieckmann suggests, authority may be seen as playing a necessary part in the unfolding and development of social co-operation. The exercise of authority, he says, is tantamount to an instinctual activity (Dieckmann 1977: 217-8). Extending Dieckmann's idea, we might remember that the genes themselves work together, they are interactive and interdependent.

Further, what ethologists tell us about animal behaviour depicts co-operation just as much as competition, sharing as commonly as ruthlessness, huddling together for warmth, hunting together, sometimes helping each other to build nests, uniting for defence (Bateson 1984). Co-operation has always co-existed with competition, both are 'archetypal'. Similarly, inhibitions upon aggression have as established a history as impulses to discharge it.

After all, what does 'animal' signify? The paradigmatic animal may be a wolf *or* a cow. Similarly, concentration camps speak to us of sadistic aggression *and* of passive compliance. The Oedipus complex is about competitive rivalry and father-murder *and* about intergenerational co-operation and lineage (see Kohut 1982). As Mary Shelley knew, man and monster are one.

But, as I have said, original morality seems to be insufficient for the leading of a moral life. In Hesse's words, 'a man may keep the commandments but be far from God'. It can be experienced as harsh, vengeful, primitive, and cold; it grapples with the appetites – in Money-Kyrle's words 'zonal bite will be reversed into moral beat' (quoted in Newton 1975: 190). In an adult, in adverse circumstances, this takes the form of a profound suspiciousness of others, a tendency to jump to the worst possible conclusions, to rejoice in the other's misery when it seems deserved, and, ultimately, to retreat into the wilderness to feed on locusts and honey. Occasionally, such a psychology may buttress social order but somewhere there will always be an inferior element in it, and occasionally, unhappily, the patient plays this part.

For the fatal flaw in original morality is its vertical perspective, its obsession with the superior–inferior dynamic. The need to maintain the vertical split (superior–inferior), which is central to original morality, fuels the horizontal split that threatens the world so pressingly just now (Russia–America). The vertical split (superior–inferior) is superimposed on the horizontal plane (self/other, them and us, Russia and America). If we ask ourselves what it is that enables such shadow projections to occur and be effective, we have to posit some hypothetical force such as original morality. For *something* enables me to take the superior position in relation to you, leaving you smelling of my shit. It's the judgemental flavour of shadow projections that gives them their power and this may be laid at the door of original morality. In its isolated, 'pure' form, original morality has helped to create our divided world, slouching towards apocalypse.

None the less, it remains vital to see beyond the developmental aspects of original morality, to value it as a lifelong capacity, as well as concentrating on what has to be achieved to overcome it. Even if original morality may be seen to dominate a certain phase of development, it contributes a potential richness of texture and quality to all phases, not merely as a 'moral defence' or 'anti-libidinal ego' (Fairbairn, 1952).

Original morality casts things in black and white, but black and white are genuine colours. In them, images of perfection and perfectibility are kept alive. It is true that they are body-less, humour-less, care-less – but, nevertheless, they are reassuringly perfect. It is true that original morality is essentially a morality of narcissism, of the uroboros, of once-and-for-all redemption. But it is precisely these problematic features that we often need. Original morality saturates behaviour, serving us as a well into which we can dip, regenerating ourselves, overcoming cynicism, recapturing enthusiasm, relieving pain. Original morality keeps alive our dreams of getting things done as planned. In pathological form, this may be an addiction to perfection but original morality also stands as a prefiguring of its partner, moral imagination, just as the self prefigures the ego, later to coexist with it.

Original morality has a function, then. As Jung noted, striving after moral perfection is 'not only legitimate but is inborn in man as a peculiarity which provides civilisation with one of its strongest roots' (*CW* 9i: para. 123). Original morality is a broad-horizon reality for all its oversimplification and certainty. 'Insight [exists] along with obtuseness, loving-kindness along with cruelty, creative power with destructiveness' (*CW* 11: para. 560). Original morality is present in the experience of being in love, when the loved one can do no wrong and in the experience of hate when the hated one can do nothing right. Even when original morality leads to experiences of persecution and guilt, this may be seen as providing an emotional foundation for thought and, hence, for maturation. A picture emerges in which the task of the one confronted with original morality – parent, friend, or analyst – is to defuse, moderate, mediate such morality, tenderize it, round it out, render it fruitful, de-idealize it, shake it up a bit – *but not to do away with it altogether*.

The point can be illustrated further by reference to primary and secondary process. Though secondary process is undoubtedly more developed, primary process continues throughout life and, without it, there is no *prima materia* for secondary process. Similarly, primitive forms of consciousness continue alongside more developed forms (Plaut 1959; Samuels 1985a: 69-83; Zinkin 1979). Moral words are amongst the first to be learned.

From this perspective, an *equation* of moral imagination with the so-called 'mature' superego or the depressive position, or an *equation* of original morality with the paranoid–schizoid position would be too hasty. Both moralities interact with each other and in both positions – and we know from Bion how it is that the positions themselves enjoy an interdependence and interplay (1965). So there are two different axes to consider:

paranoid–schizoid <——-> depressive position and
original morality <——-> moral imagination.

Moral imagination

So, by now the reader is probably asking, what is this thing called 'moral imagination'? Broadly speaking, as the moral aspect of imagination, it is moral imagination that we use when confronted with a pressing, problematic, and, especially, conflict-laden situation. Moral imagination is one means by which we apply our imagination to complex social and political issues. *Moral* because a choice may have to be made; *imagination* because that choice may have to be ingenious, less than clear-cut, a compromise or a creatively improved adaptation. Let's now look in detail at what is involved; at first, my approach is going to be an oblique one.

Right at the start of the Jewish Day of Atonement service (Yom Kippur), there is a short prayer that is of fundamental importance. So central is this prayer, that in some congregations it is not recited by the reader alone but together with two members of the congregation. In all versions of the ritual, the prayer is recited *three times* and therefore may be assumed to be of supreme significance. This is the prayer:

> All vows, bonds, oaths, devotions, promises, penalties and obligations: wherewith we have vowed, sworn, devoted and bound ourselves: from this Day of Atonement unto the next Day of Atonement, may it come unto us for good: lo, all these, we repent us in them. They shall be absolved, released, annulled, made void, and of none effect: they shall not be binding nor shall they have any power. Our vows shall not be vows: our bonds shall not be bonds: and our oaths shall not be oaths.

Our vows shall not be vows. What are we to make of this extraordinary pronouncement, the equivalent of cancelling all resolutions at the very moment of making them? Remember, this is *the* high, holy day. There are three possible understandings of the prayer. First, we must be careful not to aim too high, making promises for the future that we cannot keep because of our human limitations. Given the massive sanctions laid down in the Old Testament against those who break their vows, it is crucial to state, right at the start of the process of repentance and atonement, the possibility that it will not work out as intended in the future. Thus, reference is made to the period between this Day of Atonement and the one next year. The second interpretation of this Kol Nidrei prayer is exactly the opposite: that the vows, bonds, promises that are being annulled refer to those made last year, which experience has shown to be unfulfilled or unfulfillable. It is urgently necessary to cancel these promises for we are even now in breach of them. Finally, a third reading, by cancelling all human moral contracts, we are free to contract with God. The compulsions of original morality are anticipated and, hopefully, purged.

I have introduced these reflections on the Yom Kippur ritual to show that a recognition of the unliveable nature of original morality on its own lies at the heart of Judaism, and perhaps of all religions. Jung unfairly castigated Judaism as a source of repressive and legalistic moralism, overlooking the more generous side. What Jung failed to recognize, before the war in his *Zentralblatt* papers on racial psychology (1934) and after it in *Answer to Job* (*CW* 11), is that Judaism enjoys and suffers the tension between original morality (certainly not lacking therein) and moral imagination.

It is not a case of contrasting absolute moral principle with relative quasi-moral behaviour. Both original morality and moral imagination have principles. What follows is an attempt to outline some of the principles of moral imagination.

Moral imagination contains an intuitive and psychological understanding of what a moral principle really is. As the philosopher Philippa Foot points out, morality differs from etiquette or good manners in that:

> Moral rules are not taught as rigid rules that it is sometimes right to ignore (as in the case of etiquette); rather we teach that it is sometimes *morally permissible* to tell lies (social lies), break promises (as e.g. when ill on the day of an appointment) and refuse help (when the cost of giving it would be as we say disproportionate). So we tend, in our teaching, to accommodate the exceptions *within* morality, and with this flexibility it is not surprising that morality can seem 'unconditional' and 'absolute'.
>
> (Foot 1978: 186-7)

Accommodating the exceptions within morality is a good enough summary of moral imagination. With this perspective on moral principle, we lessen the intimidation that is attached to obligation, hence enlarging the area of choice.

If original morality is about manifestos, moral imagination is about that Mediterranean shrug of the shoulders when faced with inconvenience or even disaster. Sometimes accompanied with an exclamation 'Boh!', the gesture signifies an acceptance of imperfection, a worldly and wise reluctance to hope for too much, and sometimes it signals a creative improvisation to try to deal with things.

J. Steiner, a British psychoanalyst, makes a helpful contribution here. Discussing the question of Oedipus's knowledge or lack of knowledge of his plight, Steiner argues that 'we are meant to accept the idea that *both* can be simultaneously true, that he knew and at the same time did not know' (Steiner 1985: 165). Nothing could be further from the all-knowingness, maintaining narcissistic equilibrium, that we encounter in original morality. But if we are to avoid turning a blind eye to the plight of Oedipus, we also need that *certainty* that is the benchmark of original morality.

Continuing to search for the principles of moral imagination, let us focus on two specific themes: forgiveness and moral pluralism.

Forgiveness, and not blame, characterizes moral imagination. Forgiveness of one part of the self by another part, forgiveness of another person, or by another person, forgiveness of one group by another. Forgiveness is important because it can bring a new element into a situation; it is therefore creative (hence imaginative) and, to a degree, an autonomous force in psyche and culture. Forgiveness has much to do with suffering. For the sinner to *feel* a sinner, he or she experiences suffering. At the same time, the one who is to forgive will also have to suffer – for there can hardly be any forgiveness where there is no price to pay. Looked at in this way, the process of forgiveness rests on the ubiquity of suffering.

Forgiveness, as an image and as an experience, makes us question the operation of linear time. When forgiveness is coupled with repentance, then the present may be regarded as shaping the past. Associated promises of good behaviour in the future may be regarded as shaping the present. Forgiveness frees the imagination from the shackles of linear time. The value of forgiveness can be seen in analysis when the patient explores the possibility of forgiving his or her parents for the damage he or she feels they have inflicted. The patient leaves off his or her armour and displays hospitality towards images of the past; this process is the justification of reductive analysis.

In addition, we might query the conventional forgiveness–blame dichotomy. There is a middle position in which I partly blame the malefactor (or bad side of myself) and partly forgive him or it. We can then speak of part-punishment and part-redemption. Whatever the standing of these terms theologically or philosophically, we often encounter what is involved in an emotional form in the consulting room.

On the other hand, the patient gripped by original morality will know the moral score and will strive to become wholly virtuous before he or she forgives him/herself. As far as forgiving sinful others is concerned, the originally moral patient is unlikely to entertain the idea or, if he or she does, it will be in a form that reduces the other to nothing but a blob of contemptible and penitential stuff – hence easily pardonable from on high.

The next theme I want to pursue concerns moral pluralism. Though I intend to develop a different set of ideas here, I am thinking also of a morality of transition, liminal morality, differing moralities attached to the erotogenic zones, to specific images, to the various gods or to the stages of life. (In Chapter 8, I wrote of Hermetic morality in relation to primal scene imagery).

If one looks at the multifarious moral commandments and prohibitions that exist, it is very difficult to state the one general principle, or even a few general principles, that connect all of them. They are unavoidably plural; it is their essence to discriminate numberless kinds of approved and disapproved behaviour. This can be seen in the Day of Atonement ritual, in which enormous lists of specific sins are confessed out loud; general confession seems inadequate even though it is general absolution that is sought. The specific, the nitty gritty, the plural images of sin are thrust forward. This is so because human beings do not have a single dominating concern or goal, no one supreme interest – and the concerns, goals, and interests that may be observed are, again, innumerable, It is not a question of moral perception but of moral perception*s*. There is a need to reconcile, or to downplay, or to privilege and accentuate very different concerns, and this is true for individuals and society alike. What we admire and value in ourselves and others need not follow any logical format: warmth and openness together with careful attention to detail, driving ambition with pervasive self-doubt. Such illogical combinations occur in the external world as well: societal conflicts and political pluralism are mirror and model for the moral conflicts of the personality.

It follows that moral imagination typically requires a weighing up of conflicting claims: for example, should I support a friend whom I know to be in the wrong? My response to this kind of question, coupled with my responses to myriad others of equal difficulty, informs the dynamics of social *communitas* and of moral imagination. Here, in the weighing of claims in conflict, original morality comes into its own, vital for the workings of moral imagination. We must endeavour to *use* the moral knowledge we have always had.

Thus far, I have been pitting moral imagination against the adoption of single-criterion ethics. Here I would like to recall Jung's admonition to follow the inner voice even when this risks being shunned as a deviant (*CW* 10: paras. 825-57). I find myself undecided as to whether this constitutes a single-criterion ethic. Sometimes in his constant preference for a subjective, intuitive, and emotionalist morality, Jung can be seen as an exemplar of original morality; knowing and biased. Does sharing Jung's morality mean opening the inner ear and closing the outer one? On the other hand, the inner voice may itself be plural in its nature, expressing more than one point of view.

I have been arguing that there is a psychological value in facing a conflict of claims, something more than a mere acceptance of practical realities, that would be moral relativism or situation ethics. It is important not to see moral imagination as just the daily version of original morality, or as the relative outcome of absolute principle. *Pluralism is not the same as relativism.* Perceiving a conflict of moral principles is not the same as claiming that, in life, principle has to be watered down. Moral *relativism* implies a hierarchy in which principle is placed above and distinct from praxis. Moral *pluralism* sees no value in unlivable principle, nor takes such a pat-on-the-head, there-there attitude to moral failure, based on concessions to human appetites. There's a name for that: casuistry. The principles involved in moral pluralism embrace their own tricksterish failure in the world; we accommodate the exceptions within morality; *the exceptions make the rules.*

After all, as the philosopher Anthony Kenny points out, what we mean by 'goodness' is itself plural and may vary when discussing either a thing or a state of affairs.

> The criteria for the goodness of a thing depend on the nature of the thing in question: an earthworm who does well the things that earthworms do is a good earthworm, no matter whether anybody wants an earthworm or not. The criteria for the goodness of a state of affairs depend on what people want: good weather is not weather which is good of its kind, or

which does well the things which weather does, but weather which enables you to do well whatever it is you want to do.

(Kenny 1963: 221n)

Of course, moral imagination itself could be represented as a single-criterion ethic, with *its* value wedded to pluralism and conflict. I don't see any defence against that save to recall that one leitmotif of this chapter has been to point out the co-presence of original morality, the acme of single-criterion ethics, with moral imagination. The absolute has its place. Indeed, sometimes it is necessary to make a one-sided commitment, based on one moral criterion or a small set of criteria. Then moral imagination must cope with a tension within itself between the variety of pluralism and the intense strength of the moral absolute. This may be seen when a person makes a massive investment in a god, a profession, an art, a relationship. It is a part of human experience to be torn in this way and the rack is stretched between more than mere models of behaviour; variant self-images are at odds. Nowhere is this more marked than in the ways in which nation states present themselves to others or see themselves from within. The difficulty an individual might have in reconciling the competing claims of his inner units is multiplied when the problem is faced by the state.

The question of moral pluralism is also addressed in Diderot's brilliant dialogue entitled *Rameau's Nephew*, written *circa* 1761. The amoral, tricky, corrupt, wastrel musician challenges the validity of the moral principles by which his philosopher interlocutor is judging him. True, he says, there may be some kind of general conscience, just as there is a general grammar but, as in grammar, there are exceptions. In fact, as the Diderot scholar Peter France points out, Rameau is doing more than defending the exception against the rule; he, too, is arguing that the exception *is* the rule. It follows that 'so-called virtue is cold and unlovable, so-called vice is what makes the world go round' (France 1983: 79). In the end, like so many tricksters, Rameau 'turns the tables by casting doubts on the sanity of those who patronise him' (France 1983: 81).

In this clash of original morality and moral imagination, we should not assume that each protagonist represents one side in a clear-cut way. Both parties speak for both moralities at different times. Of course, Diderot is present in both of his creations. The point is that, in original morality, there is either no dialogue or, if there is a dialogue, it is one with overclear and unequivocal positions in it. In moral imagination, not only is there dialogue but it is difficult to say with certainty who speaks for what. The clinical parallel is with the dialogues of active imagination that become suspect when cut and dried. In *Rameau's Nephew*, we see how the relationship between the two men changes during and because of their communication.

Now, as promised at the outset, it is time to consider how depression drives a wedge between original morality and moral imagination, frustrating their dialogue and their mutual fertilization. In particular, when we reflect upon moral imagination, as an experience and in emotional terms, aggression cannot be avoided. Without aggression, 'conflict' remains a word and not a living and coruscating process. *Aggression fuels moral imagination.*

Depression

I want to present depression as a philosophy of our day, dedicated to the condemnation and suppression of aggression. As such, depression may be seen as a moral disorder and injurious to moral imagination. Depressed patients tell us of being overwhelmed by feelings of badness, destructiveness, and, above all, self-blame. Psychodynamically, the connection with aggression lies in the fantasy of having destroyed the loved object or person who was necessary for emotional survival; ambivalence was not a possibility. Alternatively, depression may be a means of guaranteeing parental love and acceptance by gainsaying the aggression that is felt not to be permitted by the parents. The reader will note that I couple these opposing viewpoints, for I believe that the real value of theoretical disagreements amongst analysts is that they point to the nub of the matter, whatever it is, and suggest a starting point for the tyro theoretician (see the opening and final chapters).

This also applies to background speculation concerning the aetiology of depression, particularly where the debate polarizes along developmental/archetypal lines. From the personal historical perspective, we have to think of the vulnerable mother, in fact or fantasy, meaning her vulnerability in psychopathological and environmental terms. The depressed mother, the unmothered mother, the too-young mother – and then the poor, ill-housed, badly educated, unsupported mother (see Brown and Harris 1978). The mother's vulnerability performs a phenomenological work upon aggression. In plain language, the child's aggression seems to the child to be worse than it really is. From an archetypal perspective, we have to think tentatively of an adverse and inborn imbalance between love and hate in an individual. This is a very hard thing to stomach: some people are born constitutionally more aggressive than others. Given an unfavourable and unempathic response to the excess of aggression, and it is clear that depression in the adult may be the outcome. Here, it does not matter whether the archetypal view is expressed in terms of the gods or in the language of biochemistry, neurology, and genetics.

One of the consequences of the moral certainty of depression is that the psychological value of aggressive fantasy is lost. Depression, functioning as a moral philosophy, promotes two well-known but seemingly intractable conflations: of aggressive fantasy and destructive fantasy – and then of fantasy and action. Let's consider these in turn.

Aggressive fantasy has its own *telos*. In saying this, I do not intend to minimize the damaging, negative, painful, perverted, controlling aspects of aggressive fantasy. However, the observation has often been made that aggressive *behaviour*, in the form of healthy self-assertion, is a necessity for survival in both an absolute and a social sense. My concern is more with aggressive images and images of aggression. Because the ground to be traversed is undoubtedly familiar, I would like to make a start by saying that the old debate about whether aggression is primary and innate, or a secondary reaction to frustration and fear, or both, has tended to mask a more significant question: what are the consequences for moral speculation if aggression *is* innate? It seems to me that there is no moral problem whatsoever with aggression as an innate factor, no need for shame or apologetics about that (but cf. Jung *CW* 5: para. 504n, where he demurs at the death instinct). After all, sex is similarly innate and is not minimized on that ground nor are attempts made to eliminate it altogether.

Aggressive fantasy promotes a vital style of consciousness (images of tearing things up, dissecting them, controlling them, playing with them, making use of them). Aggressive fantasy has much to do with our desire to know; it is not, in itself, completely bloodstained and unreflective. (Bad science is not science *per se*.) Aggressive fantasy can bring into play that interpersonal separation without which the word 'relationship' would have no meaning. In this sense, aggressive fantasy may want to make contact, get in touch, relate. For some, mainly men perhaps, it may be the only way to relate. The same is true for internal units and processes; aggressive fantasy enables separate images of the parents to emerge, and other imagos, and inner discriminations – for example, what theory refers to as the ego-self axis. As Searles says, 'at one moment a violent urge may express a striving to be free and at the next a desire to relate' (Searles 1973: 325). Aggressive fantasy forces an individual to consider the conduct of personal relations. When one fantasizes an aggressive response to one's desires on the part of the other, one is learning something about that other as a being with a different but similar existence to one's own. Without aggressive fantasy, there would simply be no cause for concern about other people and so aggressive fantasy points beyond ruthlessness to discover the reality and mystery of persons. 'It is only when intense aggressiveness exists between two individuals that love can arise' (Storr 1970: 57). Finally, aggressive fantasy is playful at times, even humorous, a continuous cartoon of ejaculatory, exploratory enjoyment, a *jouissance* – for women, perhaps one way to be 'seminal', 'thrusting', and 'penetrative'.

Since it is composed of images as much as impulses, aggressive fantasy can be approached via its specifics. An example appears in Freud's 'A child is being beaten' (1919). And Jung, writing about the treatment of depression, suggested that getting to the inherent fantasies leads to 'enrichment and clarification of the affect' (*CW* 8: para. 167). But it is clarification of the *image* that is needed in relation to aggressive imagery: biting is not tearing, nor smearing, nor cutting, nor punching, nor shooting, nor beating.

Aggressive fantasy, like incest fantasy, has a refuelling and regenerating function that is accentuated in more extreme fantasy. For aggressive fantasy returns us to basics, to evolutionary dangers just as much as to the mother's body or the father who bars our path.

When an instinctual impulse is blocked in terms of actual expression, the fantasies associated with it may be permitted space in which to take on more depth; it is not important whether we refer to this as sublimation or transformation. But if the fantasy is itself blocked, then this cannot happen. What Jung pioneered for fantasies of incestuous sexuality in *Symbols of Transformation* should be attempted for aggressive fantasy. This would mean, for example, that aggression between persons, or the aggressive fantasy of one about the other, may not only be about those two persons; its symbolic meaning as *coniunctio* as well as its literal potential engages our interest. The perversity and horror of aggressive fantasy may give it a creative capacity to nourish the soul. Just as with sexuality and spirituality, the transformation of aggressive fantasy tends to be in the *general* direction of its opposite: creativity and moral imagination – towards forgiveness and the new departure that that can bring; towards moral pluralism; and towards an acceptance of the body's irreducibly aggressive motions. We should not forget the thrill and excitement of aggressive fantasy, its action in and upon sexuality and feeding. Then there is the bliss of the calm after the storm. Aggressive fantasy, breaking taboos as it does, proposes an image of human moral creativity, shorn of idealizations and full of eros; Jacob wrestling with his angel. Transformation is never easy, sometimes destructive, and impossible to order up. Renewal and aggression are twins.

Finally, in this survey, there is the part played by aggressive fantasy in a gut response – that free play of imagination that permits one to react outside of the 'rules', leading eventually to an aesthetic sense. (The reader might recall the discussion in Chapter 5 of the father's role in the transformation of aggression.)

In myth, when Kronos turns on Uranus, one of the imaginal birth moments of Western culture, he cuts off his father's genitals with a sickle, casting them into the sea. From them, Aphrodite is born, the goddess of love. Out of the despairing, murdered, foamy ejaculate steps the epitome of beauty. Here, too, the imago of child as phallus has its archaic roots. It seems to be no accident that contemporary depth psychologists have needed to make the aggression–depression dynamic a central part of their theorizing. Nor is it coincidence that Hermann Hesse's counterpart to Narcissus, the one who leads a life of mind and spirit, is Goldmund, as often killer as fornicator. In its confusion of aggressive and destructive fantasy, a depressed ego stops the dialogue between the aggressive mind and the world.

I mentioned that depression promotes two conflations and we have just been looking at one of them, between aggressive fantasy and destructive fantasy. The other mix-up was between fantasy and action. Here the designation of depression as a moral philosophy makes sense. In depression we can see a distorted application of what, in philosophy, is referred to as intentionality. Any emotion (and that includes fantasy) will construct an object towards which it is directed, towards which it has intention. I cannot be aggressive save in relation to an object of aggression or believe without an object of belief. Such 'intentional objects' include ideas (objects of thoughts), individuals (objects of love and hate), or groups (objects of alliance and enmity).

In depression, the strength of aggressive fantasy, and the moral consequences ascribed to it by the ego, make for intentional objects of immense power. While the value of intentional objects is that they facilitate emotional expression, their coming to psychic dominance – as they do in the omnipotent, destructive fantasies of the depressed person – has absolutely the opposite effect: a paralysis of the imagination and a judgemental, landslide victory for original morality. The depressed person – or culture – is confronted with an utterly literal portrayal of the outcome of fantasy. In the language of philosophy, in depression 'intentional objects' become 'material objects'.

I am not saying that inner and outer are absolutely different or that fantasy and action are unconnected. But in depression the ego adopts an exclusively external perspective, forgetting, in Winnicott's phrase, that moral guilt belongs to inner reality (Winnicott 1958: 15). Therefore a depressed person cannot join in the dance of original morality and moral imagination.

I have been working up these ideas about depression at some length because they have particular relevance to our reactions and responses to the nuclear threat. (This is my case illustration, so to speak.) Consider: in almost every respect, the emotional dynamics of our confrontation with the nuclear situation replicate and stimulate those of depression. There is a confusion between inner and outer; inner fantasies of world destruction that have always existed are now literal fact. There is an enormous fear attached to the expression of aggression today; total war might result. Moral imagination is overwhelmed and the ego, dominated by original morality, searches for something to blame: history, the system, patriarchy, the enemy, the scientific ego itself.

The pressing issue is our powerlessness in the face of the nuclear problem. We need to distinguish between the psychological dynamics of the world political situation and the specific psychological dynamics of our inertia and impotence. Not what is felt about the Russians, nor why it is felt, but how we feel about a world in which Russians, Americans, and others are locked into a certain kind of combination. If we look at things from this standpoint, the critically disabling anxiety from which we suffer is not paranoid anxiety, hence not characterized primarily by splitting, projective identification, projection of the shadow, and so forth. In the nuclear age such concepts, often quoted by depth psychologists, do not illuminate our paralysis when what used to be regarded as an overliteral apperception of aggressive fantasy has become the plain fact. *We can destroy our adversaries* – and, from that, depression will follow, silencing the articulation between original morality and moral imagination. We back away from the creative edge of our aggressive fantasies when, in reality, it is through their free play that we can begin to realize their opposites – forgiveness and compassion (J. Kirsch, personal communication 1986).

Like depression with its delusions of self-blame, the nuclear situation forces us to stay locked into original morality. For whether we anticipate with certainty total nuclear destruction or, with equal certainty, a peaceful balance based on the fear of retaliation, it is *such certainty itself* that keys us into original morality. When depression and original morality collude, one's sense of responsibility becomes the victim; 'integration of the shadow' becomes a pious nonsense. If nuclear weapons have injured our capacity for moral imagination, they certainly show our need for it. But cultural depression will prevent the need from being met. Hopelessness has become global and there is no space for good thoughts about ourselves.

In our culture, the depressive fear of our own destructiveness, and the corresponding paucity of moral imagination in relation to that, have reached epidemic proportions. The traditional institutions for its containment have become eroded. Our culture suffers from a collective, depressive delusion that it is all-bad, all-destructive. We are therefore alienated from the possibility of forgiveness. Moreover, the process is circular; depression and original morality feed into one another so that we cannot extract the value from our aggressive fantasies. When we talk of the positive side of the shadow or of healthy aggression, we should take care not to neglect the depressive block in us that prevents such gold from being mined. There is also the possibility that interruption of the flow between original morality and moral imagination may itself lead to (further) depression.

Women in our culture experience particular difficulties in expressing aggression; one result may be their statistically greater tendency to become depressed. For women have much to feel aggressive about; they have to be nice, adopt a passive social stance, and worry about their appearance; they are said to be 'maternal' and their eroticism is limited by male preconceptions. Yet it is women who have led the way in protesting against the

212

assumptions of nuclear proliferation. Perhaps their anger and aggression at what is required of them by society has freed their imaginations and enabled them to take action. However, for men and women, the depressive fear of losing parental love makes it hard to say 'no' to the political parent-figures; it is a problem that is not usually addressed by those who want 'the people' to act.

For some, global hopelessness is itself so intolerable that trust is placed in simplistic, single-strand solutions. Using the language of this paper, this is original morality and not moral imagination at work.

Depth psychology and social analysis: a comment

It would concern me greatly if the question of the validity of applying concepts and intuitions from depth psychology to issues of a social and cultural nature was not addressed in this chapter. To begin with, psychological ideas are already part of culture. They are generated in a precise historical context even though their imagery may be recycled through the operation of the archetypes. We may find in our analyses of the internal world just what it is that is experienced in society. Conversely, how we perceive the world and what we perceive therein tells us about the psyche. The interpenetration is not an imposition; it already exists. However, it is important to carry out a necessary work of abstraction upon clinical material before applying it to social trends and issues. That is why I am interested in using theoretical *disputes* rather than single theories when discussing cultural and social matters: depression as personal–historical or as innate and endogenous; a consequence of aggressive fantasy or a learnt passivity. Focus on the debate permits a more flexible application of the psychology assuming, as it does, that psychological dialogue, discourse and dispute are cultural phenomena, reflecting cultural processes and preoccupations. We learn as much about clinical practice when we reflect upon culture as vice versa.

Another way for the analyst intent in communicating an analysis of culture to proceed is to stick close to the therapeutic method. Instead of a surreptitious identification of the culture (or an aspect of it) as the 'patient', such identification becomes open. According to M. Stein (1985: 22), this 'treatment' of a cultural phenomenon is demonstrated in Jung's approach to Christianity. Stein shows how

Jung's method used three main planks of psychotherapeutic procedure. These are: (a) historical reconstruction; (b) interpretation, both reductive and forward-looking; and (c) the transference–countertransference dynamic. Thus, when we examine a phenomenon (a case?) such as helplessness and hopelessness in the face of the nuclear threat, we are interested in how the problem has evolved, how we understand its origins, where it seems to be going, and, finally, how we relate to it on an emotional level and how it (the problem) responds to our therapy. This last subject is important: even the social analyst writes out of a personal agenda; though this may be hidden, his or her countertransference has to be considered. Social problems, like patients, respond to treatment in differing ways. The hope is to avoid the self-deception of 'objective' analysis; this would be analogous with the inhuman application of the worst kind of 'high-tech' medical approach. Using psychotherapy as the model for cultural analysis makes use of the critic's affective engagement. Looked at like this, maybe all social and political enquiry is really therapy.

A further reason for including this 'comment' is that the nuclear threat is but one aspect of a general alienation of women and men from their social world: pollution, poverty, exploitation, sexism, and racism are all part of the picture.

Coda

I had thought to stop the chapter here, with depression as 'the problem', so to speak. But, conscious that it is well known that there are many positive aspects to depression, I gradually became aware that depression, the problem, could also be visioned as a kind of solution, or at least as an ambience in which solutions could be worked upon (because there is no obvious solution).

Overcoming depression involves a reconstruction and reconstitution of the internal world so that losses are somehow made good or accommodated to; imagos of others (particularly parents) allowed fruitful life; and personal responsibility for disaster reassessed. All of these involve entering fantasy, owning the aggressive images and hence one's potential for aggressive, even warlike discharge. An alternative to discharge, though, is to be forgiven for one's aggression; by oneself or by its recipient whether friend, enemy, or analyst.

Considered in this light, depression may be seen as lying at the *heart* of moral imagination and, especially, of forgiveness. Paradoxically, depression may then actually *constitute* a link between original morality and moral imagination. For depression forces us to take fantasy seriously, if not literally. This means facing the potential outer reality of aggressive fantasy alongside its inner creativity. When that happens, depression becomes the forum for an integration of the instinctual body and the imaginative soul and our aggressive dreams show us the meaning of our despair.

Finally, I want to introduce the metaphor of depression as a *search*. For the individual, such a search may be a search of collective memory – Memory, mother of the Muses and hence of creativity generally. The work of memory is the work of mourning. In the nuclear age, we have to search in our memory for the archaic fascination with death that spawned civilization and from which we have turned our faces. The search in depression reflects a need for continuity as a fundament of imagination. Depression enables imagination to be of service. Depression may be seen as a piecing together, over time, of a solution. That is partly why the writer has to get depressed when the book isn't going well, the mother when the baby won't feed, the worker when faced with unemployment, each of us when threatened by the bomb. All have to search for a solution. The depressive process, static on the surface, is a flow of information, intuitions, and images leading to a reorganization of these. For that is all that is meant by 'solution'; it is not 'cure' or getting rid of depression. The misery of depression comes in part from the awful slowness of the search and its apparent futility.

12

The diversity
of psychology and the
psychology of diversity

The general impression I have of depth psychology is that there was a golden age that is now past. The broad outlines of the enterprise are firmly drawn (cf. Gorkin 1987: 29). If that is so, then the fertilizing challenge presented by the arrival on the scene of all-inclusive theories, forcing a person to work out his or her response, has been lost. If our generation's job is not to be restricted to professionalization and institutionalization, it is necessary to highlight one thing we can do that the founding parents and brilliant second-generation consolidators cannot. This is to be *reflexive* in relation to depth psychology, to focus on the psychology of psychology, a deliberate navel-gazing, a healthily narcissistic trip to the fantastic reaches of our discipline; a post-modern psychological outlook, redolent with the assumption that psychology is not 'natural', but made by psychologists. After that, but only after that, we can turn towards the world. My point is that when analysts look at themselves, how they think, feel, behave, organize themselves, they are, often unknowingly, also gazing at the world of psyche. So a post-modern angle, which might scorn the idea of depth, can coexist with a preoccupation with the unconscious symbolisms of the soul.

There is a need to work these opening remarks into a methodology. The rationale for this last chapter rests on the notion that the difference between making a theory and critiquing a theory is a delusive one. As Derrida (1978) says, everything is a free play of signs and metaphors. A psychological theory, or an account of a technical consideration in analysis, forms a text with no 'natural' meaning. This approach to texts may be a Gnostic one, using analytic intuition and the knowledge locked up in our reactions, our countertransferences to the text. The polemical and argumentative

216

style of most psychoanalytic discourse, reflects the competition of theories and underscores an appreciation of their suasive, rhetorical intent and content.

When theories compete, what attitudes are possible? None seem satisfactory. We can choose between them – but that may lead to blind partisanship and possibly to tyranny. We can synthesize them – but that may lead to omnipotence and an avoidance of the hard edges of disagreement rather than to transcendence. We can be indifferent to the dispute – but, as I shall argue forcefully, that leads to ennui and a subtle form of 'clinical' inflation. Of course, we can be pluralistic – but that leads to fragmentation and anxiety (as we shall see); further, it is hard to do, this pluralism.

Texts of psychological theory can constitute for the post-golden age analyst what alchemical texts constituted for Jung. A deconstruction of depth psychology parallels his of alchemy. What has motivated the (by now) vast project of depth psychology? What are depth psychologists doing? Just as the alchemists projected the workings of the unconscious into chemical elements and processes, becoming caught up in the pervasive symbolism of it all, so the texts of the depth psychologist, taken as a whole, may unwittingly provide us with documents of the soul. What was intended to be *about* psyche is *of* psyche. The conscious aim may be to plumb the past for its truths, or to connect past and present, or to reveal the workings of cumulative psychopathology. But what gets revealed, however, are the central characteristics of psyche itself. This is where clashes between theories are so useful, because the actual clash contains the definitive psychic issue. Not psychological dialectics, but psyche's discourse given dialectical form. The warring theories and the specific points of conflict speak directly of what is at war in the psyche and of what the specific points of conflict therein might be. Personal experience itself exemplifies contradictory theories; for instance, those giving primacy to innate or to environmental factors in the development of personality, or those attempting a combination. Did my mother abandon me because I am unlovable? Or was she mad? Or, unhappily for me, are both true?

The texts of depth psychology constitute, in Derrida's words, a 'world of signs without fault, without truth and without origin which is offered to an active interpretation' (Derrida 1978: 292). We are forced, no matter how earnestly we seek truth, to pay attention to those three horsemen of the post-structural apocalypse: relativity, interaction, and the absence of 'deep' structures divorced from experience. *Everything depends on the active interpretation* – even, or especially, a historical approach.

Pluralism, dispute, and depth psychology

Bearing in mind the intention to be reflexive, what follows is an attempt to work out a pluralistic attitude to dispute in depth psychology. As I suggested in the opening chapter, we can use pluralism as an instrument to help us to look at the topic of dispute in depth psychology. It should be noted that the chapter does not cover the area of scientific method, nor does it consider the scientific status or mode of construction of analytical theories, nor examine the category differences between hypothesis, theory, and model (cf. Kuhn 1970; Peterfreund 1983; Popper 1959; Zinkin 1984). As far as the theories with which I am engaged are concerned, I take a phenomenological approach to them: they are part of my natural world. I'm more interested in what we do with the theories we've got.

A pluralistic approach to depth psychology suggests that a person interested in any particular area of knowledge should seek out the conflict and, above all, the *competition* between practitioners and ideologues in the discipline. The implication is that even a beginner should try to discover what the contemporary debate is all about. This approach differs radically from the conventional, linear style of education and training. There, one is supposed to start at 'the beginning' and, when the 'basics' have been mastered, exposure to more grown-up disagreements is permitted. The pluralistic point I am advancing, strengthened by a good deal of teaching experience, is that *starting at the beginning is no guarantee of comprehension*. However, if a person were to focus on the up-to-the-minute ideological conflict, then he or she cannot avoid discovering what has gone before and 'book learning' remains a living process. In a way, this is an educational philosophy derived from analysis itself. In an analysis, the focus of interest is where the internal 'debate' is at its most virulent; and in analysis the participants do not follow a linear 'course'.

The debates within depth psychology give it life. They also serve to define the discipline generally (see Samuels 1985a) and act as access routes for those who want to learn. If you react emotionally to some argument or other, then you 'belong' to depth psychology; you share its vertices, even if you dispute what its conclusions are to be. What is important is not whether people are right or wrong (though everyone has views about that), but whether you know what they are talking about. For, in depth psychology, it is really rather hard to be completely wrong.

The attitude towards disagreement that I want to promote here has been termed 'bootstrapping'. The somewhat unfortunate term is borrowed from theoretical physics. Instead of searching for one guiding theory, we might consider using many theories in parallel up to a point where their mutual inconsistencies and incompatibilities cause this to break down. Then the breakdown becomes a focus for study. Bootstrapping is not the same as synthesizing theories nor is it a form of eclecticism, nor is it based on consensus. What is central to bootstrapping is that *no one theory, nor the level of reality to which it refers, is regarded as more fundamental than any other.* Geofrey Chew, the originator of the bootstrap approach, writes: 'A physicist [read analyst] who is able to view any number of different, partially successful models without favouritism is automatically a bootstrapper' (quoted in Capra 1975: 87). The bootstrapper knows that it may be impossible for there to be a single theory that will work. What holds the theories together is that the subject matter somehow holds together: for the physicist, the universe; for the depth psychologist, the psyche. Passion for one approach, inevitably partial, is replaced by passion for a plurality of approaches.

Clearly, for there to be any dialogue at all, some assumptions have to be permitted and agreed though consensus can become like airline food – just acceptable to everyone but truly palatable to none. However, blandness is not what I perceive as problematic with consensus. In depth psychology, and perhaps in science as well, personal allegiance and power dynamics play a part (Kuhn 1970). Orthodoxy, heterodoxy, and heresy come into being. For instance, commenting on the impact of Klein's new ideas on the British psychoanalytic community in the 1930s and 1940s, R. Steiner invites us to consider how consensus evolves and can be manipulated within depth psychology:

> there is no doubt that due to the particular manner of psychoanalysis's transmission via the personal analysis of candidates, with all the deep processes of dependence and identification which this involves, innovations can mobilize, among other things, extremely primitive persecutory anxieties connected with the inevitably confusing experience

of certainties being thrown into doubt, and connected also with fear, suspicion and envy of what is presented as new.

This can easily disturb the peaceful tendency towards a static equilibrium and that attitude of dogmatic conventionality which rests on the intellectual and, above all, emotional security that comes from more or less completely interiorized certainties.

(R. Steiner 1985: 59-60)

This state of affairs can be seen most vividly in relation to training for analysis and psychotherapy and therefore lies at the very root of depth psychology as a social institution. Though the trainee is an adult, a degree of regression seems inherent in the training situation due to the continuing entanglements of the trainee's analysis and supervision. It has been claimed that the training posture fosters regression in general and persecutory anxiety in particular, and that this is exacerbated by a confusion in the minds of the trainers between analysis and training (Bruzzone *et al.* 1985). My worry is somewhat different from that expressed by the group of Chilean psychoanalytic trainees whose views I have just summarized. It is that the whole range of careful, thoughtful experiences most analysts have been through in their training might inadvertently take the creative sting out of pluralism. I am thinking of syllabi, seminar themes, reading lists, feedback sessions, and so forth. The more 'integrated' the training programme, the greater the denial of pluralism.

I fear that this deprivation of pluralism may have contributed to the consensual formation of cultlike bodies within our little world of depth psychology. Being in a cult implies obedience. There is too much obedience in depth psychology today and a pluralistic vision of the field is set against that. There is a serious danger that training programmes will become obedience cults and that this will be rationalized by reference to the advantages of practising out of a system in which one has conviction. It is striking how many of the groups that are active in analytical psychology and psychoanalysis cluster round leader figures. The leaders may be remarkable people with an original and comprehensive vision, which would partially account for the tendency, but I think there is more to it than that. I do not think this pattern of leadership within analytic institutes results from *conscious* fostering, but would argue that its effect is to shield the trainee from the stresses and anxieties of pluralism – and from its benefits. The need for strong leader figures has a lot to do with the desire to avoid the anomalous. The leader sorts things out by arranging competing ideas in a schema of acceptance, protecting or advancing his or her own in the process. The desire to avoid anxiety and confusion when confronted with new ideas (as noted by Steiner, pp. 219-20, above) leads groups to select leaders as combination censor and safety net.

A cult is characterized by a belief system based on ideas that have become standard within the group. The group is hence relatively closed, like a secret society that controls and disciplines its members (see Rustin 1985). Indeed the key element can be summed up in that word 'membership'. There are two elements involved here: (a) the status of belonging to a group, and (b) the hurdle one must cross to obtain status (a). The quality of the status must be in part an effect of what happens at the hurdle. To cross the hurdle, the individual must pass through a series of stages or phases. For a variety of reasons, in most training institutions, these stages usually get referred to as 'years'. Now I can see that this stems from the fact that most courses run on the basis of a series of annual seminars. But this is surely woefully inappropriate for a training in the most individualistic of professions. The calendric approach ('she's a second-year trainee') can be seen as a massive disincentive to pluralistic thinking because the implication is of an orderly, logical, in-control sort of process that is headed towards a single, known goal; it signifies a dangerous tendency to mass-produce our new analysts.

And yet our courses, the course I did, are not sterile. Most depth psychologists speak warmly of their training and this cannot be exclusively ascribed to identification with the trainers, or flattery, or professional protectionism. Two developments typically occur during training, both of which have a pluralistic implication. The first is that, at some point in training, the individual starts to vary the task he or she has been assigned in an attempt to individualize it, or bring it more into line with his or her evolving interests. The second development is that, after a time, most analysts join small peer-discussion groups in which they find a somewhat freer atmosphere than in the large institute. The snag with such groups is that developments in thinking and practice stay private, escaping the hurly-burly of the marketplace; they therefore do not contribute as directly as they could to the pluralist stew pot (see Samuels 1985a: 267-9; Sandler 1983 for a discussion of 'private theory-making').

Pluralism and its constraints

I have been trying to show that pluralism is a useful attitude to take towards competing theories, and that depth psychology wants to become, needs to be, and, ironically, *is* pluralistic. But pluralism suffers from constraints. Each of these contains its own validity, richness, and utility. Hence, what follows is discussion, not diatribe. There is a general antipluralistic tenor in much modern psychological discourse. I would like to examine two constraints on pluralism: holism and numinosity.

The dynamics of holism

Personal experiences of feelings of oneness mean that I partly share the holistic ideal. But I doubt whether holism is relevant or appropriate as a bedrock for depth psychology. Singer clearly felt otherwise when she summed up the ideas behind the holistic stance, which has become the contemporary paradigm:

> that it is holistic means we see entities first as wholes and only secondarily do we examine the parts ... every science, every religion, every philosophical system ... helps those who use it to gain a holistic and organised picture, involving phenomena too vast and complex to be grasped if approached piecemeal.
>
> (Singer 1979: 10, 13)

Jung gave warning of the dangers of this. In 'Depth psychology and self knowledge' he writes:

> if the goal of wholeness ... should grow naturally in the patient we may sympathetically assist him toward it. But if it does not grow of itself, it cannot be implanted without remaining a permanently foreign body. Therefore we renounce such artifices when nature herself is clearly not working towards this end. As a medical art, equipped only with human tools, our psychology does not presume to preach the way to salvation.
>
> (*CW* 18: para. 97)

Guggenbühl-Craig is on the same track when he wonders if there is not too much said about roundness, completeness, and wholeness.

He suggests it is 'high time we spoke of the deficiencies ... of the Self. Today we have succumbed to the cult of the complete, healthy and round, to mandala-like perfection' (Guggenbühl-Craig 1980: 25-6).

The sociologist Peter Bishop (1986) joins his voice to what is, these days, a minority opinion. He feels that holism necessarily stands *outside* and *on top of* the *detail* on the world and its *dangers*. Holism is a fantasy of 'a stable global image [which] gives focus to the boundlessness of space' (Bishop 1986: 61). 'Humanity seems trapped within its own dreams of unity' (Bishop 1986: 64).

Similarly, the political theorist Kenneth Minogue has argued persuasively that approaches that see everything as connected with everything else strike at the very heart of civilization (Minogue 1986). Minogue's ideas, it seems to me, apply equally to holism. He regards culture as requiring the marking off of certain places as holy or sacred and education as 'a process in which the young learn to distinguish the different spaces and values of a complex civilization'. Barbarians, concludes Minogue, never come into contact with these complexities. When it performs a butterknife function, holism could be the new barbarism.

Holistic thinking tends to be utopian (Jung's 'preaching'). There is a certain compulsiveness that gets attached to holism. Holism can be an attempt to deny the pain of rupture, of *rupture* even. Those who measure cognitive dissonance have shown how a person aims to organize his or her inner and outer worlds as harmoniously as possible. Though I take this to be a way of dealing with anxiety rather than an authentically holistic position, there is considerable overlap. Thus the individual will give greater weight to select aspects of his or her perceptual field to fit the relatively stronger needs. For example, a deprived person will see parental figures everywhere or be overwhelmingly conscious of their absence. The perceptual field alters to avoid a sense of fragmentation or confusion; for the depth psychologist, cognitive dissonance occurs when he or she constructs the system of faith known as a metapsychology (Atwood and Stolorow 1979).

Holism attempts to use the 'holographic paradigm' or the 'new physics' to proclaim the overcoming of Cartesian dualism. For instance, from a holistic standpoint, the organic and the inorganic may be seen as quite indivisible. But this is altogether different from a pluralist version that recognizes that *sometimes* we see things as persons and persons as things (Redfearn 1982). Or the psychological and the material may be holistically elided so that matter is regarded as possessing intelligence. Again, quite different from apperceiving a degree of nonrandomness in nature. The problem with holistic mega-images such as a 'world-soul' (Whitmont 1971) is not that they are wrong. How could they be? Nor are they unrooted in (pantheistic) experience. No, the problem is that the more all-encompassing, the bigger the image, the more antipathetic it becomes to other images, to other people's images. (Pluralism, as an image, can be just as intolerant.)

The problematic aspects of holism that I have been discussing come into being when it is the macrocosm that is being surveyed. On a microcosmic level, in clinical situations perhaps, certain holistic leaps are of great importance and we do not have to believe in a whole system to make use of them. I am thinking, for example, of the relation between image and instinct as this takes place in an individual. The image evokes the aim of the instinct; the instinct generates its own imagery (see *CW* 8, paras. 397-420). So a women's dream image of a handsome man may be related to a sexual impulse and, *at the same time*, some instinctual problem may already be being worked on in the unconscious by the image of that handsome man. Similarly, microcosmic holism helps us to grasp the complicated interrelation of the human and the transpersonal – in a marriage, say. What we judge to be human and personal (husband, lover) and what we experience as transpersonal or even divine (Adonis, Christ, Eros) may be envisioned in some kind of reciprocal relationship without losing the specificity of each level. We shouldn't have to choose between holism and reductionism on a once-and-for-all basis. Pluralistic searches are for ways of overcoming rigid dualisms like those mentioned without imposing the false unity of extreme holism.

On numinosity

The second constraint on pluralism is numinosity. When Otto, in his book *The Idea of the Holy* (1917), wrote of the *'numinosum'*, he was referring to a particular aspect of religious experience. Jung summarized this as:

a dynamic agency or effect not caused by an arbitrary act of will. On the contrary, it seizes and controls the human subject, who is always rather its victim than its creator. The *numinosum* – whatever its cause may be – is an experience of the subject independent of his will .... The *numinosum* is either a quality belonging to a visible object or the influence of an invisible presence that causes a peculiar alteration of consciousness.

(*CW* 11: para. 6)

The *numinosum* defies explanation but seems to convey an individual message which, though mysterious and enigmatic, is also deeply impressive. The *numinosum* is so powerful that it orchestrates the many variables in a particular situation into one overwhelming message. This may be what happens when single themes become dominant in the thinking of certain theorists: sexuality, mothering, transference, pluralism. On the other hand, it is this tendency for certain themes to acquire numinosity that we must thank for many of the breakthroughs in depth psychology. The difficult side is that beliefs tend, if not to ossify, to become so important to the personal stability of the individual concerned that, when challenged, he or she feels threatened and persecuted in a life-or-death way. On balance, I would not want live in a world or work in a field where people did *not* feel themselves threatened if their beliefs were challenged. Nor would I want to be cut off from the feeling of being absolutely 'right', that refreshing, visionary state that overcomes doubt and inferiority to let the creative ideas emerge; ideas that others regard as 'wrong', perhaps. Nevertheless, as far as the defence of pluralism is concerned, the *numinosum* is a considerable danger.

However, I feel we can turn the problem to our advantage by working out a new way to *value* even wrong-thinking or error, both of which are, quite understandably, likely to be as numinous as truth. As S. Sayers (1985) suggests, even illusions about reality reflect reality to some degree. Kafka put it like this: 'The correct perception of any matter and a complete misunderstanding of the matter do not totally exclude one another.' John Morley, the Liberal political philosopher, on his Victorian way to a thorough rejection of even the *potential* value of error, unwittingly provides us with a helpful list of the virtues of error: (1) a false opinion may disclose useful associations and even lies might lead to creative possibilities; (2) all minds are not open to reason and, hence, some will only respond to what is less than perfectly true, some response being better than none; (3) demolishing a false opinion may do more harm than good; (4) knowing that something is true may not be helpful as regards future thought or action; (5) sometimes error is a stepping-stone to truth (Morley 1893). This list of Morley's may be coupled with a pragmatic approach to ideas (that is one that stresses that their truth is measured by the degree to which 'they help us to get into satisfactory relations with other parts of our experience' (James 1911: 157)). The hope is that even ideas that are distorted by the operation of the *numinosum* may find a use. The numinosity of psychological theories lies to a great extent in their capacity to guide future action and practice. This is in contrast to their power to provide definitive answers to fundamental and fascinating questions of human nature. James's pragmatism involved a type of democratic procedure in which a man is free to *choose* which of several conflicting theories to accept. If his examination of the alternatives cannot help him make a decision then he is free simply to follow his own inclination – that is, allow the *numinosum* to decide (and here typology will be very important). Pluralism and the *numinosum* become compatible when *the act of choice is experienced as numinous* and not simply what is chosen. Then we are free to choose, choose, and choose again; conviction and tolerance both flourish.

Pluralism, politics, and morality

Can diversity be analysed so as to reveal its special requirements and guidelines? And can we develop a vision of diversity that makes a place for unity?

We know directly from politics that *freedom* does not guarantee diversity, for freedom can lead to one element expanding to take a tyrannical hold over the whole. If I am free to do or be what I like, this will produce an unequal state of affairs between you and me. To make sure that does not happen, we may be required by political consensus or law to be more equal in some or all respects. But then an inhibition has been placed on my freedom. Exactly the same conundrum faces the depth psychologist today. If he or she acts on, lives out, holds dear, fights for his/her ideology, what is he or she to do with the differing points of view of which he or she is aware? The freedom to have a particular point of view may lead to an unhelpful, destructive denigration and abandonment of some people's ideas to the ultimate detriment of one's own position.

Nor does *equality* necessarily underpin diversity, for equality may lead to the perils of indifference and boredom. This can be seen in the attitude some practitioners have towards theoretical differences: that they don't matter when compared with clinical inevitabilities. As if everything in analysis were not suffused with theory – and, ideally, vice versa. If all views are considered to be equally valid, what is to become of the freedom to feel a special value attaching to one's own view?

So, surprising to the analyst, perhaps, if not to the political philosopher, neither the freedom to think nor an egalitarian approach to thought can be said to guarantee pluralistic diversity and avoid tyranny or ennui.

The pluralistic version of the psyche involves our seeing it and its processes as democratic. However, to ensure that this stays the case, and to bring about its own particular brand of democracy, pluralism refers to 'a system of mutual adjustment that is trying to bring off a compromise between the power of majorities and the power of minorities, between the political equality of all and the *differing intensity of feelings*' (Kelso 1978: 64, my italics). The pluralist democracy of the psyche is something other than a simple majority vote; it is not a populist democracy. Nor is the democracy of the psyche a polyarchal construction with authority concentrated and vested in the interior equivalents of elected officials. Psychic pluralism, like political pluralism, has to try to share power between such officials and 'interest groups'.

It seems to me that the key question is that of *relevance*. In politics, we have to look for the relevant citizenry for any particular issue. We juggle distance from a problem with intensity of feeling about it, along with special knowledge or information. I may feel very strongly about something that affects me greatly, like a new traffic scheme. The majority of people in my town may disagree with me but not be quite so affected. Or we may be thought to be equally affected but I happen to feel more passionately about the new scheme, believing, rightly or wrongly, that I have justifiable special reasons for this (e.g. I may work at home and so suffer a double dose of the problem compared to some others). Now, in psychology, in spite of a reluctance to use metaphors of too tangible or concrete a nature, we still speak of 'investment of libido', or of the degree of meaningfulness that has been aroused by a particular experience, or of the relative importance to the individual of his or her various self-objects. Depth psychology is, to an extent, about preference and relevance. Crucially, then, in a pluralist perception of the psyche, specificity and intensity of emotion counts as much as the crude weight of votes.

There are different kinds of pluralism – pluralism is itself pluralistic. For instance, pluralism may be characterized by a *laissez-faire* attitude. In order for no single elite group to dominate, there has to be a large number of groups functioning. Alternatively, a pluralist vision of society may see it as divided into small autonomous fiefdoms or corporations; each fiefdom having power in its own area so that noone would dominate all areas of activity (we could call these fiefdoms 'beneficial monopolies'). A third variation on pluralism is overtly change-oriented. Power is divided, as in the other two descriptions, but those without power are helped by governmental regulation of interest-group behaviour. Give and take – and live and let live – are moderated by central management with long-term planning. In sum, as Kelso says, 'in place of a unified, homogeneous public with relatively constant preferences, pluralists see a wealth of different associations with varying interests and contrasting policy preferences' (1978: 62). The notion that political theory has worried away at many of the problems psychology has also had with the One and the Many is strengthened.

We might begin to create a programme for pluralism by trying to envision spontaneity as a genre or particular style of psychological life. This means a person's putting trust in the gnostic, revelatory capacity of images and experiences, without stressing any presupposition that these are derivatives of an unknowable absolute. It is the spontaneous and autonomous nature of experience and its images that work to support a pluralist response to them. As an extension of spontaneity, we may need actively to embrace contradictory positions. Not only because opposites can lead to each other eventually, but because contradiction itself produces novel elements. Spontaneity, as a genre, challenges hierarchy because of this capacity to generate the novel and the unpredictable; it influences other areas besides those at which it is directed.

Spontaneity also challenges 'objectivity'. It turns out that a revaluation of objectivity is critical for this pluralistic programme. We know from the physicists that the *way* we perceive the world acts as a strong influence on *what* we seem to perceive and, even, on what is actually perceived. However, such observer bias needs to be balanced by thinking of a 'bias' in the objects observed themselves. Objects of perception that are not human may need to be granted a life of their own, on their own terms. If we refer to *anima mundi*, soul of or in the world, this is more than animism. As

228

the philosopher H.H. Price (1932) suggested, even material objects are not inactive in the face of our perception of them; such objects are said by Price to possess a 'sensuousness' that facilitates our appreciation of them as sensory data.

It is interesting to consider 'objectivity' and even 'coherence' as gender-influenced ideologies. When we speak of the 'hard' sciences or facts, we are also dealing with the consequences of gender-based, child-rearing practices that have relegated softness and irrationality to an inferior ('feminine') standing. In addition, the 'masculine' cast of so-called objectivity may, to some extent, be an outcrop of the needs of most boys and many girls to assert their differences from their mother. The achievement of personal boundaries and optimal separation from the mother may, for some individuals, tip over into rigidity and an accent on distance and precision – the objective attitude. Depth psychologists with such an outlook tend to be uncomfortable with transpersonal phenomena, such as mystical experience, because such things cannot be understood from a distance, from outside. Knowledge of such phenomena can only come from some kind of merger with what is perceived and that awakens latent fears of returning to suffocating symbiosis with mother.

A new role emerges for subjectivity in psychological theory: not a pathological skewing of the evidence, nor an inevitable but pitiable flawing, but a valid dimension of theory-making. That said, not all theoretical developments are the outcome of typological characteristics; in fact, theories in depth psychology have a life of their own, independent of the intentions of their creators. If I know of theories of infant development, I must see the infantile roots of the adult world. But, and this is the point, I cannot consider the question at all any more without allowing the developmental perspective an objective role in any discussion. There are no infantile roots without a theory about infantile roots – at least not now. *Theory-making is a primary psychological activity.*

Problems of 'objectivity' are highlighted when the objects of perception are human, or whatever is felt by the observer to be inside him/herself. For instance, when we refer to our bodies, we find that what we thought to be of the body cannot avoid also being psychological. Here I would like to emphasize that I am not thinking of psychosomatics, nor of a view encapsulated in Merleau-Ponty's claim to be the 'absolute source' of his own body (Merleau-Ponty 1962: 129). The body may be psychological in another, more direct and challenging way, so that it and its organs have their own specific psychologies, rendering objectivity in relation to the body well-nigh impossible.

We lack an adequate vocabulary, syntax, or linguistics with which to express and discuss the body's psychology. It seems very important to me that we continue to try to use *words* for this purpose, for they are intermediate, partaking of both body and psyche – after all, it ain't what you say but the way you say it! The word is not an enemy of the body, unless it is used purely intellectually or as an instrument of domination. Those (including myself) who have tried to use words in this area, usually end up by imposing on the body some other language, such as that of mysticism, alchemy, or part-object psychology.

To make pluralism work in relation to the body, we have to try, in Perera's phrase, to deal with things on their own 'matrix level' (personal communication 1985). Not always asking from whence, nor where to, nor into what. Analysts, in particular, have to be careful not to impose their valuable ideologies of transformation and sublimation upon bodily impulses in such a way that this becomes a requirement. Concentration on the matrix level or sphere in question will avoid facile attempts to change things into something else – in analysis, by premature and clichéd interpretation.

Coming to the end of this programme for pluralism, we have to ask ourselves what the moral function of psychological pluralism might be as it struggles to hold the tension between the One and the Many without making them into 'opposites'. Pluralism is engaged in the discovery of truths just as monism is engaged in the discovery of Truth. *The existence of diverse theories about people complements the psychological diversity within a person.* My concern has been that pluralism should not follow the logic of competition so fully that an ideological purity leading to tyranny is the result, nor allow its embracing of diversity to degenerate into a farrago of seemingly equal truths leading to ennui as much as chaos. I will stick my neck out and say that the *telos* or goal of pluralism is 'reform'. By reform, I do not mean something specially distinguished from revolution, as in 'liberal reform', but reform as a portmanteau term to include renewal, rebirth, spontaneous *and* well-planned evolutions, and imaginative productivity generally. Reform has its moral connotation and that is deliberate.

Bernard Crick once compared politics to sexuality – an activity that simply must be carried on: 'one does not create it or decide to join in – one simply becomes aware that one is involved in it as part of the human condition' (Crick 1964: 26). The moral factor that attends reformist pluralism also has to do with *involvement*. Involvement in the experience of psyche and involvement in the politics of depth psychology – which, as I have been arguing, are the same thing.

References

Abend, S., Porder, M., and Willick, M. (1983) *Borderline patients: psychoanalytic perspectives*, New York: International Universities Press.

Abrams, R. (1977) 'Genetic points of view: antecedents and transformations', *J. Amer. Psychoanal. Assn.* 25:417-26.

Achterberg, J. (1985) *Images in healing: Shamanism and modern medicine*, Boston and London: Shambhala.

Armstrong, D. (1962) *Bodily sensations*, London: Routledge and Kegan Paul.

Atwood, G. and Stolorow, R. (1979) *Faces in a cloud: subjectivity in personality theory*, New York: Jason Aronson.

Balint, M. (1968) *The basic fault: therapeutic aspects of regression*, London: Tavistock.

Bateson, P. (1984) 'The biology of co-operation', *New Society*, 31 May 1984.

Baudson, M. (ed.) (1986) *Art and time*, London: Barbican Art Gallery.

Bentley, A. F. (1926) *Relativity in man and society*, New York: Knickerbocker.

Bion, W. (1965) *Transformations*, in *Seven servants*, New York: Jason Aronson (1977).

Bion, W. (1970) *Attention and interpretation*, in *Seven servants*, New York: Jason Aronson (1977).

Bishop, P. (1986), 'The shadows of the holistic earth', *Spring*, 1986.

Bly, R. (1986) Statement at conference at Hofstra University on 'C.G. Jung and the Humanities', unpublished.

Bohm, D. (1980) *Wholeness and the implicate order*, London: Routledge and Kegan Paul.

Broverman, I., Broverman, D., and Clarkson, F. (1970) 'Sex-role stereotypes and clinical judgements of mental health', *J. Consulting and Clin. Psych.* 34:1.

Brown, G. and Harris, T. (1978) *Social origins of depression*, London: Tavistock.

Bruzzone, M. *et al.* (1985) 'Regression and persecution in analytic training: reflections and experience', *Int. Rev. Psycho-Anal.* 12:4.

Buber, M. (1931) *Jewish mysticism*, London: Dent.

Calder, J. (1986) 'The Prophet Samuel', *The Guardian*, 12 April 1986.

Capra, F. (1975) *The Tao of physics*, London: Wildwood House.

Carotenuto, A. (1982) *A secret symmetry: Sabina Spielrein between Jung and Freud*, New York: Pantheon.

Carr, E.H. (1964) *What is history?* Harmondsworth: Penguin.

Casement, P. (1986a) 'Countertransference and interpretation', *Contemp. Psychoanal.* 22:4.

Casement, P. (1986b) 'Interpretation: fresh insight or cliché?' *Free Associations* 5.

Chodorow, N. (1978) *The reproduction of mothering: psychoanalysis and the sociology of gender*, Los Angeles: Univ. of California Press.

Cooper, D. and Tinterow, G. (1983) *The essential cubism: Braque, Picasso and their friends 1907-1920*, London: Tate Gallery.

Corbin, H. (1972) '*Mundus imaginalis*, or the imaginary and the imaginal', *Spring*, 1972.

Corbin, H. (1978) Preface to D. Miller, *The new polytheism*, Dallas: Spring Publications.

Corbin, H. (1983) 'Theophanies and mirrors: idols or icons?' *Spring*, 1983.

Crick, B. (1964) *In defence of politics*, Harmondsworth: Penguin.

Davies, P. (1984) *God and the new physics*, London: Dent.

Davis, M. and Wallbridge, D. (1981) *Boundary and space: an introduction to the work of D.W. Winnicott*, London: Karnac.

Derrida, J. (1978) *Writing and difference* (trans. A. Bass), London: Routledge and Kegan Paul.

Dieckmann, H. (1974) 'The constellation of the countertransference', in G. Adler (ed.), *Success and failure in analysis*, New York: Putnam's Sons.

Dieckmann, H. (1977) 'Some aspects of the development of authority', in A. Samuels (ed.), *The father: contemporary Jungian perspectives*, London: Free Association Books 1985; New York: New York Univ. Press 1986.

Dobbs, B. (1975) *The foundations of Newton's alchemy, or 'The hunting of the Greene Lyon'*, Cambridge: Cambridge Univ. Press.

Eichenbaum, L. and Orbach, S. (1982) *Outside in...inside out: women's psychology: a feminist psychoanalytic approach*, Harmondsworth: Penguin.

Fairbairn, W. (1952) *Psychoanalytic studies of the personality*, London: Tavistock.

Foot, P. (1978) *Virtues and vices*, Oxford and New York: Oxford Univ. Press.

Fordham, M. (1957) *New developments in analytical psychology*, London: Routledge and Kegan Paul.

Fordham, M. (1970) 'A reply to Plaut's "Comment" ', in M. Fordham *et al.* (eds), *Technique in Jungian analysis*, London: Heinemann (1974).

Fordham, M. (1974) 'Jung's conception of transference', *J. Analyt. Psychol.* 19:1.

Fordham, M. (1976) *The self and autism*, London: Heinemann.

Fordham, M. (1978) *Jungian psychotherapy: a study in analytical psychology*, Chichester: Wiley.

Fordham, M. (1979) 'Analytical psychology and countertransference', in L. Epstein and A. Finer (eds), *Countertransference*, New York: Jason Aronson.

Fordham, M. (1985) *Explorations into the self*, London: Karnac.

France, P. (1983) *Diderot*, Oxford and New York: Oxford Univ. Press.

Freud, S. (1905) *Three essays on the theory of sexuality*, std edn 7, London: Hogarth.

Freud, S. (1910a) 'The future prospects of psycho-analytic therapy', std edn 11, London: Hogarth.

Freud, S. (1910b) '"Wild" psychoanalysis', std edn 11, London: Hogarth.

Freud, S. (1913) 'The disposition to obsessional neurosis', std edn 12, London: Hogarth.

233

References

Freud, S. (1916-17) *Introductory lectures on psycho-analysis*, std edn 15-16, London: Hogarth.

Freud, S. (1917) 'Mourning and melancholia', std edn 14, London: Hogarth.

Freud, S. (1918) 'From the history of an infantile neurosis', std edn 17, London: Hogarth.

Freud, S. (1919) 'A child is being beaten', std edn 17, London: Hogarth.

Freud, S. (1920) *Beyond the pleasure principle*, std edn 18, London: Hogarth.

Freud, S. (1923) *The ego and the id*, std edn 19, London: Hogarth.

Freud, S. (1933) *New introductory lectures on psycho-analysis*, std edn 22, London: Hogarth.

Freud, S. (1940) *An outline of psycho-analysis*, std edn 23, London: Hogarth.

Galenson, E. (1986) 'Some thoughts about infant psychopathology and aggressive development', *Int. Rev. Psycho-Anal.* 13:3.

Gilligan, C. (1982) *In a different voice: psychological theory and women's development*, Cambridge, Mass.: Harvard Univ. Press.

Glover, E. (1950) *Freud or Jung*, London: Allen and Unwin.

Goldberg, A. (ed.) (1980) Introduction to *Advances in self psychology*, New York: International Universities Press.

Goodheart, W. (1984) 'Successful and unsuccessful interventions in Jungian analysis: the construction and destruction of the spellbinding circle', *Chiron*, 1984.

Gordon, R. (1965) 'The concept of projective identification: an evaluation', *J. Analyt. Psychol.* 10:2.

Gorkin, M. (1987) *The uses of countertransference*, Northvale, New Jersey and London: Jason Aronson.

Greene, L. (1984) *The astrology of fate*, London: Allen and Unwin.

Guggenbühl-Craig, A. (1971) *Power in the helping professions*, New York: Spring Publications.

Guggenbühl-Craig, A. (1980) *Eros on crutches: reflections on psychopathy and amorality*, Dallas: Spring Publications.

Gunderson J. and Singer, M. (1975) 'Defining borderline patients: an overview', *Amer. J. Psychiatry* 132:1.

Hamilton, V. (1982) *Narcissus and Oedipus: the children of psychoanalysis*, London: Routledge and Kegan Paul.

Happold, F. (1963) *Mysticism: a study and an anthology*, Harmondsworth: Penguin.

Hartocollis, P. (1983) *Time and timelessness*, New York: International Universities Press.

Heimann, P. (1950) 'On counter-transference', *Int. J. Psycho-Anal.* 31.

Hillman, J. (1973) 'The great mother, her son, her hero, and the *puer*', in P. Berry (ed.), *Fathers and mothers*, Zürich: Spring Publications.

Hillman, J. (1975a) *Revisioning psychology*, New York: Harper and Row.

Hillman J. (1975b) *Loose ends*, Dallas: Spring Publications.

Hillman, J. (1977) 'An enquiry into image', *Spring*, 1977.

Hillman, J. (1979) *The dream and the underworld*, New York: Harper and Row.

References

Hillman, J. (1980) 'On the necessity of abnormal psychology: Ananke and Athene', in J. Hillman (ed.), *Facing the gods*, Dallas: Spring Publications.

Hillman, J. (1983) *Archetypal psychology: a brief account*, Dallas: Spring Publications.

Hofstadter, D. and Dennett, D. (1981) *The mind's I*, Harmondsworth: Penguin.

Hubback, J. (1973) 'Uses and abuses of analogy', *J. Analyt. Psychol.* 18:2.

Hudson, L. (1983) Review of A. Storr (ed.), *Jung: selected writings*, London: Fontana, 1983; *Sunday Times*, 13 March 1983.

Jacoby, M. (1985) *Longing for paradise: psychological perspectives on an archetype*, Boston: Sigo.

Jaffé, A. (1979) *C.G. Jung: word and image*, Princeton: Princeton Univ. Press.

James, W. (1909) *A pluralistic universe*, London: Longmans, Green; Cambridge, Mass.: Harvard Univ. Press (1977).

James, W. (1911) *Pragmatism*, London: Longmans, Green; London: Fontana Library of Philosophy (1962).

Jones, E. (1927) 'Early development of female sexuality', in *Papers on psychoanalysis*, London: Baillière, Tindall and Cox (1950).

Jung, C.G. Except as below, references are to the *Collected Works (CW)* and by volume and paragraph number (see Acknowledgements).

Jung, C.G. (1934) 'Zur Gegenwärtigen Lage der Psychotherapie', *Zentralblatt für Psychotherapie* 7: 1 & 2; also as 'The state of psychotherapy today' (*CW*: 10).

Jung, C.G. (1963) *Memories, dreams, reflections*, London: Collins; Routledge and Kegan Paul.

Kelso, W. (1978) *American democratic theory: pluralism and its critics*, Westport, Connecticut and London: Greenwood Press.

Kenny, A. (1963) *Action, emotion and will*, London: Routledge and Kegan Paul.

Kermode, F. (1985) 'Freud and interpretation', *Int. Rev. Psycho-Anal.* 12:1.

Kernberg, O. (1967) 'Borderline personality organization', *J. Amer. Psychoanal. Assn.* 132.

Kernberg, O. (1975) *Borderline conditions and pathological narcissism*, New York: Jason Aronson.

Kernberg, O. (1979) 'Some implications of object relations theory for psychoanalytic technique', *J. Amer. Psychoanal. Assn.*, supp. vol. 27.

Kernberg, O. (1984) *Severe personality disorders: psychotherapeutic strategies*, New Haven, Connecticut and London: Yale Univ. Press.

Keutzer, C. (1984) 'The power of meaning: from quantum mechanics to synchronicity', *J. Humanistic Psychol.* 24:1.

Klein, M. (1929) 'Infantile anxiety situations reflected in a work of art and in the creative impulse', in *The writings of Melanie Klein*, vol. 1, London: Hogarth (1975).

Kohlberg, L. (1968) 'Moral development', in *Int. Encyc. of Soc. Science*, New York: Macmillan Free Press.

Kohut, H. (1971) *The analysis of the self*, New York: International Universities Press.

Kohut, H. (1977) *The restoration of the self*, New York: International Universities Press.

Kohut, H. (1978) *The search for the self*, New York: International Universities Press.

Kohut, H. (1982) 'Introspection, empathy and the semi-circle of mental health', *Int. J. Psycho-Anal.* 63:4.

Kohut, H. (1983) 'Selected problems of self psychological theory', in J. Lichterberg, S. Kaplan (eds), *Reflections on self psychology*, Hillsdale, New Jersey and London: The Analytic Press.

Koss, J. (1986) 'Symbolic transformations in traditional healing: perspectives from analytical psychology', *J. Analyt. Psychol.* 31:4.

Kris, E. (1952) *Explorations in art*, New York: International Universities Press.

Kugler, P. (1982) *The alchemy of discourse: an archetypal approach to language*, Lewisburg, Delaware: Bucknell Univ. Press; London: Associated Universities Press.

Kuhn, T. (1970) *The structure of scientific revolutions*, Chicago: Chicago Univ. Press.

Lacan, J. (1949) 'The mirror stage as formative of the function of the I as revealed in psychoanalytic experience,' in *Ecrits* (trans. A. Sheridan), London, Tavistock (1977).

Lambert, K. (1981) *Analysis, repair and individuation*, London: Academic Press.

Langs, R. (1978) *The listening process*, New York: Jason Aronson.

Langs, R. (1979) 'The interactional dimensions of countertransference' in L. Epstein and A. Feiner (eds), *Countertransference*, New York: Jason Aronson.

Laplanche, J. and Pontalis, J.-B. (1980) *The language of psychoanalysis*, London: Hogarth.

Lauter, E. and Rupprecht, C. (1985) *Feminist archetypal theory: interdisciplinary re-visions of Jungian thought*, Knoxville: University of Tennessee Press.

Lemaire, A. (1977) *Jacques Lacan*, London: Routledge and Kegan Paul.

Leonard, L. (1982) *The wounded woman: healing the father–daughter relationship*, Ohio: Swallow Press.

Lewis, C. and O'Brien, M. (1987) *Reassessing fatherhood: new observations on fathers and the modern family*, London: Sage.

Lipnack, J. and Stamps, J. (1986) *The networking book: people connecting with people*, London and New York: Routledge and Kegan Paul.

Little, M. (1957) '"R" – the analyst's total response to his patient's needs', *Int. J. Psycho-Anal.* 38.

Little, M. (1960) 'Countertransference and the patient's response to it', *Int. J. Psycho-Anal.* 32.

Lopez-Pedraza, R. (1971) 'Comment on psychology: monotheistic or polytheistic?', by J. Hillman, *Spring*, 1971.

Lopez-Pedraza, R. (1977) *Hermes and his children*, Zürich: Spring Publications.

Lowndes, J. (1987) *Eve's secrets*, London: Bloomsbury.

McEwan, I. (1981) *The imitation game*, London: Picador. (Orig. London: Cape, 1981.)

References

Mahler, M. (1971) 'A study of the separation–individuation process', *Psychol. Stud. Child*, 1971.

Malcolm, J. (1982) *Psychoanalysis: the impossible profession*, London: Pan.

Masson, J. (ed.) (1985) *The complete letters of Sigmund Freud to William Fliess 1887-1904*, Cambridge, Mass. and London: Harvard Univ. Press.

Mattinson, J. (1975) *The reflection process in casework supervision*, London: Institute of Marital Studies.

Meier, C. (1949) *Ancient incubation and modern psychotherapy*, Evanston: Northwestern Univ. Press (1967).

Meltzer, D. (1973) *Sexual states of mind*, Strath Tay, Perthshire: Clunie Press.

Meltzer, D. (1978) *The clinical significance of the work of Bion*, part 3 of *The Kleinian development*, Strath Tay, Perthshire: Clunie Press.

Meltzer, D. (1981) 'The Kleinian expansion of Freud's metapsychology', *Int. J. Psycho-Anal.* 62:2.

Melzack, R. and Wall, P. (1982) *The challenge of pain*, Harmondsworth: Penguin.

Merleau-Ponty, M. (1962) *Phenomenology of perception*, London: Routledge and Kegan Paul.

Miller, D. (1981) *The new polytheism*, Dallas: Spring Publications.

Milner, M. (1977) *On not being able to paint*, London: Heinemann.

Minogue, K. (1986) 'Keeping out the new barbarians', *The Times*, 26 September.

Mitchell, J. (1974) *Psychoanalysis and feminism*, London: Allen Lane.

Money-Kyrle, R. (1971) 'The aims of psychoanalysis', in D. Meltzer (ed.), *Collected papers*, Strath Tay, Perthshire: Clunie Press (1978).

Morley, J. (1893) *On compromise*, London: Macmillan.

Neumann, E. (1954) *The origins and history of consciousness*, London: Routledge and Kegan Paul.

Neumann, E. (1973) *The child*, London: Hodder and Stoughton.

Newton, K. (1965) 'Mediation of the image of infant–mother togetherness', in M. Fordham *et al.* (eds), *Analytical psychology: a modern science*, London: Heinemann (1973).

Newton, K. (1975) 'Separation and pre-oedipal guilt', *J. Analyt. Psychol.* 20:2.

Newton, K. (1981) 'Comment on the emergence of child analysis' by M. Fordham, *J. Analyt. Psychol.* 26:1.

Oakeshott, M. (1933) *Experience and its modes*, Cambridge: Cambridge Univ. Press.

Ogden, T. (1987) 'The transitional oedipal relationship in female development', *Int. J. Psycho-Anal.* 68:4.

Otto, R. (1917) *The idea of the holy*, Oxford: Oxford Univ. Press.

Padel, J. (1985) 'Was Shakespeare happy with his patron? One psychoanalytic view of the relationship', *Psychoanalytic Psychotherapy* 1:3.

Paolino, T. (1981) *Psychoanalytic psychotherapy*, New York: Brunner Mazel.

Parker, R. and Pollock, G. (1987) *Framing feminism: art and the women's movement 1970-1984*, London and New York: Pandora.

237

Peterfreund, E. (1983) *The process of psychoanalytic therapy*, Hillsdale, New Jersey and London: The Analytic Press.

Peters, R. (1985) 'Reflections on the origin and aim of nostalgia', *J. Analyt. Psychol.* 30:2.

Plaut, A. (1956) 'The transference in analytical psychology', in M. Fordham *et al.* (eds), *Technique in Jungian analysis*, London: Heinemann (1974).

Plaut, A. (1959) 'Hungry patients: reflections on ego structure', *J. Analyt. Psychol.* 4:2.

Plaut, A. (1970) 'Comment: on not incarnating the archetype', in M. Fordham *et al.* (eds), *Technique in Jungian analysis*, London: Heinemann (1974).

Plaut, A. (1973) 'The ungappable bridge: numbers as guides to object relations and to cultural development', *J. Analyt. Psychol.* 18:2.

Plaut, A. (1975) 'Object constancy or constant object?', *J. Analyt. Psychol.* 20:2.

Plaut, A. (1977) 'Jung and rebirth', *J. Analyt. Psychol.* 22:2.

Pontius, A. (1986) 'Crime as ritual', unpublished.

Popper, K. (1959) *The logic of scientific discovery*, London: Hutchinson.

Popper, K. (1963) *Conjectures and refutations: the growth of scientific knowledge*, London: Routledge and Kegan Paul.

Powell, S. (1985) 'A bridge to understanding: the transcendent function in the analyst', *J. Analyt. Psychol.* 30:1.

Pribram, K. (1971) *Languages of the brain*, New York: Prentice-Hall.

Price, H. (1932) *Perception*, London: Macmillan.

Priestley, J.B. (1947) Author's note to *Three time plays*, London: Pan.

Racker, H. (1968) *Transference and countertransference*, London: Hogarth.

Redfearn, J. (1978) 'The energy of warring and combining opposites: problems for the psychotic patient and the therapist in achieving the symbolic situation', *J. Analyt. Psychol.* 23:3.

Redfearn, J. (1979) 'The captive, the treasure, the hero and the "anal" stage of development', *J. Analyt. Psychol.* 24:3.

Redfearn, J. (1982) 'When are things persons and persons things?' *J. Analyt. Psychol.* 27:3.

Redfearn, J. (1985) *My self, my many selves*, London: Karnac.

Rickman, J. (1951) 'Number and the human sciences', in *Selected contributions on psycho-analysis*, London: Hogarth (1957).

Riviere, J. (1952) General introduction to *Developments in psycho-analysis*, London: Hogarth.

Rustin, M. (1985) 'The social organization of secrets: towards a sociology of psychoanalysis', *Int. Rev. Psycho-Anal.* 12:2.

Rychlak, J. (1984) 'Jung as dialectician and teleologist, in R. Papadopoulos and G. Saayman (eds), *Jung in modern perspective*, Hounslow, Middlesex: Wildwood House.

Rycroft, C. (1972) *A critical dictionary of psychoanalysis*, Harmondsworth: Penguin.

Samuels, A. (1980) 'Incest and omnipotence in the internal family', *J. Analyt. Psychol.* 25:1.

Samuels, A. (1985a) *Jung and the post-Jungians*, London and Boston: Routledge and Kegan Paul.

Samuels, A. (1985b) (ed.) *The father: contemporary Jungian perspectives*, London: Free Association Books; New York: New York University Press (1986).

Samuels, A., Shorter, B., and Plaut, A. (1986) *A critical dictionary of Jungian analysis*, London and New York: Routledge and Kegan Paul.

Sandler, J. (1983) 'Reflections on some relations between psychoanalytic concepts and psychoanalytic practice', *Int. J. Psycho-Anal.* 64:1.

Sayers, J. (1982) *Biological politics: feminist and anti-feminist perspectives*, London: Tavistock.

Sayers, J. (1986) *Sexual contradictions: psychology, psychoanalysis, and feminism*, London: Tavistock.

Sayers, S. (1985) *Reality and reason: dialectic and the theory of knowledge*, Oxford: Blackwell.

Schwartz-Salant, N. (1982) *Narcissism and character transformation: the psychology of narcissistic character disorders*, Toronto: Inner City Books.

Schwartz-Salant, N. (1984) 'Archetypal factors underlying sexual acting-out in the transference/countertransference process', *Chiron*, 1984.

Schwartz-Salant, N. (1986) 'On the subtle-body concept in clinical practice', *Chiron*, 1986.

Searles, H. (1959) 'Oedipal love in the countertransference', in *Collected papers on schizophrenia and related subjects*, London: Hogarth (1968).

Searles, H. (1973) 'Violence in schizophrenia', in *Countertransference and related subjects: selected papers*, New York: International Universities Press (1979).

Searles, H. (1975) 'The patient as therapist to his analyst', in *Countertransference and related subjects: selected papers*, New York: International Universities Press (1979).

Segal, H. (1973) *Introduction to the work of M. Klein*, London: Hogarth.

Sheldrake, R. (1985) 'Collective memory, time and evolution', in C. Rawlence (ed.), *About time*, London: Cape.

Shorter, B. (1983) 'The concealed body language of anorexia nervosa', in A. Samuels (ed.), *The father: contemporary Jungian perspectives*, London: Free Association Books (1985); New York: New York Univ. Press (1986).

Shorter, B. (1987) *An image darkly forming: women and initiation*, London and New York: Routledge and Kegan Paul.

Siann, G. (1985) *Accounting for aggression: perspectives on aggression and violence*, London and Boston: Allen and Unwin.

Singer, J. (1979) 'The use and misuse of the archetype', *J. Analyt. Psychol.* 24:1.

Statham, D. (1987) 'Women, the New Right and social work', *J. Soc. Wrk. Practice*, 2:4.

Stein, L. (1958) 'Analytical psychology: a modern science', in M. Fordham *et al.* (eds), *Analytical psychology: a modern science*, London: Heinemann (1973).

Stein, M. (1985) *Jung's treatment of Christianity: the psychotherapy of a religious tradition*, Wilmington, Illinois: Chiron Publications.

Stein, M. (1987) 'Looking backward: archetypes in reconstruction', *Chiron*, 1987.

Stein, R. (1974) *Incest and human love*, Baltimore: Penguin.

Stein, R. (1987) 'Reflections on professional deformation', in M. Spiegelman (ed.), *Jungian analysts: their visions and vulnerabilities*, Phoenix: Falcon Press.

Steiner, J. (1985) 'Turning a blind eye: the cover up for Oedipus', *Int. Rev. Psycho-Anal.* 12:2.

Steiner, R. (1985) 'Some thoughts about tradition and change arising from an examination of the British Psychoanalytical Society's controversial discussions (1943-1944)', *Int. Rev. Psycho-Anal.* 12:1.

Sterba, R. (1934) 'The fate of the ego in psychoanalytic therapy', *Int. J. Psycho-Anal.* 15.

Stern, D. (1985) *The interpersonal world of the infant: a view from psychoanalysis and developmental psychology*, New York: Basic Books.

Stevens, A. (1982) *Archetype: a natural history of the self*, London: Routledge and Kegan Paul.

Stewart, L. (1987) 'Affect and archetype in analysis', *Chiron*, 1987.

Stokes, A. (1972) 'The image in form', in R. Wollheim (ed.), *Selected writings*, Harmondsworth: Penguin.

Stone, M. (1981) 'Borderline syndromes', *Psych. Clin. N. Amer.* 4:3.

Stone, M. (1986) (ed.) *Essential papers on borderline disorders: one hundred years at the border*, New York: New York Univ. Press.

Storr, A. (1970) *Human aggression*, Harmondsworth: Penguin.

Sullivan, L. (1947) *Kindergarten chats*, New York: Wittenborn, Schultz.

Taylor, C. (1982) 'Sexual intimacy between patient and analyst', *Quadrant*, 15:1.

Tuby, M. (1982) 'The search and alchemy', *Guild of Pastoral Psychology Lecture*, no. 210, London: Colmore Press.

Ulanov, A. (1979) 'Follow-up treatment in cases of patient/therapist sex', *J. Amer. Acad. Psychoanal.* 7.

Underhill, E. (1961) *Mysticism*, London: Methuen.

von Franz, M.-L. (1978) *Time, rhythm and repose*, London: Thames and Hudson.

Wallerstein, R. (1983) 'Self psychology and "classical" psychoanalytic psychology – the nature of their relationship: a review and overview', in J. Lichtenberg and S. Kaplan (eds), *Reflections on self psychology*, Hillsdale, New Jersey and London: The Analytic Press.

Walzer, M. (1983) *Spheres of justice: a defence of pluralism and equality*, Oxford: Blackwell.

Whitmont, E. (1971) 'Nature, symbol, and imaginal reality', *Spring*, 1971.

Willeford, W. (1985) 'How unitary is one? How dual is two?: *unus mundus*, polarity and the mother–infant relationship', *Harvest* 31.

Williams, M. (1963) 'The indivisibility of the personal and collective unconscious', in M. Fordham *et al.* (eds), *Analytical psychology: a modern science*, London: Heinemann (1973).

References

Winnicott, D.W. (1945) 'Primitive emotional development', in *Collected papers: from paediatrics to psychoanalysis*, London: Tavistock (1958).

Winnicott, D.W. (1949) 'Hate in the countertransference', in *Collected papers: from paediatrics to psychoanalysis*, London: Tavistock (1958).

Winnicott, D.W. (1958) 'Psycho-analysis and the sense of guilt', in *The maturational processes and the facilitating environment*, London: Hogarth (1965).

Winnicott, D.W. (1962) 'Providing for the child in health and crisis', in *The maturational processes and the facilitating environment*, London: Hogarth (1965).

Winnicott, D.W. (1963) 'Communicating and not communicating leading to a study of certain opposites', in *The maturational processes and the facilitating environment*, London: Hogarth (1965).

Winnicott, D.W. (1967) 'Mirror-role of mother and family in child development', in *Playing and reality*, Harmondsworth: Penguin (1974).

Winnicott, D.W. (1974) *Playing and reality*, Harmondsworth: Penguin.

Winnicott, D.W. (1987) *The spontaneous gesture: selected letters of D.W. Winnicott*, F. Robert Rodman (ed.), Cambridge, Mass.: Harvard Univ. Press.

Winterbotham, F. (1974) *The ultra secret*, London: Weidenfeld and Nicolson.

Young-Eisendrath, P. (1987) 'The absence of black Americans as Jungian analysts', *Quadrant* 20:2.

Zaehner, R. (1957) *Mysticism: sacred and profane*, Oxford: Oxford Univ. Press.

Zinkin, L. (1979) 'The collective and the personal', *J. Analyt. Psychol.* 24:3.

Zinkin, L. (1984) 'Is there still a place for the medical model?', *Spring*, 1984.

Zoja, L. (1987) 'Analytical psychology and metapsychology of feeling', *J. Analyt. Psychol.* 32:1.

Index

Compiled by Albert Dickson

242

Bateson, P. 198
Baudson, M. 37
Beckett, S. 39
Bentley, A. 14
biology 34–5
   women and 75, 92–3
Bion, W. 159, 167, 169, 200
bisexuality 90, 105
Bishop, P. 223
Bleuler, E. 115
Bly, R. 80
body (soma) 105, 110, 229
   analyst's xii, 152, 164, 175,
   184; and image 45, 157, 165,
   174; male/female 101, 103,
   187; and mind 29, 40; and
   psyche 26, 101–2, 104, 170,
   230; and soul 164, 215;
   subtle 171, 172, 192
Bohm, D. 178
border, boundary 110–11
   as image 110
borderline disorder 39, 57, 74, 81
   aggression and 107–8,
   111–16, 117–19; debate on
   107, 111–14; depressive
   psychosis in 108; father's
   role in 67, 82, 87, 89, 111;
   gender and 67, 97, 107–22;
   hereditary factor in 94, 107,
   114–17; incest and 118
Braque, G. 47
Broverman, D. and I. 73
Brown, G. 207
Bruzzone, M. 220
Buber, M. 32, 166, 167
Buddhism 138

Calder, J. 39
Calvino, I. v
Capra, F. 178, 219
Carotenuto, A. 190
Carr, E. H. 25, 36, 54
case histories: borderline
   disorder 57–8, 81–3;
   depression 144; difficulty in
   relationships 59–61, 83–5;
   guilt feelings 155–7;
   homosexuality 140–2;
   inadequate parenting 61–2;

phobia 87–9
Casement, P. 158, 159
castration 86, 210
   of sex offenders 93
castration anxiety 86
causality 17, 35–6
Chew, G. 219
child abuse 68, 113; *see also*
   incest; sexual abuse
Chodorow, N. 74
Christianity 138, 180, 182, 213
Clarkson, F. 73
cognition 40, 162
cognitive dissonance 223
collective unconscious 168, 176
communication 177
   countertransference and 144,
   145, 153, 168; interpersonal
   173–4; patient's, to analyst
   50, 144–5, 150, 160;
   symbolic 145
complexes, archetypal core of
   24, 25, 28
confession 59, 190, 204
conflict 1–2, 6, 11, 129, 205
   and aggression 207; in
   archetypal states 31, 32–3; in
   borderline disorder 122;
   intergenerational 85–6, 87
conflict psychology 11, 112
*coniunctio, coniunctio
   oppositorum, see*
   conjunction, conjunction of
   opposites
conjunction 129, 131, 180, 184,
   209
   and alchemical imagery 172,
   181; of opposites 124,
   127–8, 134–5, 173, 181–2
conscience 86, 94, 196–8
conscious 40, 55, 179, 183–4
consciousness 69, 129, 165,
   189, 200
   alteration of 225; and archaic
   ego 25; moral 139; and
   reality 43–4
containment 11, 22, 88, 127, 178
   analytical relationship and
   181
Cooper, D. 46, 47

145; and self 200, 209;
splitting of 149; and
unconscious 28, 110, 181
ego-ideal 60, 100
ego psychology 111, 112
Eichenbaum, L. 74
Einstein, A. 14
Elwes, C. 105
emotion 22, 80, 104, 178, 200
of analyst 145–6; imagery
and 43, 172; investment of
24; time and 39; *see also*
affect
empathy 67, 112, 146–7
of analyst 31, 113, 171, 184
endocrinology 93, 101
eros 50, 210
and agape 190–2; in analysis
187–90
Eros 188, 224
eroticism 188, 189, 212
eroticization 69, 190
ethics 197, 205, 206
ethology 198
evil 196
good and 130, 139

facilitating environment 170
Fairbairn, W. 199
Fallopio, G. 103
false self 29
fantasy 79, 110, 181
aggressive/destructive 85,
91, 108, 113, 207–11; and
borderline disorder 113; of
creating 29, 32; of
dismembering women 87; of
fusion 32, 130, 132, 171,
172; grotesque 134, 140; and
image 123–4; incestuous 66,
68, 80, 127, 209;
masturbation 140;
omnipotent 29–31, 211;
parthenogenetic 138, 140;
primal scene 126, 132, 134,
141; and reality 124, 164–5;
reparative 190; sexual/erotic
53, 76, 140, 189, 190; of
suffocation/being swallowed
31; voyeuristic 190; of world

destruction 211
father 58, 64, 141
absence of 62, 83, 118;
aggression and 49, 81, 140;
alcoholism in 62, 79;
apperception of 74;
archetypal 27; authority of
27, 67; and borderline
disorder 67, 82, 87, 89, 111;
and child 70–5, 77–91, 102,
104, 132; as cultural
phenomenon 27, 71–2, 75,
86; and daughter 62–6,
77–85, 91, 156, 161; death of
59, 60, 141; depression in
87–8; in depth psychology
66, 67, 70, 71, 77; erotic
playback from, to daughter
66, 80, 82, 85, 91; and
gender identity 72–5;
idealized 90; identification
with 86, 91; intergenerational
conflict/alliance with 85–6,
87, 89; and mother 29, 73;
parenting function of 68;
physical contact with 60–1,
68, 82, 102; as a relation
66–76; self-image of 87;
sexual abuse by 67, 159; and
son 59–61; 66, 85–91; and
transformation of aggression
88–9, 90, 91; violence in 59,
79, 82
father-image 27, 72, 87, 123
negative 50, 67–8; as
warrior-hero 60
feminine; *see* masculine and
feminine
feminine principle 66, 78, 83,
94–100, 188
feminine psychology 83, 94,
95–100, 101, 175
femininity; *see* masculinity and
femininity
feminism 71, 98, 100, 106
fermentatio 182–3
Fliess, W. 17
Foot, P. 202
Fordham, M. 16, 20, 37, 173,
176; and archetypes 162; and

spirituality 160; on trickster
136–7; on wholeness 222; as
pioneer x
Kafka, F. 225
Kant, I. 38
Kelso, W. 227–8
Kenny, A. 205–6
Kermode, F. 15–16
Kernberg, O. 75, 114; and
borderline debate 111–13
Keutzer, C. 9
Kinsey, A. C. 103
Kirsch, J. 212
Klein, M. 9, 197, 219; and
primal scene 134, 135; and
projective identification 169;
and psychic reality 171
Kohlberg, L. 195
Kohut, H. 5; and borderline
debate 111–13; and empathy
112, 115, 146–7, 152
Kol Nidrei 201–2; *see also*
Atonement, Day of
Koss, J. 166
Kris, E. 68, 74, 145
Kugler, P. 34, 157, 180
Kuhn, T. 218, 219

Lacan, J. 5, 42, 71, 178, 185–6
Lambert, K. 176, 190, 191
Langs, R. 145–6, 149
lapis 180
Laplanche, J. 126, 139, 188
Lauter, E. 99
Lawrence, D. H. 167
Leach, E. 139
leadership 94, 220–1
Lemaire, A. 186
Leonard, L. 67
Lewis, C. 67
libido 160, 188, 192, 197
incestuous 82, 86;
withdrawal of 24
life instinct 188
Lipnack, J. 40–1
Little, M. 145
logos 188–9
Lopez-Pedraza, R. 12, 138, 140
love 69, 178, 200, 208
Lowndes, J. 102

Machiavelli, N. ix
Mahler, M. 70
Malcolm, J. 190
mandala 137, 223
manhood 73
marriage 21
parental 62–3, 84–5, 123,
127–8, 133–4; *see also*
hierosgamos
masculine and feminine 97, 104,
136, 188, 229
masculine principle 188
masculine psychology 85, 94,
101, 175
masculinity and femininity 75;
and gender difference 96; as
metaphors 95, 104
massa confusa; *see prima
materia*
Masson, J. 17
masturbation, Pan as god of 138,
140
Mattinson, J. 156
McEwan, I. 120–1, 122
McManus, A. 105–6
Meier, C. 148
Meltzer, D. 136, 140, 159,
169–70, 171
Melzack, R. 44–5
memory 37, 215
mendacity 136, 137–8, 139
menstruation 105
Mercurius, Mercury 125, 131,
136, 183; *see also* Hermes
merger 129–31, 132, 134–5,
156, 177–9
Merleau-Ponty, M. 229
metaphor 3, 9, 138, 179, 216
alchemy and 175–8, 180–4,
192–3; anatomy as 103–4,
187; core of 56;
direct/indirect 177–9;
literalism and 27–8, 46–7,
68–9, 78, 104; masculinity
and femininity as 95, 104
metapsychology 111, 136, 223
mid-life crisis 35
Miller, D. 8
Milner, M. 197
Minogue, K. 223

229
separation-individuation 70
sex
    difference 92–3, 95–6, 101,
    105; versus gender 95
sex organs 102–3
sexual abuse 53–4, 67, 81, 159
sexual intercourse 185, 187
    parental 64, 87, 123, 126,
    131, 133, 138; posterior 127,
    140
sexuality 42, 55, 65, 134, 160
    and aggression 58; genital
    187–8; Hermes and 140–2;
    symbolization and 185,
    187–8, 190
shadow 25, 82, 184, 190, 196
    integration of 212; projection
    of 50, 199, 211
Shakespeare, W. 165
Sheldrake, R. 34–5
Shelley, M. 199
Shorter, B. 99–100
Siann, G. 93–4
sign 43, 177, 216
sin 204
    original 138, 194
Singer, J. 222
Singer, M. 109
Smith, Adam ix
social analysis 14
social organization 41, 96, 120
society 98, 228
Society of Analytical
    Psychology 176
soror mystica 182, 185–6
soul 100, 151, 174, 186–7, 217
    alchemy and 180–1; and
    body 164, 215; ego and 195;
    and image 45; psychology
    and 21, 167; symbolism of
    216
soul guide; *see* psychopomp
spirit 86–7, 167
spirituality 40, 42, 162, 189
splitting 19, 25, 60, 211
    of ego 149; of personality
    51–2, 170; of psyche 155
Stamps J. 40–1
Statham, D. 105

Stein, L. 26
Stein, M. 26, 213–14
Stein, R. 158, 191
Steiner, J. 203
Steiner, R. 219–20, 221
Sterba, R. 149
Stern, D. 23
Stevens, A. 92, 94, 95, 101, 198
Stevens, C. 100
Stewart, L. 26
Stokes, A. 46
Stolorow, R. 223
Stone, M. 114, 116–17, 118
Storr, A. 209
sublimation 87, 209, 230
suicide 57, 58
Sullivan, L. 13
superego 2, 29, 200
    as archetype 195, 197–8
symbiosis 70, 85, 229
symbol(s)
    and image 43; king and
    queen as 184; metaphor and
    177, 179; sign and 43, 177;
    see also image
symbolism 217
    dental 130; and sexuality
    185, 187–8, 190; of soul 216
Symington, N. 151
synchrony 16, 25
    and depth psychology 24; in
    developmental psychology
    17, 19, 23–4, 27–8, 30, 35–7,
    65; diachrony and 16, 37, 49
syzygy 127

Taylor, C. 190
teleology 17, 35, 133
telos 23, 48, 81, 88, 208, 230
temenos 148
theft 136, 138, 139
theology 167
therapeutic alliance/relationship
    184, 193
third area (Winnicott) 40, 167–8
threeness 28–9, 31–2, 73, 125,
    132
three-person psychology 19, 74
time 19, 20, 25, 36, 203
    and emotional development